BILL WALTON'S TOTAL BOOK OF BICYCLING

BILL WALTON'S TOTAL BOOK OF BICYCLING

**BILL WALTON
AND
BJARNE ROSTAING**

Bantam Books
TORONTO • NEW YORK • LONDON • SYDNEY • AUCKLAND

BILL WALTON'S TOTAL BOOK OF BICYCLING
A Bantam Book / April 1985

Library of Congress Cataloging in Publication Data

Walton, Bill, 1952–
  Bill Walton's Total book of bicycling.

  Includes index.
  1. Cycling. 2. Bicycles. I. Rostaing, Bjarne.
II. Title. III. Title: Total book of bicycling.
GV1041.W25 1985   796.6   83-46000
ISBN 0-553-34075-1 (pbk.)

Published simultaneously in the United States and Canada

PRINTED IN THE UNITED STATES OF AMERICA

DH   0 9 8 7 6 5 4 3 2 1

This book is for Adam, Andrew,
Christopher, Luke, and Nathan—and
kids all over the world who will learn
to love the bicycle

The authors gratefully acknowledge the help and guidance of the following people: Alison Acker, Michael Aisner, Kim Allis, Dr. Robert Arnot, Jock and Win Boyer, Sheldon Brown, Nancy Campbell, Lurelle Cheverie, Connie Clausen, Sal Corso, Dennis Donohue, Gary Fisher, F. X. Flinn, John Francis, Bob and Barbara George, Patricia Gormond, Dr. Clifford Graves, Cyrille Guimard, Peter Guzzardi, John Krausz, Craig Kuhl, Barbara La Fontaine, Bob and Greg Le Mond, Jurgen Leth, Bruce Martin, Fred Mengoni, Peter Mooney, Michael Neel, Nick Peck, Neil Quinn, Jack Simes, Lynn Volkman and Bill Woodul.

Also the following organizations: Bikecentennial, The League of American Wheelmen, National Off-Road Bicycle Association, U.S. Cycling Federation, and U.S. PRO.

Finally, without the patient assistance and expert guidance of our technical consultant, John C. Allis, this book would not have been possible. May the wind be always at his back.

CONTENTS

INTRODUCTION

I wasn't surprised when U.S. riders swept half the cycling events at the Los Angeles Olympics and took more medals than anyone else. I had trained with members of the 1980 team in San Diego, and it wasn't easy keeping up with them. Anyone could see the sport here was taking off and I was glad of it, being a lifelong cyclist and enthusiastic member of the so-called "bike boom" of the seventies. Bicycles have been part of my life for a long time.

I was six years old when I rode a bicycle the first time, and I still remember that experience clearly. The bike belonged to my older brother Bruce, and I'd been watching him ride it long enough that I had the idea. As I recall, I just got on, Bruce gave me a push, and I rode it away. I'd been doing it in my imagination for some time, and it came naturally.

We lived on a hill, so I rode down the hill, and then I learned something else about bicycles when I rode back up. It really made an impression on me because it was a whole new way of moving, completely different from walking or running. It was a lot of fun—faster and more exciting, the kind of thing you tend to remember. It gave me a feeling of independence I really liked.

After that I was into bikes. As soon as my folks would allow it, I was riding all over San Diego, back and forth to the beach, everywhere. After a while I couldn't find bikes to fit, but I always owned one. I rode to get where I wanted to go, but also because it felt good. These were one-speed bikes I was riding, your basic bicycle, nothing expensive, and it wasn't until years later, when I was at UCLA, that I started riding nice ten-speeds. I really appreciated the way this kind of bike responded, and expanded your range. Cycling became my alternate sport, though I didn't think of it that way. It was a pure pleasure activity, and a healthy and productive one, I might add. Also it was to some extent an escape from the pressures of life. I could work things out on a ride.

My first derailleur bike was a green Bertin, which I bought because it was the tallest bike I could find—about a 25½" frame, I think. It came from Hans Ort's Westwood bike shop, and they fixed me up with an extra-long seatpost which let me stretch out my legs for the first time in years. It also gave me a pretty radical position on the bike, since the handlebars were about five inches below the seat. After buying this Bertin, I took to dropping in at Hans's shop when I had free time, and it was there that I found out about more serious cycling. I went out on rides with the guys who were racing, and through this I learned to respect the sport and the people involved in it. On the bike I was no star, just one of the group.

In college I got in the habit of riding quite frequently, especially in summer. Usually 40–60 mile rides, long enough to loosen up and unwind. I would do that probably four days a week during the summer. A couple of hundred miles a week, probably. I never consciously rode for fitness, but I know now that those rides were very beneficial in a variety of ways. I'm sure they gave me stamina and leg strength without putting stress on my knees and feet, and it never felt like work. It was the kind of activity that settled me down. I've always had to respect what a good ride can do for my mood. Going out on a bike is my idea of an excellent way to enjoy a sunny day. Being outside, getting into the movement and joy of the bike—it's very satisfying to me, that feeling of freedom.

I took advantage of something else about the bicycle then, too: the privacy. There were a lot of basketball fans at UCLA and it could be difficult to cope with this at times. Between playing basketball and attending classes, I needed to get away, so I rode around campus rather than walking. On the bike I was a lot less vulnerable, you might say; I was moving too fast for conversation. The bike gave me time by myself to digest the experiences I was having, and this was really important to me.

I finally hammered that poor Bertin to the point where I needed something new, and was lucky enough to meet a British professional rider named Norman Hill. He runs the Vancouver velodrome now, but at the time he was associated with the Falcon team. He arranged for me to get both a road and a track bike. These Falcons were a necessity, actually; my size and weight were wrong for any stock bike. They were made of stronger tubing and had less flex; and I could feel the difference, especially when hammering a big gear or climbing hills off the saddle. My first ride with the track bike was a completely new experience, and I found I was still learning a lot about bicycles. These bikes were still a little on the small side, though; manufacturers aren't geared up for out-size frames, basically. I measure out to a 29½″ frame, which creates all sorts of problems for the builder.

I might still be riding those Falcons except for a coincidence that brought me in contact with the 1980 Olympic track team, which moved to San Diego for quite some period of time to be near our velodrome. Harve Nitz, Eric Heiden, Mark Gorski, Brent Emery, John Beckmann, Dave Grylls—I can't remember all the names—they were at a hotel near my house, and I'd go out with them, riding my Falcons. I learned a lot chasing them down the road, and missed them when they left. At that time, Eddie Borysewicz, the National coach, did me an important favor, by measuring me and arranging for Ted Kirkbride, who also built the American Masi bicycles, to build me a pair of bikes that really fit. Ted sent to England for special heavy tubing normally used on tandem bicycles, then built me both a road and track bike, and they were just fine. It was my first experience with what it's like to be on a bicycle that really fits and has good rigidity, and I can vouch for the advantages of this. These aren't neighborhood bikes though, and I also have a stock Nishiki with butterfly handlebars that I knock around on.

Over the years I've thought about what is so different and unique about riding a bicycle. It's not easy to define; I have to compare it to other things I really like, such as rock music and basketball. A bicycle gives me a special combination of rhythm and speed that is continuously exciting, and it's different all the time. There's a freshness to it.

I rely on my bikes for this, and often wished to communicate these feelings, but I never did anything about it until Bjarne Rostaing spoke to me about the possibility of doing a book several years ago. Not a specialist's book, but an introduction to the bicycle with basic useful information about all aspects of the bicycle and how to enjoy it, rather than just purely mechanical things. It passed from my mind until half a year later, when Bjarne wrote me about the idea. I spoke to some cycling people we knew in common, and I got a positive impression. This is the book we came up with, and I think it covers the territory. I could definitely have used a copy back when I was learning things the hard way.

BILL WALTON

1.
FITNESS AND PHYSIOLOGY

Fitness is the natural condition of the body, and throughout history, more or less constant physical activity was part of life as we knew it. The human body has not changed in the century since the Transportation Revolution, and while millions of people have shifted from an active to a sedentary lifestyle, movement is still essential to good health—preferably sustained, relatively unforced movement that does not endanger joints or pull muscles.

Deprived of vigorous activity, the body sends warning signals. Its ability to circulate fluids is reduced; the lymphatic system slows down; flexibility and resilience are lost; the glands secrete less vigorously and organs age prematurely. With time and disuse, the body often becomes chronically half sick, and this changes the way you feel about yourself. It takes the fun out of life.

THE NATURE OF FITNESS

Having plenty of oxygen available to the brain and the muscles is closely connected with a capacity for sustained mental and physical effort and a general sense of confidence and well-being. The bicycle is one of the best possible ways to bring this about. In cycling, large volumes of oxygen pass through the lungs and into the bloodstream for long periods. Irvin Faria (*Cycling Physiology for the Serious Cyclist*, Charles C. Thomas: Springfield IL, 1978) compares the volume of air breathed during a minute by athletes in various sports, and shows a high of 203 milliliters for cyclists. (Rowers and swimmers came next,

APPROACHES TO THE BICYCLE
There's more than one approach to the bicycle; these folks have all found their own very different ways (and bicycles).

followed by cross-country skiers.) Elsewhere, Faria cites a study of German national teams in which both amateur and professional cyclists show greater heart volume than athletes in other sports. This suggests why cyclists always score at or near the top on ergometer tests (tests that measure work performed) when compared to other athletes.

But tying the value of riding a bicycle to the achievements of an elite group of competitive athletes is not very relevant to the needs and goals of recreational cyclists and commuters, many of them beyond competition age and not athletes to begin with. Swimming, running, skiing, and rowing can all accomplish the same thing. What is special about cycling is its combination of convenience, utility, and compatibility with body mechanics: It doesn't hammer the joints.

Ernst Van Aaken, the legendary German "runner's doctor," makes this point clearly in the Van Aaken Method (*Runner's World*: Mountain View, CA 1976). Speaking about runners with training-induced injuries, he says that a layoff is not usually necessary and that bicycle training should be substituted: "The basic principle is that stress is taken off the legs, but the circulatory system is kept working. . . . This has the advantage of continuing to train the endurance functions of heart and circulation." He adds that "No other sport is so complementary to running." When Olympic gold medal marathoner Joan Benoit was unable to run some months before the '84 Olympics, she chose this means of maintaining fitness—obviously it helped.

A leading theorist in endurance physiology who has coached Olympic medalists and world record holding runners, Van Aaken also has a broad-based practice of nonathletes, children, and older patients. Known as the father of long, slow distance training, he speaks with authority. Many trainers in other sports agree that the bicycle is a conditioning device par excellence and a work-cure for "pains in knees, feet, shins, hips, etc.," as he puts it. This explains why so many professional football, soccer, basketball, and baseball players work out on bicycles. It also suggests why more people continue cycling past the age of 35 than run, jog, ski, or play tennis (1983 Simmons Market Research Study).

HOW IT WORKS

The bicycle accomplishes its therapy/conditioning by substituting a similar but more fluid leg motion for that of running. At the same time, it also shifts the major effort from the muscles at the back of the leg to the quadriceps ("quads"), at the front, which are the biggest and strongest in the body. By supporting the rider's weight, the bicycle eliminates weight-bearing stress and direct shock to the feet, knees, and hips. It has the further advantage of allowing an extremely wide range of effort; a bicycle in basically flat terrain moving 8–10 mph requires about as much energy as walking, while at sustained near-maximum effort a bike offers a very high, continuous work level to the system for those who want it, which is how long-distance cyclists become so incredibly fit.

BREATHING AND CIRCULATION

Cardiologist Paul Dudley White described what happens in a bike rider's body as well as anyone. A lifelong cyclist who attended President Dwight Eisenhower and who lived into his late seventies, Dr. White could observe the process in himself: "Cycling helps the lungs to bring oxygen into the body and pump out carbon dioxide," he said. "As bipeds, we need something to help us keep the blood circulating up

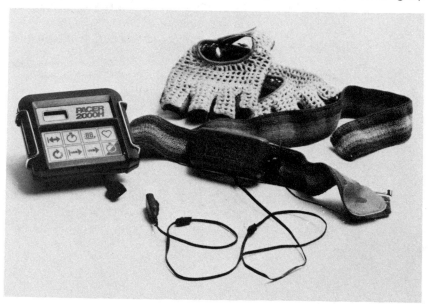

THE PACER 2000
This was the original device for keeping track of pedal rpms, pulse, speed, and distance traveled. It is not cheap ($110–115 complete with pulse monitor) but for those who feel the need to monitor body function carefully this is a useful accessory. Other companies now make many similar items.

from the lower part of the body. When the leg muscles contract, they squeeze the veins and actually pump blood toward the heart."

This increased flow of blood has many results, all good. Most essentially, it carries oxygen where it is needed. Deeper breathing provides much more oxygen; the pulse rises; most body functions are mildly stimulated. Continued over a period of time, this kind of activity becomes aerobic (oxygen dependent) exercise, and there is little question that it is highly beneficial.

Dr. Jean-Pierre de Mondenard, another man with long cycling experience, provides further details. In Krausz's *The Bicycling Book* (Dial: NY, 1982) Mondenard notes classic signs of cardiovascular strength: improved respiration, increased pulmonary capacity (ability to absorb oxygen), and a larger, stronger heart, which beats more slowly but delivers more blood on each stroke. The cyclist's heart is steadier under stress, says Mondenard, as well as having improved endurance and quicker recovery. Not specified by Mondenard is the general refurbishing of veins, arteries, and capillaries, which many doctors consider the best possible insurance against heart attack and the best basis for real recovery from one. Equally important, cholesterol is reduced, and lipid (blood fat) balance is improved.

OTHER EFFECTS

In his work with cyclists, Mondenard also observed improved digestion (more nutrients absorbed, wastes eliminated more quickly and completely), sweat and urine stimulated (along with their ability to carry away toxins), large muscles oxygenated and developed, hip and ankle joints benefited rather than overstressed, sleep improved, and obesity reduced. Even allowing for the century-old French love affair with the bicycle, this is a formidable list, touching on many of the most basic psycho-physical human functions. They are also functions that tend to deteriorate in civilized man—or sedentary man, as he might be called.

Mondenard specifically recommends cycling for many cardiac patients, victims of high blood pressure and hypertension, diabetics and arthritics. Obviously, such exercise therapy should take place under medical supervision, but Mondenard clearly indicates that the bicyle can improve fitness in a wide range of people from athletes to near-invalids, helping restore the body to its natural condition.

Dr. Bob Arnot, CBS Morning News consultant on health and fitness, and author of the book *Sportselection* (Viking: NY, 1984), regards some claims by cycling enthusiasts as somewhat exaggerated. A member of innumerable Olympic medical committees (and an active cyclist himself), Arnot observes that, "You can do virtually no exercise and live to be a hundred; you just won't feel very well. Without exercise, you get creaky and feel old much sooner. This is what bothers so many sedentary people; they're not actually sick, but they're not on a very high plane of wellness. They get enough oxygen for what they do, but there's not much surplus.

"But there are some definitely established medical considerations that are often ignored. Many people ride bicycles for the feeling of well-being created by the release of painkilling endorphins, and because this kind of exercise can balance the manic and depressive cycles, the ups and downs of life. Also, blood sugar level is stabilized by regular exercise, which is beneficial for everyone, and especially so for diabetics. Another thing is that you lose bone calcium after your mid-forties without a reasonable amount of exercise, and this is a problem for women even more than men, because they begin with less calcium.

"The final thing, of course, is the reduced risk of heart attack. According to Ralph Paffenberger's well-accepted study of 17,000 Harvard graduates, if you've been steadily burning 2,000 calories a week in exercise, you're 63% less likely to have a heart attack. That's about three or four hours a week of cycling, jogging, rowing, swimming, or cross-country skiing. Fast racquetball, squash or basketball can do the same thing . . . ." Other recent studies support this.

AEROBICS AND CYCLING

THE NATURE OF AEROBIC ACTIVITY

Exercise in which the body metabolizes glucose stored in the liver and the muscles by using oxygen is described as *aerobic* exercise. It can be sustained for long periods of time, and it effectively combats the general atrophy caused by sedentary life. Aerobic exercise does no violence to the body, which goes through successive warm-up thresholds as blood flows more and more freely, until the system reaches a level it can sustain. Energy is released on a relatively stable curve, and painful exercise by-products in blood and muscles are a minor problem.

ANAEROBIC EFFORT

Short-duration, high-intensity effort is very different. This kind of exercise is *anaerobic*; it metabolizes glucose *without* using oxygen, creating a completely different situation for the body. Anaerobic metabolism gives the violent energy of the sprint, of the punch, of weightlifting, and of throwing a discus, shot, or ball. For a short period of time, a very high level of energy is released, but the process is inefficient; anaerobic activity produces an abundance of waste products such as lactic acid, which cause pain and leave the body slowly. Heart attacks during exercise tend to occur at these high levels.

Another result is so-called oxygen debt, which causes dizziness, tunnel vision, and other reactions as the body catches up with the demand for oxygen. The sudden, heavy stress on joints, tendons, and muscles is hard on older and less fit bodies. Paradoxically, one way to get rid of anaerobic by-products is light aerobic exercise, and racing cyclists will often pedal around easily for a while after a sprint.

WHAT HAPPENS IN THE CYCLIST'S BODY

As the cyclist moves up through various levels of effort, the adrenal glands release the chemical compounds epinephrine and norepinephrene into the bloodstream. Respiration quickens, the heart beats faster, and moves more blood with each contraction. The change is very marked, especially during strenuous effort. The normal resting body uses approximately six to eight liters of air per minute, from which it extracts about three-tenths liters of oxygen; a good athlete in full effort takes in as much as 180 liters of air in the same period, extracting up to five liters of oxygen from this. At the same time, carbon dioxide is released in much greater quantity, along with other waste products. Gauging your effort accurately is not easy, and the best indicator is your pulse, which gives a good estimate of cardiovascular effort.

PULSE

Pulse is a classic indicator of both fitness and health, but it is also very individual. There is no basic norm. Some people have a resting pulse below 40; others are close to twice that. Likewise, reaction to

COSMETIC FITNESS

Along with the fitness boom and the sudden popularity of participation sports came another, very different, "cosmetic-fitness" boom for those who don't want to bother. Looking fit is in, and so is a whole miniindustry of health clubs, sunlamps, and gadgets intended to make you look lean and mean. In a burst of honesty, one New York operation defined their product as Passive Fitness.

There is no passive fitness, though you can get a tan, firm up flab, or tone muscles on a fit body with some sessions at a spa. If you're really lazy, you can also have your muscles stimulated electrically while reading the paper, but your passive fitness program will be strictly cosmetic. Fitness works from the inside out; when your heart muscle is healthy and circulation is good, you feel different. And it is a proven fact that you can lift absolutely humongous weights while actually losing *cardiovascular fitness. (Faria's weight lifters actually had about the same heart volume as the man on the street, and less than average when figured against body weight—a shocking statistic.) If you're fool enough to take steroids while pumping iron, you can increase your risk of heart failure.*

This is not to say that any or all of the above activities are bad, just that they put the cart before the horse. Cardiovascular fitness is basic; the other stuff is icing. After you're in shape, take a musclebound friend for a nice ride in the hills. If your basic abilities are comparable, you'll be stunned, and so will he or she. Just look out for cross-country skiers and distance runners; those folks are fit.

effort varies greatly. Added to this is the sometimes misleading evidence of some sports doctors and physiologists who generally work with fit, motivated young athletes, and tend to lose perspective on the capacities of more typical people. There is, for example, a fairly widespread notion that "training effect" (cardiovascular improvement) takes place at 135–145 heartbeats per minute, and that anything less is a waste of time. Actually, this is only the most obvious of several thresholds. It is easy to spot, because this is the point above which lucid conversation becomes difficult or impossible for most people.

TAKING PULSE AT NECK
The pulse is easiest to find at the neck; use a finger rather than the thumb, which has its own pulse.

PULSE MYTHOLOGY

The mythology is extensive and misleading. Macho slogans like "no pain, no gain" are applicable only to those trying to squeeze every last bit out of their systems, and who have ample recuperation time, near-perfect diet, and uncomplicated lives. (Bike racers have their own version: "No brain, no pain.")

Van Aaken disputes the necessity for high-intensity training for endurance sports, saying that even world-class distance runners can do much of their training at around 125 beats per minute, and that breathing is most efficient in this range. Except for the dedicated competitor, this is definitely the beginning of sanity.

USING PULSE TO ASSESS HEALTH AND FITNESS

The most useful aspect of the pulse is not its resting or exercising count or its maximum (unless you are into violent effort). What matters most are its *variations*, and the patterns of those variations, which should become predictable. Your pulse rises not only with physical effort, but with many kinds of stress, and it also can become slightly elevated when you are overtired or not yet recuperated from exercise or illness.

When your morning (resting) pulse goes down a few beats, it is generally a good sign. Another good sign is your postexercise pulse coming down quickly and reliably to a similar level each time. Both are among the most basic signs that you are becoming reasonably fit without risking your health. When your pulse comes down slowly or stays high for no apparent reason, you have probably been pushing yourself too hard and/or are slightly sick.

Overall, lowered pulse and quick recovery indicate improved fitness and health; the heart has improved its capacity and is delivering more blood with each beat. A lowered pulse combined with lethargy, dizziness, or depression is not a good sign, however.

Base (waking) pulse, if taken daily over a period of months, should gradually decrease with systematic exercise. Another useful index is the difference between this pulse and the pulse taken a few seconds after rising and moving around. Current thinking is that if the difference is small, you are gaining fitness; if pulse shoots up when you stand up, it's probably time to rest, take a day off, or otherwise ease up. But don't rely on pulse alone as a guide to your general condition. Bloodshot eyes often indicate too much exercise, as do lethargy, nervousness, and persistent fatigue.

LIMITS

For those curious about limits, the formula for maximum pulse is usually figured as 220 minus age in years, though this is not the only formula. But for a relatively unathletic person interested in an aerobic workout, this is very misleading. An overweight, out-of-shape, 38-year-old office worker who puts his or her pulse up to 182 is not only loading up with lactic acid and drastically shortening the workout, but may well be at some risk. It is wise for older and/or less fit people to have a stress test before experimenting in this range. A few minutes of this high pulse rate create stresses that much longer periods at 120 beats per minute would not even approach. Maximum pulse is of interest mainly to serious young athletes.

FITNESS AND HEALTH

Fitness has a lot in common with health. It raises resistance to infection by improving circulation and stimulating glandular functions. Work capacity and concentration increase as energy level rises. Mentally, fitness stabilizes and builds confidence because you sense that you are functioning better and are ready for stress. Properly used, the exercise leading to fitness also provides a constructive outlet for stress. In the zone between mental and physical, such characteristics as aggressiveness, relaxation, coordination, and animal alertness are improved. And according to Dr. Rokuro Koike, writing in *The Bicycling Book*, cycling stimulates male sexuality through increased activity of Cowper's glands, although prolonged cycling can depress it. No parallel study was done on a female cyclist.

HYPERFITNESS

Hyperfitness is another matter. Here, bodily systems are operating at near-maximum capacity, and the athlete must be monitored carefully. This kind of "form" requires careful diet with plenty of rest, and the hyperfit athlete spends lots of time either in exertion or recuperation. Body fat is maintained at the lowest possible level. This is not health in the usual sense, and it is not a stable condition. Hyperfitness is an edge sport in itself, with the athlete in constant danger of pushing too far. The peaking athlete's body is always close to red-line. Like any machine being driven close to its limit, the hyperfit body needs special care and maintenance.

EXERCISE ADDICTION: THE PERILS OF PERSONAL BEST

Many people are capable of psyching themselves into overtraining in search of hyperfitness, at least for a while. It has its kick and definitely creates a sense of exhilaration and achievement; that sweet spot of top performance is hypnotic. Not many can arrange the necessary care and maintenance though, and methodically overextending yourself can be debilitating for those with jobs, families, and other interests.

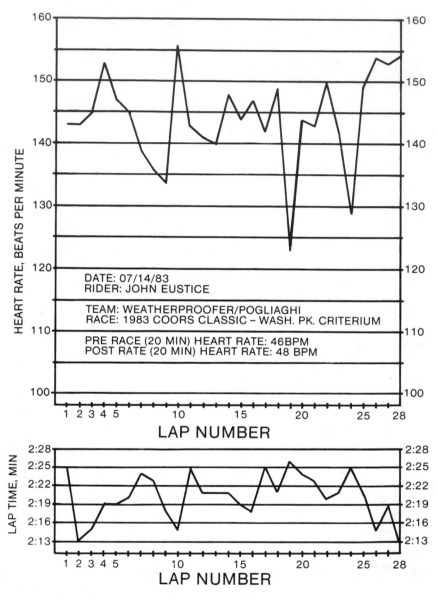

DATE: 07/14/83
RIDER: JOHN EUSTICE

TEAM: WEATHERPROOFER/POGLIAGHI
RACE: 1983 COORS CLASSIC – WASH. PK. CRITERIUM

PRE RACE (20 MIN) HEART RATE: 46BPM
POST RATE (20 MIN) HEART RATE: 48 BPM

TRUE FITNESS

The correlation of beats per minute (bpm) and lap times of 1982 U.S. professional champion John Eustice during competition is very close, and varies more than 32 bpm. Even more interesting is his quick recovery—all the way down to 48 bpm within 20 minutes of finishing the event. Our thanks to Wyoming Biotelemetry.

Maintaining a balance between exercise and the rest of your life is a real problem for some people, and a realistic sense of your capacities is very helpful. Variation in human physical capacities is very wide, falling on the same bell-curve distribution as intelligence and most human attributes. Thus one person's warm-up is another's workout, and accepting standard competitive goals can do more harm than good. The point for most people is not competition or the continually striving for "personal best" performances; this can take the pleasure out of any sport. The point for most of us is being healthy and feeling good, which means, for many people, building up gradually from a level no serious young athlete ever has to deal with.

WARM-UP

Warming up is an excellent idea because it reduces stress on the cardiovascular system, muscles and joints when you begin to exercise. While the warm-up process is not yet completely understood, it definitely takes longer for some people to warm up than suggested by those medical authorities who believe that all systems are fully operational in two or three minutes. The body continues to change its response for a much longer period. And if your warm-up is gradual, the likelihood of muscle and joint pain is reduced.

Professional racing cyclists are well aware of this. Although they ride faster and cover much longer distances than amateurs, the first 30–60 kilometers of a professional road race (which often lasts 200–300 kilometers) is often one long warm-up. On a bicycle, the trick to warming up is to stay in low gears that keep your legs moving at fairly high rpms; a fast-moving leg gets plenty of oxygen and does not send strain up into the back. You may want to go harder after 10 or 20 minutes, but holding back and trying to pedal smoothly in the lower gears will extend the warm-up, and ultimately your fitness.

SWEAT

At some point in your warm-up (it varies considerably from person to person) you will break a sweat, which is a general indication that you are accomplishing something. This threshold is below that much discussed 135–140 pulse for most people, and you will find that it is not constant. Out-of-shape people often sweat quickly and profusely, but as their fitness improves, they usually sweat less easily. Also, the amount of sweat and its secretions change with fitness, as the body learns to conserve minerals and water.

One thing medical authorities agree on: Dehydration is dangerous. Replace the water you lose. This means drinking before, during, and after a ride. The point cannot be stressed too much; thirst is *not* a reliable measure of dehydration.

BODY AWARENESS

Approaching physical activity in an aware state allows you to get an accurate sense of where you really stand, as athletes learn to do. Pulse gives one kind of information, performance another; the third is best described as mood or affect. To feel strong and calm usually indicates an approaching peak; feeling edgy suggests a peak has arrived, and that it may be time to back off. If you are tired, indifferent, or negative, it may be time for a day off and more sleep. The body has its own rhythms, and if you can learn to exercise really hard only when you're healthy, you tend to stay healthy.

Maintaining this level of effort is an art that takes self-knowledge, but it is crucial in terms of integrating exercise with the rest of your life. People don't turn away from exercise when it works for them, and it works best when keyed to one's own basic rhythms. This is another kind of sweet spot, and the feedback comes back loud and clear. Plunging in blindly and forcing yourself into fatigue each day is not the answer.

HARD AND EASY DAYS

Rest and recuperation are enormously important, especially if you tend to throw yourself into things. If you're not used to exercise, you can figure that an hour of it will throw you off a little; you'll feel different, having used up energy that would normally have gone elsewhere. If you're not ready for this every day, don't push it; it doesn't matter that much. Many athletes follow a hard-day/easy-day pattern. For beginning cyclists over 30 this often translates into riding every other day. Three or four hour-long rides a week are enough to make a difference; your body will use the days off to stabilize your gains.

If you find yourself riding every day, try to alternate the hard and easy rides, or figure on reduced energy and needing more rest for a while. If you are hardy and/or young, you probably won't notice any adverse effects, but if you come from an average genetic background and are coming back from years of sloth, the sharp rise in physical demand combined with insufficient rest can bring on a cold or a chronically fatigued state. The bicycle can draw you into excessive effort (old European coaches used to call it bicycle hunger), and when it goes too far, it stops being fun.

STAYING LOOSE

Keeping your pulse around 120–125 and going easy on the hills the first few weeks will minimize the pain of "going anaerobic" and the feeling of exercise hangover. If you haven't been exercising at all, the idea is to sneak up on fitness. It also helps to take it easy after a hard ride and to time exercise so that you don't go into a meeting or other demanding situation when you're overtired. Runner-doctor George Sheehan recommends aspirin for athletic aches, and while this disagrees with some stomachs, hot tubs definitely help loosen the painful knots in hard-worked bodies. Massage is great, too.

Finally, don't get locked into a compulsive program. Even the very best racers follow the suggestions of their bodies rather than a mechanical pattern. "I ride the way I feel," observes 1983 Professional World Champion Greg Le Mond, whose six World championship medals establish him as the finest American racer in half a century. "I don't push myself in training if I'm not feeling well; I back off. My team gave me several vacations during my first season, and that was really crucial to my success. . . . No matter who you are, your strength ebbs and flows, and you have to accept that, and work with it."

This is totally different from the lockstep many people impose on themselves or accept from coaches, and it is the best kind of advice for any rider, because it is based on the realities of the human body.

FLEXIBILITY

Flexibility is basic to being comfortable on a bike, and swimming is one way to get it. Equally good are yoga and yoga-derived stretches, which do not build muscle, but can widen the range of physical movement by stretching muscles, tendons, and ligaments. Yoga can also help control the compulsive urge toward overactivity mentioned earlier. Numb hands (and sometimes crotch), lower-back ache and shoulder aches all respond to stretching if you have patience.

The problem lies in doing stretches or yoga *asanas* right. Every fitness-sport magazine runs a brief article on the subject from time to time, and almost every participant has had the experience of forcing or "bouncing" a stretch, followed by pain, sometimes injury.

You may not find what you need at the local health spa though. Of the established systems to teach flexibility and breath coordination, the Nickolaus Method may be the most basic and easily available. Long familiar to professional dancers, it has also been used by athletic teams to eliminate unnecessary, inefficient body motion; it is a very good way to get your body more supple and better coordinated.

IMPROVEMENT

How long does it take to develop enough strength and endurance to enjoy rather than suffer through a half-day's ride? It is common knowledge in cycling that last season's miles (and winter activities) pay off in this season's performance. Developing real fitness is a long slow process and it comes in definite thresholds. A month shows a difference, but it probably takes a good half year of regular exercise before the body fully responds. Sometimes it overresponds and needs extra rest. Short vacations from exercise, provided they don't go beyond a week or so, can be as beneficial to the casual rider as to a Greg Le Mond. The slight theoretical loss in fitness is balanced by relaxation. There are certain kinds of repair the body must take time for; ignore this and you can slip into a persistent fatigue that turns many people away from exercise. It's just not much fun.

CROSS-TRAINING: THE SECRET OF THE TRIATHLON

Finally, while hard-core racing cyclists may disagree, most people find that alternate or supplementary activity, sometimes called *cross-training*, maximizes both general fitness and the pleasure of riding. The popularity of triathlons is closely linked to this, and to the mental effects of variety. While the cardiovascular system, lower, and middle body are all well exercised on a bicycle, the upper chest, shoulders, and arms are not, and long rides can create aches and pains in the neck and spine. Good position on the bicycle, smooth pedaling, stretching, and massage all alleviate this, but so do other forms of exercise. One clue is that formerly specialized athletes often remark that the triathlon, by using different muscle groups and postures, tires them less than they expected. So says John Howard, who went from five national cycling championships to a Hawaii triathlon title in 1981. Dr. Arnot says that mixing in some other exercise is "completely appropriate and beneficial for most people—all except the tiny percentage specializing for high-level competition."

What it comes down to is that some thrive on the bicycle as a steady diet and some don't. It's an individual thing.

SPINE AND BREATH

Ian Jackson combines athletic expertise with thorough knowledge of yoga, massage, Rolfing, the Nickolaus method, autosuggestion and other approaches to relaxation, and body re-alignment. He has studied with Milton Erickson, foremost clinical hypnotherapist of his time, and yoga expert B.K.S. Iyengar—"and anyone who had useful knowledge."

Jackson thinks that the key to both relaxation and performance lies in seeing that "dance and sport are not so far apart as people think. There is a lot to be said for smooth, controlled movement; it's definitely basic to riding a bicycle well."

His work with athletes is impressive. 1981 Hawaii Ironman Triathlon winner John Howard, current holder of the 24-hour cycling distance world record (513 miles) says, "I improved my performance substantially through Ian's help. The man knows what he's doing." During Jackson's stay at the Colorado Springs Olympic Training Center he worked with 1984 Olympic Gold Medalist Alexei Grewal, whose reaction can be seen in these excerpts from a letter:

"The breathing techniques work! Much time and practice will be needed for me to unlearn old patterns, but the start is there . . .

". . . between you and me I will win. I won't be able to stay in complete focus between now and then, but when the time comes I will win!"

(continued)

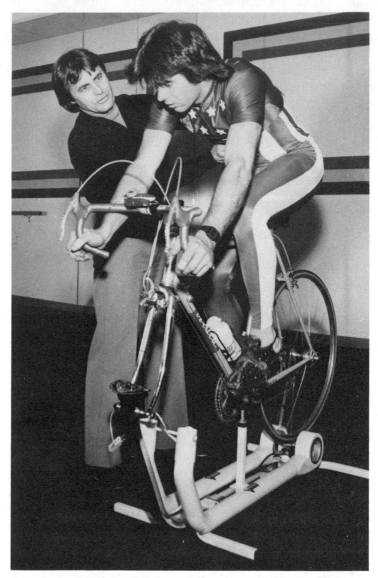

CHAMPION SKATER DONNIE VANPATTEN WITH IAN JACKSON

Bill Watkins, who qualified for the Olympic time trial but withdrew because of a knee problem, wrote:

"My performances at the (Olympic) Trials were the best I have ever done; it was nice they came when they did . . . . much of this may be credited to your help—thanks for providing me the tools to focus my energies."

(continued)

Jackson is no elitist, though at triathlons he is greeted and thanked by all ranks of competitors, top to bottom. He thinks the similarities between athletes and ordinary people are more significant than the differences.

Jackson does not think uncoached yoga or stretching is the best way of preparing and/or relaxing the body for cycling. "The problem involves both spine and breathing, as yoga teaches, and they should not be considered separately. But yoga is not basically an action-oriented discipline, and it's too sophisticated for most people to approach without help. You can hurt yourself by forcing the asanas (positions), especially if you have the determination that people tend to bring to athletic activity. The same goes for yoga-derived stretches that are recommended by many people who don't even know their source. Simple awareness of basic functioning is the first step, and the second is equally simple exercises. I'm talking now about people 'off the street,' so to speak, as well as athletes.

"What I would recommend for almost anyone is to start by lying on the floor. In this position, the lumbar area [small of the back] and neck are off the floor. Without any stress and strain, you accept the floor as your guide. I make jokes about the floor being the teacher, but it's really true.

"You start by pulling your heels toward your buttocks until your feet can rest flat on the floor; as your knees rise, the space under your back will close up. In that position, concentrate on the out breath. As you breathe out, bring your back down toward the floor. You use the out-breath to press the lower spine back against the floor. This lengthens and relaxes the spine.

"At the same time you're breathing out and bringing your spine to the floor, drop your chin into the notch of your collarbone, which will further lengthen and straighten your spine. Use your breathing to establish a rhythm of stretch and release in the spine. You are loosening and stretching your spine as you breathe without any complicated or potentially damaging body twists. When you have a physical sense of this process, concentrate on squeezing the air out each time it is expelled, and relax completely on the in-breath. The air will come in by itself.

"Dancers have been doing this for years; and it is good
(continued)

for just about anyone. I don't tell people how long to do this or when; I tell them to do it until they feel more relaxed and in tune with their bodies. It takes something like five minutes for most people to get into it, and while it's good to do before riding, it is also good to do at almost any time. It brings you into contact with the two most basic realities of this (cycling) activity. What do most riders complain about? Breathing hard and aching backs or necks.

"The classic complaint of new riders is that the back of the neck and shoulders bother them during and after a ride. I told one woman to think about the way a kitten dangles from its mother's mouth: the chin goes in rather than sticking out, and the spine falls into a smooth curve with the tail tucked under, as if you were hanging from the nape of your neck, letting your shoulders drop. I'm wary of absolutes, but my experience indicates this is a comfortable and effective position for most bodies on a bicycle.

"I also believe that effort can and should be coordinated with the out-breath, that exhaling can be shifted rhythmically from side to side rather than always synchronizing with one side, which people definitely tend to do. This can prevent injuries of the type described by Dr. Dennis Bramble, whose research at the University of Utah indicates that most people tie the out-breath effort to one side of the body—and injure that side."

Jackson is now working on a book tying together the various endurance sports. Those who want to know more about his approach can write him at P.O. Box 7601, Little Rock, Arkansas 72217

FOOD AND DRINK: GENERAL

Aerobic metabolism demands air, water, and plenty of calories. A cyclist can lose quarts of water on a hard day's ride, and use up to 6,000 calories. Running out of food is bad, not drinking is worse, and the combination is devastating. The Frenchman Velocio (Paul de Vivie), probably the most knowledgeable cyclist of his time, enunciated the cardinal rule: "Eat before you are hungry, drink before you are thirsty."

Few statements about the sport are more accurate and succinct. Velocio also suggested avoiding meat and any kind of alcohol while on the bike; most riders would agree with this, though many feel that a meat-free diet lacks something, and that a glass of wine or beer in the evening does no harm.

LIQUID REPLACEMENT

Racing cyclists used to have a saying that dry is fast, but this is one case where their advice should be ignored; all contemporary research disagrees emphatically: *Flirting with dehydration is dangerous*. Any sports doctor will tell you so.

Liquid replacement is critical, because biological processes are expedited by water. Body cooling, a crucial process for the rider, is largely accomplished by perspiration, which requires water; moreover, the blood itself thickens in dehydration, placing a strain on the heart, and basic processes within the cell also require water. Occasionally, people who ride to reduce weight will be misled by the loss of water weight; the result is dehydration. Unfit or semifit riders lose water fastest, and unless your rides are restricted to an hour or less, you need a water bottle. Tourists and racers in training often carry two.

WATER

There is nothing like water, and the hotter the weather the better it goes down. On desperate climbs you can also pour it over your head,

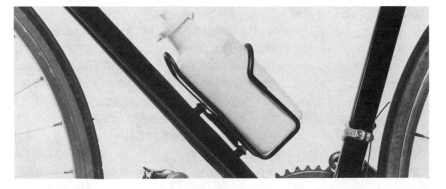

BOTTLE IN CAGE
On a hot day this is your best friend. For long summer rides, carry two; you'll need them.

which feels better than it sounds. Inside or out, water is your cooling system. It bypasses the digestive process and takes effect quickly. Tepid water sounds terrible, but it's just fine when you need it, and it goes into the system painlessly. Very cold water sounds better, but some stomachs react to it with aches and cramps. There is also a simple way to cool a water bottle: stuff it into a wet sock. Wind created by the motion of the bike will evaporate water in the cloth and reduce the temperature enough to make a difference. (Children's socks fit better and thick socks work best.)

TEA

Water is not the only thing to drink, and many riders like some calories, especially in cool weather. Tea is popular in all weather, and it's worth noting that the caffeine in tea is not a simple stimulant; the right amount can also trigger the release of glycogen (the form sugar takes when stored in muscles or liver), and there is evidence that caffeine in moderation also helps the body to burn fats. This is probably the reason for tea's century-long popularity with racers and tourists.

No one adds milk to their tea, because it is commonly thought to create phlegm, but lemon and honey (or sugar) are common additions. Generally tea is brewed weaker in summer, stronger in winter. Because tea represents the wisdom of many generations, it should not be ruled out on theoretical grounds. If you dislike the idea of caffeine, brew it weak; but the millions of riders over the decades who have found tea effective and compatible can't be ignored. The same caffeine that bothers you at the office may affect you favorably on the bike.

ELECTROLYTIC REPLACEMENT

Electrolytic-replacement drinks (E.R.G., Pripps, Gatorade, etc.) are the new wave. A number of studies have been done, apparently proving their superiority to tea, water, and each other. The jury is still out, but the basic idea is reasonable; these drinks more or less approximate sweat, with some sugar added. Exercise depletes the body of certain salts, and these drinks replace those salts. The sugar is not a bad idea either, particularly for out-of-shape riders, whose blood-sugar levels tend to be less stable. The optimal ingredients are yet to be established, but experienced riders invariably dilute these potions more than manufacturers recommend.

NUTRITION: THE NEED YOU CAN'T IGNORE

Cyclists are legendary eaters, especially those who ride long distances. They need to be; failure to replace nutrients has a variety of unpleasant effects. The first is glucose deprivation, known to Europeans as hunger-knock; in America it's called the bonk. Both terms describe what happens when blood-sugar levels drop too far. Bonking out is quite an experience, and in some circumstances can actually be dangerous. Lack of blood sugar not only weakens you physically but affects perception, reaction time, and coordination. Your mind wanders, and so does the bike.

The long-term effects of poor nutrition are more subtle. As vitamins and minerals are used and not replaced, there is a general feeling of depletion and the body becomes more vulnerable to disease.

FOODS FOR THE ROAD

What to eat is a matter of hot debate in sports-medicine circles. On the bike, the first rule is easy digestion, and beyond that it is very difficult to generalize. Some riders eat just about anything. Lon Haldeman destroyed his food-faddist competitors in the epic Race Across America, getting from California to New York in less than ten days largely fueled by such delicacies as burgers and pizza. Greg Le Mond likes hot Mexican and Oriental foods, and former national champion John Allis does not have dinner without wine if he can help it. Five-time Tour de France winner Eddy Merckx and his team ate countless little sandwiches made of a roll, butter, ham, and jam, in addition to plenty of fruit. If you live on the bike, the rules are different. They also differ from one person to another, so take advice with a grain of salt.

THE VIRTUES OF FRUIT

For reasons discussed elsewhere, less fit riders tend to run out of liquids and sugars much faster than the rider with some miles in his legs. Fruits meet this need more completely and quickly than other foods. This makes them extremely popular with both racers and knowledgeable tourists; it's no exaggeration to say that fruit is the most universally accepted on-bike food. Fruits offer liquids, complex carbohydrates, and other nutrients that are essential over the long haul—vitamins, minerals, and trace elements.

They are also both convenient and refreshing. Fructose is released into the system more slowly than the refined sugar in candy and junk food, offsetting the up-and-down blood-sugar syndrome in which the body is first deprived of sugars, then overloaded. (As hypoglycemics know, this is bad news.) Pears and bananas are top favorites, followed by peaches, apples, and oranges (which should be sectioned and wrapped beforehand).

Those who follow racing know that Fausto Coppi won race after race on bananas; the next generation went to the pear. Both are good, and both contain potassium, an important electrolytic salt; lack of potassium can lead to muscle cramps, as can lack of calcium.

CARBOHYDRATES AND CARBO-LOADING

Most current research about sports nutrition centers around carbohydrates. Five to six thousand calories a day are required by athletes in serious training for cycling, running, and cross-country skiing, and the assumption is that carbohydrates are the best source of glucose, which is assumed to be the ideal fuel. Another assumption is that complex carbohydrates (fruits, grains, vegetables, cereals) are preferable to, say, cupcakes washed down with cola. The idea is to supply bulk, fiber, vitamins, and minerals at the same time as calories, and to require the body to break down these complex carbohydrates rather than just pour calories into the system.

So far so good. Less good is the practice of "carbo-loading," which involves starving the body of carbohydrates for several days, then loading up on them before a long ride. There is evidence that while the practice may increase the body's carbo storage capacity, it can also lead to abnormal water storage and other annoying side effects. Beginning cyclists preparing for a race still play this game, but, like the vegetarian approach, it has been largely dropped by serious competitive riders, who are the last word on factors affecting performance.

Endurance research has tended to be based on runners, with the 26.2-mile marathon event implicitly considered the ultimate endurance event by many researchers. This is misleading; the best runners run this distance in a little over two hours, and fair athletes who prepare themselves well do it in well under three. Equally significant, a runner's training time is limited by mechanical problems with the joints of knee, foot and hip. Two hours is a longish run, but a relatively short time on a bicycle. Both racing cyclists and tourists routinely ride for five, six, and seven hours a day, and they do it day after day. This often ignored fact has major nutritional significance.

Carbohydrates are in vogue because of research that shows them to be high in energy and easily assimilated, but they are not the only important body fuel. Each decade brings its own theories; protein was a nutritional buzz word in the not too distant past (and still is with football players). Fats are rarely discussed as endurance fuel, but they have their place, particularly in long-distance riding.

FREE-FATTY-ACID METABOLISM

Why do so many riders include meat (and fish and chicken) in their diet? Because they provide good fuel. There are two kinds of metabolism; the human body can burn either carbohydrates or fats, and fats provide several times more energy per ounce; if your system is good at metabolizing them (it varies), this can mean less volume to be digested, and digestion itself takes energy.

Although there is copious research on carbohydrate metabolism, less is available on free-fatty-acid (F.F.A.) metabolism. Meat is decried despite its formidable concentration of amino acids, which are not duplicated in any other single food and which help metabolize other foods. Over the years many cyclists have found meat very compatible, and not without reason:

"Fat in the form of free fatty acid is a primary muscle fuel at rest and during light to medium work" (60 percent effort) according to Faria, "and [the ability to use it] appears to be higher in trained than untrained cyclists." Like most bodily processes, F.F.A. metabolism is somewhat idiosyncratic; some authorities feel that certain athletes burn fats at effort levels up to 80 percent—i.e., most of the time. Women may be more efficient than men at it, according to Dr. Joan Ullyot (though this is disputed), and it is also linked to both heredity and fitness. Few people recommend meat as an on-bike food, though; it takes longer to digest than carbohydrates and is best eaten several hours before riding.

BALANCED DIET

The phrase "balanced diet" has been used so often it has little impact, but the racing cyclist, whose living depends on his performance, follows something very close to this. There is some variation from country to country, but not a great deal, and crank diets are extremely rare. Fish and chicken are in vogue, and milk is usually avoided, but the men who ride the Giro d'Italia and Tour de France eat the usual vegetables, meat-fish-fowl, fruits, and salads. Rice is popular. Fried foods are out, along with rich sauces, spices, and dairy products (calicum is taken from other sources), but the food is not much different from what school nurses have been recommending for decades. Indi-

vidual variation is important, though; Tour de France star Jacques Anquetil was forbidden salads during competition.

OFF-SEASON EXERCISE

Cyclists often prefer indoor pedaling-type exercise during the off-
season (and bad weather) because it offers general fitness plus specific preparation for the muscles needed in riding. The basic choice
used to be between some kind of exercycle (expensive and uninspir-
ing) and "rollers," a simple device that allows the bike to rest on an
arrangement of cylinders so that it can be pedaled without going anywhere. The choice was also between skill and strength; rollers demand
skill but offer relatively little resistance, while good stationary bicycles
have variable loads. The late seventies changed these options abruptly
with the appearance of "wind-resistance" trainers like the Turbo-trainer
and Racer-mate. These mount the bicycle on a stand and use the rear
wheel to drive an ingenious turbine fan, which creates higher resistance as wheel-speed increases. When the rider shifts into higher
gears, the fan spins faster, increasing resistance on an exponential
curve quite similar to that encountered by riders using similar gears on
the road. Most riders prefer this to mechanical friction-type resistance.

The latest variation is turborollers. These have two turbofans, and
when both are in operation, they provide enough resistance for anyone.
Like any rollers, they are tricky, and build skill as well as strength.

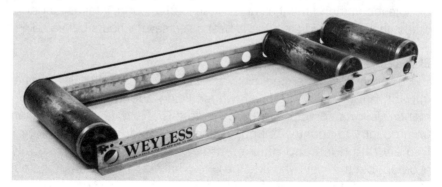

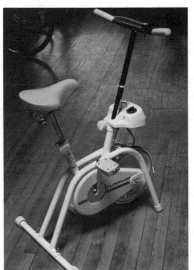

RAINY DAY EXERCISE

Exercise bikes like this Tunturi (left, about $275) are standard equipment in the training rooms for many professional sports because they build fitness and have no adverse side effects. Many cyclists use devices that allow them to ride their own bike indoors, like the Turbo-trainer (top, about $150) and rollers (page 26, from under $100 up); these let you ride your own bike in your preferred position, which exercycles do not. Turbo-trainer's fan-produced wind-resistance is smooth and variable; rollers teach you bike handling in a hurry, but many people can't quite handle them.

EFFORT PARAMETERS

Any attempt to quantify human potential is doomed to failure, but it does help to start with some idea of where you stand. Fitness, age, and general athletic talent are the basic performance and recuperation factors in this rule-of-thumb approach. Score yourself 5 points for each category where you are at the top, 4, 3, 2, and 1 as you descend. Eleven and above is very good; 7 and below suggest caution, at least until you've added subjective knowledge and some mileage. Obviously, indications of heart or blood-pressure problems would override these suggestions.

AGE:

18–27	*5 points*
28–36	*4*
37–47	*3*
48–57	*2*
58–67	*1*

FITNESS: *(Current weekly hours of exercise at pulse 125 +)*

5 +	*5*
4	*4*
3	*3*
2	*2*
1	*1*
0	*0*

TALENT:

Natural Athlete w/good endurance	*5*
Athletic	*4*
Decent at sports	*3*
Below average	*2*
Never bothered	*1*

2.
MORE THAN MEETS THE EYE

The evolution of the bicycle is the story of man's attempt to replace the horse, which from time immemorial was the fastest and classiest way to get around. Like any history, the chronicle of the bicycle is full of claims, counterclaims, confusion, and hard feelings, but no engineer will ever deny that the bicycle is an amazingly clever invention. By any objective evaluation it overwhelmingly outdoes the horse. It is infinitely cheaper to buy and maintain, it is faster at anything except standing-start acceleration, and it can go much farther in a given length of time. No horse has come close to a hundred miles in four hours, but racing cyclists do it all the time, and even touring riders do it in six or seven.

This is not to knock the horse. By multiplying human efficiency by a factor of about five, the bicycle makes man the most energy-efficient creature on planet earth. It is also very efficient at hauling loads; a cyclist can carry up to a third of his body weight many miles each day. The point is best proven in those parts of the world where the economy will not support motor vehicles. During the Southeast Asian wars of the 1960s and 1970s, the North Vietnamese military transport consisted mainly of heavily loaded bicycles running on dirt roads and jungle paths. The system was effective enough to prompt Senator Fulbright to make his famous "bomb the bicycles" remark. (They turned out to be difficult targets.)

ORIGINS

Early ancestors of the bicycle began to appear around 1800, give or take a few years, but it's uncertain who came up with the idea first. In 1790 a French craftsman named Sivrac was said to have made something with two wheels that could be kicked along with one's feet. Others claim that the pioneer balloonist Blanchard also pioneered the bicycle, in 1799. Blanchard did describe "an experiment in mechanics" concerning a horseless carriage, where a man "is either seated or remains standing, with his legs partly hidden in a sort of trunk or chest in which the springs are fixed." Whatever it was, Blanchard's strange device remained "an experiment," and the early "velocifere" was no immediate threat to the horse. It was heavy (70–90 pounds), and could not be steered. By the early 1800s, though, there were a number of these items around, both in France and England. Builders often paid respects to the competition by placing a carved horse's head at the front of this creation. But in 1818 a Baron K. S. Drais von Saurbronn of Baden, Germany, made something similar, sacrificing the horse's head for a steering arrangement. More puzzling is a similar device pictured in a stained glass window made nearly two centuries earlier (circa 1642), in Stokes Pogue, England.

However it came into being, the *draisienne* or hobbyhorse, also known as the Dandy Charger, had numerous problems, starting with the roads of that time, which were largely dirt, no one having built serious roads since the Romans. With or without horsehead or steering, the hobbyhorse was inefficient, very heavy, and lacked brakes or any kind of springs; you couldn't even pedal the thing. It was a novelty and nothing more.

THE DA VINCI BICYCLE

Joining a pair of wheels to make something you could kick along down the road is not a complicated idea; the Stokes Pogue window is at least plausible. But the bicycle drawing in Leonardo Da Vinci's notebooks is something else again. Basically, it is the Safety bicycle developed in 1885, and the coincidence is a little too perfect.

It took some of the most original and creative thinkers in Western technology almost a hundred years of constant experiments to refine the hobbyhorse into the modern "Safety" bicycle. Design features we take for granted took decades to evolve. Da Vinci was both genius and polymath, able to conceive future realities as unlikely in his time as the parachute and the submarine, but it must have taken a very clear view of the future to come up with pedals, chain drive, handlebars, and approximately equal-sized, spoked wheels. Many regard the disputed Da Vinci drawing as cycling's Piltdown man—a very clever hoax.

MACMILLAN INVENTS PEDALING; MICHAUX CASHES IN

After the *draisienne* eliminated the horse's head and introduced steering, the most sophisticated development was Kirkpatrick Mac-Millan's rear-drive machine of 1839. With people still kicking their hobbyhorses along with their feet, just the concept of a drive system was a very big breakthrough. Rear drive was on the money too, but MacMillan had two problems. First, he opted for a kind of treadle-and-rod rather than chain-and-sprocket drive, and second, he was isolated up in the northern British Isles during a time when people and ideas traveled slowly. He became a well-known local figure, setting speed records from town to town and picking up the first traffic ticket when a child ran into his path and was slightly injured. But his invention didn't catch on. Neither did R. W. Thompson's original pneumatic tire of 1845; no one is sure if it actually worked or was just patented.

MACMILLAN'S BICYCLE
This looks much like a draisienne, but pedals and rear drive made it very different.

VELOCIPEDE
This pedal-drive system caught on, and in modified form it's still with us. Michaux was still making a wood-and-metal boneshaker, but it was good enough to set off a second (and larger) bike boom.

The next development came in 1851 (some say earlier) from the French Michaux brothers' shop; their creation had front-wheel pedal drive like a child's tricycle. This direct-drive system kept gearing pretty low, so your legs were spinning madly at very low speeds, but this wasn't noticed at first, because you needed a low gear to get one of these 75-pound babies rolling. Early models were available in 1855, and very soon the Michaux *velocipede* kicked off the first bike boom, complete with enthusiasts, publications, and clubs. As the money rolled in, so did hard feelings. According to an employee named Lallement, the Michaux brothers had been making the usual *draisienne* novelties before he, Lallement, worked out the pedal and crank-arm drive. Getting nowhere with his claims, Lallement quit, came to the U.S., and started his own company, complete with patents. Despite Lallement, the French anointed Ernest Michaux father of the bicycle, and it was unquestionably the Michaux machines that broke the ice. By 1868 the French were racing them, and business boomed until the war of 1870, by which time a number of state-of-the-art velocipedes had found their way to England.

THE BRITISH TAKE OVER

It was good timing. Great Britain was in the grip of a creative ferment that put her in the forefront of the industrial revolution, and ultimately gave Britain control of world markets. Superior technology was the basis for the British industrial empire, and much of that technology came from men working with the bicycle. The British, who had been sidetracked into four-wheel man-powered vehicles, took the velocipede and looked at it as only sophisticated, hands-on engineers can look at a thing, sensing both its problems and its potential.

Working with what became the bicycle, British engineers and inventors developed the ball bearing (invented by the Frenchman Surnay) and the pneumatic tire (reinvented by Dunlop). They built incredibly strong, light, wire-spoked wheels, made chain drive workable, worked out a variable gearing transmission and devised the basic system of control cables used later in aircraft. They also invented the differential, later used in all automobiles, and were pioneers in the sophisticated metallurgy of lightweight steel tubing and aluminum alloy. Most important, they developed an approach to design and construction that is never wrong. They grasped the principles of building strong, light, and simple. This was how the Wright brothers, who understood these principles from running a bicycle shop, were able to construct a flying machine that worked—one with a high power-to-weight ratio.

ENTER THE STARLEYS

The British brought the bicycle to its modern form in about 20 years, largely thanks to James Starley of the Coventry Sewing Machine Company, who, with members of his family, contributed more to the bicycle's evolution than anyone else. The changes came fast. First, the front wheel got bigger and bigger. Starley and others had observed that a velocipede went faster with a bigger front wheel, which gave a higher gear. (You traveled further each time the pedals went around.) Right from the beginning, the British noticed that going fast was a definite possibility. Downhills were dangerous but fun, and with a big enough front wheel you could also roll right along on the flats. The result was the "Ordinary." But as the front wheel got bigger, the rear wheel withered away, unbalancing the machine, making the Ordinary inherently unstable. A look at the Humber Beeston makes it obvious that on some Ordinaries you were damn close to riding a unicycle. But people were willing to take the chance. Like a spooky horse, the Ordinary was a challenge.

PROBLEMS OF THE ORDINARY

As the front wheel got bigger, it developed problems. It got heavier, and it got weaker, and the solid rubber tires of the period did not ab-

ORDINARY
The craving for high performance brought about this dangerous but exciting British variant. The big front wheel created higher gearing, which allowed more speed. The British had already sharpened their technology building 4-wheeled foot-powered vehicles; their best ordinaries were beautifully made and unbelievably light. This Humber Beeston racer weighs 24 pounds.

sorb road shock. Engineers worked out lightweight wire spoking, but wheels still fell apart. Starley solved the problem with tangential (overlapped) spoking which gives a much stronger, shock-absorbent wheel and is still used today. Competition led to more sophisticated metallurgy, and as tubing and construction techniques improved, the frame kept getting lighter. Racing Ordinaries could weigh as little as 20 pounds. But no matter how you looked at it, the thing was a killer. The brake dragged hopefully on a tire, but definitely could not stop the beast. And there was no freewheel, which meant that you took your feet off the pedals on a descent because the pedals were spinning too fast for feet to keep up with.

RADIAL AND TANGENTIAL SPOKING
Spokes on the left (radial) wheel come out straight from the hub; on the right wheel they come out on a tangent to the hub, and each spoke reverses direction, so that they overlap. The latter results in much more strength and flexibility. Typical Starley engineering.

That was all she wrote for some riders, because the center of gravity was way up in the air, making the machine unstable. Going over the bars for a "header" was so common that the word became part of the language. Going over sideways was common too, and just getting the thing under way was a problem in itself. You didn't ride an Ordinary unless you were nervy, strong, and well coordinated. Despite the Victorian notion that one should keep one's knees together, some women mastered this elegant monster and even raced. It was a sign of things to come.

Despite its inherent flaws and the daredevil skills it required, the Ordinary became the main line of bicycle development for more than a

STARLEY'S ROYAL SALVO
This was Starley building for the market. It looks Victorian, and it should; Queen Victoria herself endorsed it. Intended as a lady's machine, it was obviously heavy enough to handicap the rider. Within a few years women were on two-wheelers.

decade, with the Starley leading the field. But while the Starleys were knocking out Ordinaries, they were also experimenting. Tricycles were considered the thing for women, and the Starleys' Royal Salvo series was a big success, partly because of Queen Victoria's endorsement. Pedal power was officially gentrified, and the tricycle emerged as the rich man's machine.

Working out the problems of the tricycle, Starley noticed that one rear wheel always dragged when you went around a corner; to solve the problem he invented the differential, without which automobiles would also drag wheels going around corners. But the real breakthrough was moving to rear wheel drive, more or less ignored since MacMillan's machine about half a century before.

THE ROVER SAFETY—FIRST MODERN BICYCLE

When Starley opted for chain drive to the rear wheel, the Ordinary was doomed, because now you could get any gear you wanted with any size wheel. All you had to do was vary the size of the sprockets. When Dunlop developed a reliable pneumatic tire, everything that really mattered in the modern bicycle was in place. Starley's 1885 Rover had it all: roughly equal-sized wheels (soon to be fitted with pneumatic tires), tangential spoking, chain drive with sprockets that gave a reasonable gear, ball-bearing hubs—and a spring saddle. There were still changes to come, but it was close enough for jazz.

SOCIAL REACTION

In a few years, Safeties were very hot stuff on both sides of the Atlantic, and the shock waves were profound. It was much harder now for people on horses to feel superior; everyone was on a bike. People still rode horses and used them to haul carts and carriages, but in about fifteen years the Safety bicycle had created a new equality, blowing apart social conventions that had lasted for centuries. In the U.S., "scorchers" (fast and reckless riders) were all over the place, going like hell and making people nervous. Special police squads tried to keep them under control.

ODDITIES
These strange machines never went into production, but they illustrate just how differently people were thinking about pedaled vehicles before the basics were worked out. These are only two of the wild rigs proposed in the early days.

As social attitudes leaped forward, so did the quality of American roads. The millions of cyclists, working primarily through The League of American Wheelmen, were able to bring enormous pressure to bear. They became the greatest single influence in the development of paved roads in the U.S.

WOMEN AND THE BICYCLE

The farthest-reaching social effect of the bicycle was its contribution to women's independence. It was extremely difficult to keep women off the new Safeties; the demand was so strong that special "drop-frame" women's models intended for use with skirts were soon available. Amelia Jenks Bloomer argued for a woman's right to wear pants, and despite angry opposition, she won. Soon the new equality included more and more women; it was no longer daring or eccentric to ride. Coming well before such historic confrontations as the right to vote, birth control, and abortion, the bicycle simply cracked open the idea that women were frail and delicate. When Marthe Schotte, riding one of the new experimental three-speed bicycles, defeated the well-

ROVER SAFETY
Starley wasn't the only one working out a safer, lower bicycle, but his had the jump on the market. The Rover looks quaint, but it's surprisingly modern; it set off a third boom in bike sales.

known racing cyclist Eduard Fischer in a mountain road race, the impact was enormous. Very quickly the bicycle ushered in a new attitude: it made athletic coordination and fitness chic for men and women alike.

The convenience and smooth efficiency of the new Safeties appealed to women, and many of them also wanted to wear pants like Schotte and Bloomer. Enough of them did these things to provoke clergymen and other conservative forces to threats of hellfire and social censure. The bicycle was an explosive force, socially. There was no telling who you might meet or what might occur on a bike ride, and this was definitely perceived as a threat to the status quo. Threat or blessing, the bicycle definitely changed some basic behavior in very few years.

COMPETITION

Racing also became a major amateur and professional sport during the nineties, and with it came some important refinements allowing greater efficiency. First came dropped handlebars which improved

MAJOR TAYLOR AND HIS BAR EXTENSION
Taylor was not only faster than his rivals on most days, he was smarter. Early dropped handlebars came in all sizes and shapes, usually creating a cramped position like that of the Ordinary. Taylor's handlebar extension (now called a stem) allowed him a very modern and efficient position. The stem soon became standard equipment.

aerodynamics, followed by the freewheel, which permits coasting (and prompted the development of serious brakes). Then Major Taylor invented the handlebar extension—an adjustable version of what is now called the stem. As seen in the illustration, Taylor, one of the first of the great black American athletes, had figured things out to a nicety. The position allowed by his modernized bar and stem arrangement gave him great efficiency. (Along with the style points award of his day, hands down.) White riders combined against Taylor again and again. In spite of their efforts he was World Champion in 1899, set many records, toured Europe, and established himself as the greatest sprinter since his cigar-smoking mentor, Arthur "Zimmy" Zimmerman, 1893 World Champion.

Taylor rode a Safety, where Zimmy had ridden everything from Ordinaries to Stars (which had the small wheel in *front*). Taylor's preference was a sign of the times. The modern bicycle had truly arrived, and it made the sport popular enough to be allotted seven events in the 1896 Olympics.

FURTHER INNOVATIONS

The technical spin-offs were equally extensive. Bicycle-developed drive and control systems, construction methods, and metallurgy solved all the major mechanical problems presented by the gasoline engine for use on land, sea, and air by 1900. Even before that, Pierre Michaux, Gottlieb Daimler, and Carl Benz were experimenting with steam engines on tricycles. Out of their work came the motorcycle and the automobile. Evolution split into several branches, of which the bicycle continued to be the most energy-efficient. Now it was time for the final refinement that would maximize that efficiency: variable gearing.

VARIABLE GEARING

As a human-powered vehicle, (0.1–0.2 horsepower, depending on how it's figured) the bicycle benefits enormously from proper gearing. Through its ability to adapt to differences in terrain, wind, and rider strength the advantage was clear in Schotte's victory over Fischer in the mountains—Fischer had one gear, Schotte three.

PIERCE SHAFT DRIVE
Shaft drive is slightly heavier and less efficient than chain drive, but the neatness of this design is very appealing to anyone who has ever ruined a pair of pants on a dirty chain. Today's steels would make this system viable. Put a hub gear on it and you have the perfect commuter bike.

HUB GEARS

Experiments were now going on everywhere, but again it was the British Isles that produced the first reliable product. In 1902 three Englishmen developed the classic three-speed internal hub. Henry Sturmey and James Archer got their names on the thing, but for some reason Alfred Pellant never gets credit for having conceived the idea with Sturmey. Their neat little planetary gear system arrived just in time for Henry Ford to use it in his Model T. Alas, Sturmey-Archer and their imitators have basically stuck with the three-speed, although today five and more speeds can be had with the system, making it much better for the long-distance rider.

THE DERAILLEUR

The story of the derailleur (external gear) system is not so neat. Pioneered by the legendary "Velocio" (see page 45) it evolved slowly over the decades, always opposed by purists. Engineers understood the importance of riding in the best possible gear at all times, though. After the idea of multiple cogs caught on, dozens of odd, cumbersome and unreliable methods of shifting the chain from cog to cog came and went. Some required the rider to pedal backward, others required dismounting. Naked, vulnerable, and a little clumsy, the derailleur is a 19th-century concept that still works better than anything else, because it allows a wide selection of gears that make optimum use of a rider's ability. By allowing the rider to pedal at a favorable rhythm almost all the time, the derailleur reduces stress and substantially increases efficiency.

FRAME DESIGN

Although the triangulated "diamond" frame was understood by 1900 to be the strongest design, a look at pictures of old and new bicycles side by side reveals a general trend in geometry toward a more compact and "upright" design over the years. This overall distribution of angles and measurements is known as the geometry of the bicycle, and is an important factor in performance and handling. The most basic factors are *frame angles* (which may be "steep" or "shallow"), *rake* (the amount of curve in the fork), and *wheelbase*—the length of the bike, axle to axle.

Since the early 1900s bicycles have gradually evolved toward steeper angles, less fork rake, and shorter wheelbase, largely because of improved roads and a desire for quicker response, and geometry has become specialized for different uses, as explained in more detail in Chapters 3 and 4.

LINES OF DEVELOPMENT

Gradual improvements in metallurgy, better wheels and tires, and multigear systems were the most important developments from World War II to the present. Three distinct types of bicycles emerged. In Britain and the Low Countries, heavy, reliable, thick-tire (26" × 1⅜" or 1½") utility bikes with one speed drive or three-speed hub gears were very popular. Equipped with steel rims, raised bars, and rod or caliper brakes, they would go on forever despite poor roads.

The major continental style was the lighter, narrow-tired, dropped-handlebar, derailleur bike. For touring, a 700-centimeter, or 27" × 1¼," conventional "clincher" tire like that of an automobile was used; for racing a special and expensive glued-on "tubular" tire was developed with its own type of rim. These derailleur bikes really began to take hold after they were accepted in the Tour de France during the thirties, and they became even more widely accepted after World War II.

In the U.S., where distances are long, the automobile quickly supplanted the adult bicycle, and the single-speed "ballooner," riding on fat 26" × 2.125" tires, became the rural and suburban boy's basic transportation. Even heavier (around 50 pounds) than the European thick-tire bike, this "newsboy" bike used an enclosed rear-hub coaster brake and underwent whimsical design changes based on adolescent fantasies. Spring forks, tanklike construction, foxtails and electric horns came and went. These fat-tire heavyweights completely dominated the U.S. market until Americans who had been to England during World War II brought back what were called English Racers (lighter three-speeds), which began to revive the adult market. The derailleur infiltration began later, and exploded into the bike boom of the early seventies.

IN RETROSPECT

How smart were bicycle people? For nearly a century they were the cutting edge of applied modern science and technology. If a design engineer can be a genius, James Starley qualified; he was a figure at least equal to the legendary automotive Porsche family. Nor was it any accident that the Wright brothers built and flew the first airplane. Riding and working with bicycles, they developed a keen sense of the complexities of motion, gravitational effect, torque, stall-speed, and the changes that occur during acceleration and turning. It laid the groundwork for a more sophisticated sense of the infant science of aerodynamics than they were given credit for. Orville Wright's remark that ". . . because we were bicycle people, we understood that to turn you must also bank" is a classic Yankee understatement of a first principle in aerodynamics.

But the bicycle is more than a stage in the transportation revolution or an instrument of social progress. It goes on and on with amazing tenacity, continuing to evolve new forms. Like the bark canoe or the sailplane, it is a gorgeous, original creation, an engineer's dream that exists at the edge of poetry, a complex experience, a thing to fall in love with, elusive in its demands, satisfying in a truly unique way, hypnotic and seductive once you get past its defenses. Do right by a bicycle, and it gives you something back. It is an oddity in this smash-and-grab modern world—it can't be bullied any more than a musical instrument can. And it has its favorites. There are those who are ordinary mortals off a bicycle, but who somehow rise above themselves on one, through a sense of its rhythms and how it is meant to be used. Just as a Sterling Moss or Richard Petty was born to drive a car, an Eddy Merckx or Velocio fulfills the bicycle.

Where the bicycle goes from here is an interesting question. What the bicycle is in present form and what it means to people may be the better question, and this has been dealt with by some of the very best European and American writers. Ernest Hemingway is famous for his observations on bullfighting, but he understood bicycle racing enough to write well about it in short stories, and in his famous novel *The Sun Also Rises* he accomplishes a significant change in tone after the bull-fight episodes when the narrator happens upon a racing team in the middle of the Vuelta de España—Spain's Tour de France. The gulf between bullfighting and bicycle racing becomes the difference between a stylistic confrontation with death and the all-suffering determination of the riders, whose test spans weeks rather than minutes.

Less dramatic but deeper is F. Scott Fitzgerald's treatment of the bicycle in *Tender Is the Night*. Here the hero's detachment from the artifice and complexity of his wife's rich and selfish world is signified by the persistent individualism of his bicycle trips. At the end he rides right back to his obscure American roots.

James Joyce, Samuel Beckett, Leo Tolstoy, Bertrand Russell, George Bernard Shaw, and T. E. Lawrence (of Arabia) were all committed cyclists who recognized and wrote well about the mystique of the bicycle and its pleasures, but none gets to the point better than Irish novelist Flann O'Brien. A droll streak of observations about the relationship of man and machine runs through his novels. Various characters express views on the ethics of multiple gearing, whether or not bicycles might perhaps eat food left overnight on the table, and the possibility that with long use a bicycle and rider may exchange *molecules* (as a country constable explains it), creating a legal problem as the one becomes indistinguishable from the other.

VELOCIO

Of all the millions of cyclists since Sivrac and von Drais, none was better known and respected among the riders themselves than Paul de Vivie, better known as Velocio. Born in 1853, he rolled on to the ripe age of 77, and his relationship to cycling was somewhat like that of Louis Armstrong to jazz; he was there almost at the beginning and lived to see modern times. And like the immortal Satchmo, he cut a figure that cannot be ignored. In his seventies he wiped out a young rider named Philippe Marre on an overnight ride of 400 kilometers, which Marre duly recorded as one of his most amazing experiences on or off a bicycle.

Unlike some of his followers, Velocio shrewdly anticipated modern developments and looked forward to them. His memorial plaque describes him thusly: "Apostle of the Multi-gear system"—the derailleur. A classics scholar in his youth, he became the foremost cycling journalist of his time,

**VELOCIO AND
A FAVORITE BIKE**

(continued)

but his writing never diverted him from the bicycle itself. He remained interested in technical innovations all his life, never losing perspective in the sea of gadgets that came and went.

Velocio was an odd mixture of leader and recluse, and his influence was pervasive. After his start as a scholar he worked as representative of a silk manufacturer for a while, but by 1885 he was involved in bicycle manufacturing. A few years later he started a magazine, Le Cycliste, *and took on the pen name that eclipsed his own. But Velocio was the exact opposite of most cycling journalists in many ways. Not only was his education far superior, he was also a legendary rider of long distances in the aggressive "cyclo-sportif" style, which gave him opportunity to test theories and equipment ruthlessly. When something passed his test, he became its advocate, and his extremely forthright views were respected for their wisdom and accuracy. His notions on gearing could not have been more on target; as discussed in Chapter 8, they are still applicable today.*

His personal reputation was such that there is a worldwide school of Velocio fans who still meet each year at the top of a small mountain near Saint-Étienne, France where he lived. Like Velocio, they are sportif; they climb hard and time themselves up the hill. If there is an aristocracy of touring cyclists, it is these people, and they ride by what some call the Seven Commandments—Velocio's rules for cycling. These are sacred for some, but as with all religious doctrines, there is room for sects and interpretations owing to a bit of ambiguity. On the other hand, these are the best set of cycling rules ever put together for general use, and they provide a much better starting point for the inexperienced cyclist than leafing through magazine articles by narrower minded and less experienced enthusiasts caught up in passing fads.

The best thing about the rules, and the man himself, is that they look past the hardware at the experience itself. Velocio's sense of the mental and physical aspects of riding a bicycle comes from almost infinite experience examined by a very sharp mind.

VELOCIO'S COMMANDMENTS

1. *Stop briefly and not too often, so as not to chill or lose your rhythm.*
2. *Eat frequently and lightly; eat before you are hungry, drink before you are thirsty.*
3. *Don't push yourself until you're too tired to eat or sleep.*
4. *Add clothing before you are cold, take it off before you are hot; but don't avoid sun, air, and rain.*
5. *Avoid alcohol and meat, at least while on the road.*
6. *Ride within your limits. Learn your pace and don't be tempted to force yourself during the first hours of a ride, when you are fresh.*
7. *Don't show off ("ride out of vanity").*

3.
TODAY'S BICYCLES

During the bike boom of the early 1970s, America fell in love with the dropped-bar derailleur bicycle, otherwise known as the ten-speed. Sales of these bicycles rocketed, and imports took a big share of the market. Along with the sales boom came what might be called the real boom. Not only did bicycles begin to reappear in larger and larger numbers, but pedal power evolved to produce such unexpected events as human-powered flight, a motor-paced speed record of 138 mph (see page 66), and exotic human-powered vehicles (HPVs) that can break 60 mph. Even the drivetrain has been modified, as in the cam-drive device of inventor Larry Brown.

At the same time bicycle racing began to rouse itself from years of dormancy and American racers emerged on the international scene again, notably Greg Le Mond, world champion first as an amateur in 1979, then as a professional in 1983. Ecology, rocketing fuel costs, and a sports/fitness boom combined to make the bicycle attractive. National and international cycling organizations mushroomed, as did publications in the field, and U.S. advertisers found they could sell all kinds of products by associating them with the bicycle.

The bicycle itself has changed significantly, too. Along with such engineering dead ends as oval tubing and aerodynamic brakes came stronger, lighter frames and components. Some of the new bicycles are significantly different too. They are adaptations to new demands made by very creative designers.

BALLOONERS: THE BMX

If the ten-speed boom of the early 1970s was the most obvious sign of renewed interest in cycling, the subsequent BMX "mini-ballooner" wave has turned out to be the beginning of a whole new "fat-tire" boom. The BMX (short for bicycle moto-cross) is essentially a kid's bike, but it is light-years from the unsafe banana-seated "hi-rise" mini-clunker that dominated the juvenile market for over a decade. Designed for dirt-track short-course racing by kids as young as seven, the BMX is also a neighborhood fun bike that will perform miraculous acrobatics in the hands of a good rider. Some of the finest shots of bikes in action have been taken of young BMXers doing "radical maneuvers." The design evolved out of attempts to prepare young children for dirt-track motor-cycle racing, grew very quickly into a fad, and soon attracted a nation-wide network of riders, complete with tracks, federations, and over 100,000 registered participants.

BMX is California all the way, in concept, design, and execution. These bikes take tremendous punishment, but the good ones rarely fail under stress. Not since the turn of the century, when U.S. technical

RADICAL ACTION, CALIFORNIA STYLE
The new seventies style in juvenile bikes was set because kids could do things like this with a BMX bike; innovative adult ballooners followed.

creativity in the field was second to none, has American design shown such excellence and originality. The proof is in the BMX sweep of world juvenile markets, and in its spin-offs, the off-road bicycle and the cruiser.

ADULT BALLOONERS

These full-size, "fat-tire" bikes have caught on solidly. Ballooners are safe, steady bicycles, somewhat slower and less efficient than dropped-bar derailleur bikes, but much more adaptable. They thrive on terrain that defeats the ten-speed. The adult ballooner came into being as young riders outgrew the BMX, which is essentially a sprint bike, not suited to distances. They were looking for something with a similar feel but greater range and flexibility. California designer-builders came up with the high-performance all-terrain bike and the low-priced short-range cruiser.

CRUISER

The simple, inexpensive cruiser is good for knocking around the neighborhood and having fun, and because of the wide (26″ × 2.125″)

CRUISER
The Ross Curb Crusher sells for under $200. This is low-cost, short-distance transportation, with the basic appeal of simple, rugged, balloon-tired equipment. Not a bad deal for knocking around town.

tires, it handles beaches and dirt roads better than anything with narrow ones. It's also an excellent city bike (except when being carried up stairs), and short-distance commuters find this bike an interesting and reliable alternative to the three-speed. Offered with anything from coaster-brake or three-speed hub to a wide-range derailleur system, the cruiser does not usually have expensive components, and is not a preferred target for bike thieves. If you are looking for the odd hour of exercise combined with trips to the mall, the cruiser is something to think about. With a quick-release device on the seatpost to allow easy adjustment, it can be used by anyone in the family. Passable ones start below $200.

THE MOUNTAIN BIKE

Also called the off-road or all-terrain bicycle, the mountain bike is the most radical departure in concept since the BMX and its ability to leave cars and trucks behind appeals to something very deep in many people these days. Sophisticated design has produced bicycles that are stronger than any other kind, yet weigh little more than conventional touring bikes. If you're willing to pay for it, a state-of-the-art specimen can weigh in as low as 26 bulletproof pounds, though it will cost you close to $2,000. For about $600, you can get one that won't let you down, and it will still be under 30 pounds. Designers have also created regional variations, including a whole separate "Colorado style" of all-terrain bicycle adapted to rocky terrain.

The beauty of the mountain bike is that it brings riders to territory that was previously available mainly to motorcyclists—but it does so without tearing up fragile wilderness areas. It would take dozens of off-roaders doing their worst to equal the damage inflicted by an off-road motorcycle, for which high-power wheel spin is the big kick. Even horses do more damage than these mountain bikes.

For years riders had been modifying conventional bicycles to get off paved roads, but the inherent limitations of the dropped-bar derailleur (ten-speed) and the three-speed created problems. The all-terrain design provides the ideal solution. Handling, traction, and ruggedness are the strong points, and there is a whole new generation of components designed to take the punishment. These bikes feel good going down a grassy hill at 40 mph or climbing a pebbly gulch at walking speed. They have something to offer a wide range of riders, from backcountry camper-tourists to competitors. By leaving powered vehi-

MOUNTAINBIKE
This is the MountainBike Montari; price about $650. Other models go for up to
$2,000. Any resemblance to the Cruiser is superficial; all-terrain bikes are not cheap,
but they are the most adaptable two-wheelers around, and have opened up a new
world for many riders.

cles behind, the all-terrain bicycle can take you as far from civilization
as you want to get.

CONSTRUCTION

There is no such thing as a good, cheap, off-road bike because it
costs money to build frame and components that take sharp, repeated
stress from every angle. Bars, stem, seatpost, wheels, tires, fork, and
frame have been redesigned from scratch, and the result is a handsome beast that you have to respect. Wheels are usually 26″ × 2.125″
or 1.75″ and tires are cleated for off-road, smooth for highways. Gearing
is wide-range, with as many as 18 or 21 forward gears or "speeds".

How does an off-roader do on the road? Better than a three-speed, because of lighter wheels and better gearing; better yet with the 1.75″ rims and smooth tires. All-terrain bikes are truly what the name implies, and as one hard-core conventional road racer remarked, "this thing is hard on prejudices." MountainBike designer and manufacturer Gary Fisher has ridden century (hundred-mile) road runs with dropped-bar addicts and lived to laugh about it.

THE DROPPED-BAR DERAILLEUR

This very different design is the basic mass-market bike, and it is still the most popular U.S. bike in terms of units sold. The basic design is adaptable to touring, racing, or any kind of long-distance riding on paved roads. It is the most efficient design for most uses because it couples the human body to the bike in a way that makes very good use of the big thigh and lower-back muscles, and creates (via the dropped bars) a relatively aerodynamic position. A strong, skilled rider on a well-fitted machine can cover more ground on this kind of bike than any other. Even with loads in the 30–50 pound range, tourists routinely cover 50–75 miles daily, and 1981 Iron Man triathlon champion John Howard was on a dropped-bar derailleur bike when he rode the record 513 miles in the 24-hour Central Park Pepsi Bikathon of 1983. Lon Haldeman used a basically similar machine to cross the U.S. in less than ten days.

Howard and Haldeman rode these epics on light, competition-level equipment, machines only superficially similar to the typical low-priced ten-speed. This brings home a good point—the dérailleur bicycle can be anything from a $2,000 work of art to a $90 waste of time and money. The similarity is only in general design; supermarket bikes are built with different materials, often with nonstandard components. They are unreliable, difficult to repair, and generally a bad experience. Good bike shops avoid them. Better derailleur bikes fall into three categories: general purpose or mass market, racing, and touring.

MASS-MARKET BIKES

Most mid-price ($200–$300) derailleur bikes are more or less touring bikes, at least so far as gearing, wheels, tires, and general design are concerned, and they offer outstanding value. Recently there has been more choice in design, so that you can now buy a mid-price machine with relatively tight, responsive geometry. Contemporary drop-frame women's models usually come in the "mixte" style, which allows a lower seat.

Because the dropped-bar derailleur is so popular, mass production and competition for this lucrative market keeps prices down. You can get a reliable but heavy steel-component derailleur bike for around $200, and for another $100 you can find a lighter one with good alloy components and better tubing. The bike of the 1980s is a better machine than that of the 1970s for several reasons, the primary one being a determined effort by Oriental manufacturers to improve their bikes and sell more of them. By attacking this market with reliable, low-price components and superior quality control, they have accomplished their aim, and raised standards generally for mid-price bikes. The eighties have revealed a countereffort by U.S. and European manufacturers. All of this has been very beneficial for consumers; competition has removed most of the really poor equipment from the market.

With minor modifications, many bikes in the $280–plus range are

MASS MARKET TEN-SPEED
The $260 Schwinn Le Tour, a mid-price "ten-speed." Dollar for dollar this class of bike gives the most for your money.

MIXTE
Fuji's Royale is a 12-speed upper mid-price (about $365) derailleur bike that fits smaller riders. The mixte is the best of the drop-frame designs, and is found with both raised and dropped handlebars. The twelve speeds (rather than ten) are a plus.

adaptable for touring, training, and simply riding medium to long distances for pleasure. Iron Man Howard has pointed out that this class of bike is adequate for most triathlon competitions if suitably modified, and there are now bikes specially designed for this kind of hard, fast riding (see page 56). If you are athletically inclined, or want to ride long distances, the dropped-bar derailleur is probably what you want. Chapters 7 and 8 describe how to get the most out of it.

TOURER

There is as much variation in touring bike design as there is in tourists, but the term generally indicates medium to wide (1⅛″–1⅜″) tires, a wheelbase of 40″ or more, and fairly laid-back geometry that handles well under load; stability is important. One thing all real tourers share is inconspicuous brazed-on fittings that make it easy to attach racks, mudguards, etc. Another thing they share is quality. Good stock touring bicycles run in the mid–$300 range and up, and custom models cost as much as good racing bikes ($1,000–plus). Tubing for a custom tourer is slightly different from that of the racing bike but of the

TRIATHLON BIKE

This Miyata 710 (about $350) is a good example of the trend to more diverse design in recent upper mid-price bicycles. It is a performance machine. Its narrow one–inch rims and tires have low rolling resistance; its tubes are high-quality chrome-molybdenum steel, and it has a general neatness of design and construction that appeals to the performance-minded purchaser who is not ready to spend a fortune on a pure racing bike.

Most important, it has quite a stiff frame, with 73-degree

parallel frame angles (explained in the next chapter) and what is called a "tight rear triangle" in racing circles. (This simply means that the rear wheel is close to the crank axle, so that less energy is wasted in frame-flexing when the bike is pedaled hard.) At the same time, the fork is not so straight that it sends road shock directly to the wrists. Current models are upgraded with Dia-Compe GX 500 brakes, Sanshin hubs, and SunTour Cyclone dérailleur.

This bike and others like it are the result of a new and growing market created by the triathlon, which includes a bike leg along with the swim and run, and also by growing sophistication on the part of the fitness buff, who wants a crisper feel.

same quality, and usually from the same manufacturers. (Chapter 11 goes into the fine points.)

Gearing is different from that of a racing bike, though. It's wider in range, to allow for the weight of panniers (the bicycle equivalent of saddlebags). For heavy touring, very low gears are required, along with a wide-range derailleur to handle them, as per Chapter 8.

TOURER
Schwinn's reputation for reliability goes way back, which is important to a touring bike. This Voyageur has stable geometry plus front and rear racks. Brazed-on fittings make it easy to mount water bottle and fenders. In the mid-$400 range, it is a good buy, not really too different from bikes costing two and three times as much. The panniers (packs) and bar bag are by Kirtland.

ROAD RACER

This machine is state of the art when it comes to covering ground fast. Constructed of the best possible steel, aluminum, and titanium alloys, it is one very uncompromised piece of equipment, riding on special, very light tubular wheels and tires. The road-racing bicycle has tight geometry—a shorter wheelbase than that of a touring bike, with more upright angles and a straighter fork. With the typical padded plastic saddle, this gives a hard but well-controlled ride.

These are very exciting bicycles, very responsive to hard pedaling,

ROAD RACER

Not for everyone, but a fine piece of equipment that can be adapted for street use. This one is by Peter Mooney, price about $1400, depending on components. Except for the lightweight tubular tires and rims, racing bikes are very tough. Bike thieves prefer them above all else.

TRACK BIKE

The track bike speaks for itself; it's for going fast. It's also the purest, most elegant form of classic design. Antique stem from the John Allis collection. Stock models run as low as $400; custom models about three times as much.

with sensitive steering and 12 or 14 gears. These are arranged in a close ratio that allows the rider to make precise adjustments for wind, terrain, and other conditions. But this is not just anybody's bike. Usually priced in or near the $1,000 range, it is eminently stealable. Its tires are frail, only the strong can cope with its gearing, and its steering may be too sensitive for the casual rider to handle when he or she is getting tired. None of which changes the fact that if you love fine machinery and performance, there is enormous pleasure to be had from a racing bike, especially after it has been modified to fit your needs and abilities. There are lots of people who won't ride anything else, and with good reason. It can be an excellent all-around bike for the athlete, or for someone who appreciates the feel of good equipment.

TRACK BIKE

Many noncyclists immediately sense the truth about a classic track bike the first time they see one. It is the quintessential bicycle, with absolutely nothing to mar its beauty. Very upright angles combine with short wheelbase to express the imminent possibility of swift movement. The absence of derailleur, brakes, and all other impedimenta make the message perfectly clear. If Starley had a dream, this was it. As purchased, the track bike has no brakes; it is controlled by the single "fixed" gear, which has no freewheel, hence no coasting. You slow a track bike down by resisting the motion of the pedals, and controlling one is a skill not easily mastered. Even with a brake it's tricky.

Track bikes are specialized for different events, and some strange new creations have been developed for individual events run against the clock, where aerodynamics are crucial (pg 322). The classics, though, are those designed for the match sprint and six-day events, described in Chapter 12. The former is beefier, with very deep bars; the latter is designed with an eye toward the smoother ride required by longer distance. Some people ride track bikes on the street, usually with a front brake—high style in New York City circa 1984—but don't try it unless you already know everything in this book and have plenty of track-racing experience. With anything less than an expert on board, the track bike has a mind of its own, and it does not suffer fools gladly.

THREE-SPEED

Every year people talk about a revival of three-speed sales, and every year it fails to happen. Partly this is because the three-speed is virtually indestructible. You don't sell three-speeds again and again to the same customer; the proven design, all-steel construction, enclosed gearbox and very solid rims and tires (26″ × 1⅜″) add up to a bike that can take punishment and go on forever. Less expensive than a good derailleur bike (prices for most models range between $150–$250), the three-speed is very practical, especially in urban and suburban areas. It is the basic commuter bike for short runs, and the upright riding position lets you see everything in traffic. Another advantage is that you can shift gears when stopped at a light, which you can't with a derailleur bike. And the gears are just about completely trouble-free.

The three-speed's nemesis is the long hill. Here its gearing is simply not adequate, and its weight begins to tell, though there are strong and determined people who knock off 60–70 hilly miles in a day on a three-speed. But if you need an inexpensive bike you can rely on every

THREE-SPEED
Raleigh has made all manner of three-speeds right from the beginning. This is the Roadster, priced under $200. These bikes don't change a great deal because the kinks were worked out years ago. Good ones aren't cheap, but they are definitely cost-effective.

day without worrying about it, the three-speed is it. Like the old Volks-wagen Beetle, it is a tenacious piece of engineering that works better than it looks. Its comeback will probably occur whenever someone gets around to putting a reliable five-speed in that rear hub, takes a few pounds off the thing, and updates the geometry. Current Japanese models show signs of significant change: 27″ wheels with alloy rims, alloy components, and different frame sizes are available, though still with the usual three-speed hub. Fuji, Miyata, and Sekai all make mod-els in the low to high $200. range.

FOLDERS

The first thing you want to know about a folding bicycle is whether the thing can be ridden without annoyance. Some are so precarious and flimsy that you're forced to invent a whole new way of riding. Basic stability depends largely on wheel size (usually 16″ or 20″), geometry and rigidity; other considerations are reliability, weight, ease of folding and setting up, size when folded, and price. If you have long legs, make sure the seatpost and stem are long enough.

Prices for the small-wheel folder range from under $200 for inex-pensive heavy ones, to around $400 for exotica, but regardless of price most people find this type of bike best adapted to short distances.

FOLDING BICYCLE
This $300 Hon folder is one bike you can get in the trunk of your car. Made of stainless steel and aluminum alloy, it weighs 27 pounds and is rigid enough to be stable under hard pedaling. Racer George Mount has jumped into races on a Hon and stayed with the field long enough to surprise people.

Bickerton, Brompton, De Blazi, Hon, Peugeot, Pocket Bike, and Raleigh are among the current manufacturers. Some ride and handle far better than others, so try before you buy; a flimsy or unstable bike is trouble.

There are also folding bicycles built on standard (27" or 700cm) wheels. The large-wheel folder is rare, but it can be done well; the famous Rene Herse built collapsible tourers, and today the Montague Company (3042 Newark Street N.W., Washington, DC) makes a 22" frame, 27" wheel dropped-bar derailleur folding bike that weighs 26 pounds and sells for $600. It does not fold as compactly as those listed above, but is comfortably ridable for longer distances.

TRICYCLES

Exactly why anyone would add a third wheel to something that functions perfectly on two is a legitimate question.

Obviously the heavier, more wind-resistant trike will never be quite as fast as a bicycle, but there are people who swear by the experience.

ADULT TRICYCLE
The adult recreational trike definitely has its uses. This $275 Worksman has three speeds. Florida is full of trikes like these; senior citizens who don't want to risk a fall can go out on one without worrying.

Most people assume that the trike is easier to ride because it is inherently more stable, but this changes at high speeds, and anyone who ever took a fast corner on one would have second thoughts about that idea. Pictures of racing tricycles going through corners fast show strange and unusual contortions of the human body. The handling basics are totally unique, and five-time Tour de France winner Jacques Anquetil took a celebrated spill while learning the art.

THE NEIGHBORHOOD TRIKE

Completely different from this high-performance machine is the low-speed neighborhood trike intended for suburban transportation. While the racing trike is a high-strung, high-performance animal rarely seen outside the British Isles, the inexpensive, low-speed, utility tricycle is quite popular in some sections of the U.S. It's just about perfect for hauling a few bags of groceries a few miles. The upright position is easy to master, and the trike is very visible in traffic. These ballooner-tricycles are very popular in retirement villages, even with people who never rode bicycles; the car stays in the garage while the tricycle provides both moderate exercise and short-distance transportation for rider and packages.

One- and three-speed models are available, in the $180–$275 range, and the three-speed is much the better choice, especially for the less athletic rider. Going up through the gears improves acceleration (helpful in traffic), and you have the three-speed advantage of being able to shift while stopped at a light. You can also roll right along with a tailwind in high gear.

TANDEMS

The tandem bicycle has been around for a long time and has enduring appeal. It's a fun machine, but it's also a much more complicated piece of machinery than it seems to be, and is very different from the ordinary bicycle. The parts all look familiar, but very little about it is standard. Because the load is doubled, and because the frame is longer, stress levels are much higher. This means that a reasonably good tandem requires different tubing, brakes, wheels, tires, etc. Tandems made of standard tubing and components are much too flexible and don't stand up very well—which means, in practice, an annoying

THE TANDEM
This well-engineered Sovereign is the top of the Santana line: about $2600. Their basically similar Arriva sells for about $1800. Good tandems are expensive, and usually come from outfits that specialize in this type. "There's not much point in a cheap tandem," says John Allis, "Over the miles it will tend to give persistent problems."

and unreliable piece of equipment, unless you limit yourself to easy day trips. Tandems are also expensive because fewer are manufactured, offsetting the normal advantages of mass production. What it boils down to is this: while you can buy a very decent bicycle for about $300, you will pay many times that for a good tandem.

This suggests that the tandem is not a good choice for a first bicycle, but it definitely does not mean that you should stop thinking about a tandem, because a good one is really a pleasure to ride. The solution is to beg, borrow, or steal the use of a tandem for at least a weekend before making the commitment; a given pair of riders tends to be either more or less compatible on one of these things than they are on separate bikes, and you definitely don't want to take the plunge if your partner isn't into it.

MAINTAINING A TANDEM

No one should buy a tandem without being ready to do at least basic repairs. Because of the higher stresses involved, there tend to be more popped spokes and other minor failures on a tandem—except for the best ones. Nor is every bike shop ready to provide heavy-duty extra-length cables, heavy straight-gauge spokes, etc. A tandem is a project, not something to trifle with, and your best guarantee of satisfaction is to buy a really good one, which runs roughly in the area of $2,000. If price is the downside, the upside is that a well-coordinated tandem team can run the wheels off most riders on standard bikes in flat and rolling country. They are less terrific on sustained climbing, but not really as bad as some people think, so long as the gearing is right. Rapid descents will release all available adrenaline and convince you of the need for special brakes and substantial tires. Talk to experienced tandem owners before buying.

NEW DEVELOPMENTS

The recumbent bicycle strikes many cyclists about the same way early Safeties struck experienced riders of the Ordinary—not quite the real thing. When they first appeared in Europe half a century ago and showed signs of outracing the conventional bike, they were outlawed from competition. This is one reason why the idea of pedaling from a seated-reclining position has never caught on as a mass-production item. Now there are signs that this may change, perhaps because the recumbent does deal with a root problem of the bicycle, which is wind resistance.

There are face-forward recumbents in which brave people lead with their chins in the interest of greater speed, but the main line of

RECUMBENT
M.I.T.'s Dr. David Gordon Wilson, noted cycling authority and proponent of recumbent design, seen here on the Avatar recumbent bicycle. NASA scientists observe. Recumbents were a rare item for years, but recently several companies have begun production.

development is feet first, which has the advantage of not throwing you over the bars in a spill. With no streamlining, the reduction in wind resistance over a conventional dropped-bar bike is usually estimated to be somewhere around 20–30 percent at road speeds—a considerable breakthrough when you consider that wind resistance is by far the major energy drain even at medium (12–18 mph) cycling speeds.

If the recumbent has a weakness, it is evident on certain types of hills. You cannot use the out-of-saddle climbing position used with a conventional bike on steep climbs, which deploys muscle groups differently. But the controversy is far from settled according to M.I.T.'s David Gordon Wilson, a leading designer of street-legal recumbents. Coauthor of the excellent book *Bicycling Science* (MIT Press: Cambridge, MA 1982), Dr. Wilson is notorious for tooling around the Boston-Cambridge area at remarkable speeds.

HPVs

Wind resistance being as critical as it is to bicycle performance, people have been streamlining bikes for at least half a century. The small Zzipper Fairing (Chapter 10) reduces drag about 20% at 20 mph, and a full-enclosure Fairing slices drag radically.

Fully enclosed, highly streamlined tandem recumbents known as Human Powered Vehicles (HPVs) have broken 60 mph for short periods under favorable conditions, which included top competitive athletes to crank them, no severe sidewinds, and flat terrain. These are unusual conditions though, and there are practical drawbacks. HPVs cost thousands of dollars, are vulnerable to sidewinds, and are several times heavier than conventional bikes. Climbing a long hill on a hot summer day inside one can be something like pedaling in a sauna—uncomfortable and even dangerous.

LAND SPEED RECORD

Ever since discovering the importance of wind resistance, racing cyclists have had "paced" events and records. At first riders would tuck into the draft of a tandem, triplet, or quadricycle ahead of them, and this would get a rider up around 50 mph for short periods. Mile-a-Minute Murphy broke 60 mph behind a train, and with motorcycles speeds rose further. Then came an increasingly wild sequence of record attempts going past 100 mph and leading to the creation below, pictured with its inventor and rider, John Howard, built for a go at the 138 mph record set on the Bonneville Salt Flats by Dr. Allan Abbott. The gearing is preposterously high, and it takes forever to get rolling, but Howard rode it at 125 mph for a measured mile on a bumpy Mexican highway, which may be one of the riskiest things ever done on a bicycle.

This is a specialty, and a dangerous one. In his attack on Abbott's record, Howard nearly spilled at 110 mph, the bike leaning over so far that he scraped a pedal on the road. Long-time world record holder José Mieffret broke nearly every bone in his body and sustained four separate skull fractures in one attempt; he put himself back together and raced again.

JOHN HOWARD AT 125 MPH

HPV
(left) Interesting but very expensive and not too practical, the Human Powered Vehicle can really fly under the right conditions. Wedged into this one before a record run is speedskater-cyclist Eric Heiden. This is definitely not a commuter vehicle.

4.
FRAME AND COMPONENTS

Unlike the automobile, which is a more or less integral unit, the bicycle is simply a frame with various components attached to it. The options are almost unlimited, posing a great temptation to the mechanically inclined, but the two basic criteria for selecting components are simple: they should meet your particular needs, and they must be reliable. Few bikes are perfectly suited to their owners as purchased, but modifying them is not a big problem.

This is a good thing. Most riders eventually become dissatisfied with one or more components, often with reason. Choosing replacement parts can be difficult though, and the inexperienced buyer is lost without some basic knowledge. Recent technology has flooded the market with new options, some legitimate, some cosmetic. Experienced riders are the best source of accurate information, and magazines like *Bicycling!* (Emmaus PA) and *Bicycle Guide* (Allentown PA) *Cyclist* (Torrance CA) can keep your information current.

CURRENT DEVELOPMENTS

Some of the seemingly dramatic changes of recent years don't make much difference. Oval frame tubes may reduce wind resistance marginally in some competitive events, but a recent U.S. team found that such tubes affected handling characteristics for the worse—and in any case, the rider stays the same shape, and continues to provide most of the wind resistance. Likewise a ten-year-old Campagnolo Nuovo Record derailleur remains an excellent and desirable piece of

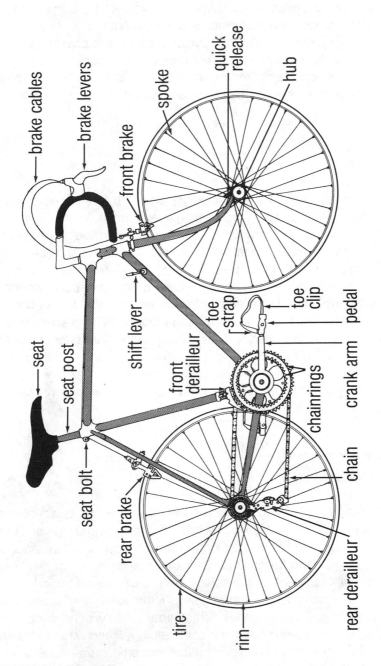

THE DERAILLEUR BIKE

brake cables

brake levers

front brake

spoke

quick release

hub

seat

seat post

shift lever

front derailleur

toe strap

toe clip

pedal

crank arm

chainrings

chain

seat bolt

rear brake

rear derailleur

tire

rim

equipment; some things evolve to the point where improvement is difficult to measure. On the other hand, today's much wider range of rim and tire options can change the whole feel of your bike. Sometimes the search for improvement has produced equipment that is flaky and potentially dangerous, or absurdly overpriced. Plastic brakes, titanium axles and $200-freewheels are not the answer, except in record attempts. Steel and aluminum (known in bike circles as *alloy*) are basic construction materials you can trust and afford.

WEIGHT

Space-age technology means *light,* and with careful design it can also mean *strong,* but the combination is expensive. Weight in itself is not always critical. Like any wheeled vehicle the bicycle has two kinds of weight—*static* (frame, seat, handlebars, etc.) and *rolling* (which the rider must turn with each pedal stroke). This includes tires, rims, spokes, pedals, cranks, and chains. Even a pound of static weight is not really important, but rolling weight is critical, and the further the weight from its turning center, the more it counts. This makes tire and rim weight *extremely* important, especially to the light rider. It used to be said by racing cyclists that an ounce in the wheel (i.e., tire and rim) was worth a pound in the frame, and while this is an exaggeration, it does clarify an important point—avoid clodhopper wheels unless you are sure you can live with them.

COMPATIBILITY

One of the annoying realities of the bicycle is that basic international standards for such things as bolt threading, tube diameters, etc., are still evolving. Bike building began as a cottage industry, and the French, British, and Italians had their own standards for generations. Because of this, you buy a machine built to one standard, and stick with this. The alternative is to have things rethreaded, which can create serious problems. Italian and British standards are widely accepted in the U.S., and they also have some compatibility; French standard parts are harder to find and are not compatible with others; even tube diameters are different. Complete details of this international fricassee are available in *Sutherland's Handbook for Bicycle Mechanics*. (Sutherland Publications: Berkeley, CA)

For most U.S. buyers, Italian/British standards are the way to go, partly because of semicompatibility (if you know what you are doing), partly because the Japanese usually follow this pattern, and partly because the parts are more available. It is extremely exasperating to find that you can't find parts to fix your bike. With low-price supermarket/department store bikes it happens all the time, because the manufacturers will use whatever they can purchase cheaply. The result is a disposable bicycle. Some manufacturers change designs frequently for no valid technical reason; dealers cannot keep up with the need for replacement parts and there are serious repair problems.

FRAME AND FORK

The frame is the heart of the bicycle, and frame design is an art. In the search for perfection, frames have been made of everything—aluminum, titanium, boron, graphite, plastic, bamboo, and steel. For all but a few riders, steel tubing is still the best in terms of strength-to-weight ratio, durability, and cost, though aluminum is now gaining favor.

Likewise, the truly wild constellation of frame geometries explored since the *draisienne* has been reduced by research and experiment to a relatively narrow range of angles and tube lengths. Early bicycles had many curved tubes, and sometimes double sets of small tubes rather than single bigger ones. Some tubes were more important than others, and as research and experiment continued, the triangulated diamond frame all but eliminated other designs, because it is stronger and lighter. The basic design is varied to fit almost any need, from BMX dirt-track racing to long-distance touring. If the diamond frame has a weakness, it is the fork, which is its only unsupported element. Careful blade and crown design compensate for this on good bikes.

Of the so-called women's ("drop") frames, the mixte is the best engineered; it solves the problems of a lower seat for smaller riders and is superior to the conventional drop frame, which is an inherently weak design. Purists say bad things about the slightly heavier and more flexible mixte, but when it is well designed and constructed with quality tubing, it is perfectly all right except for competition.

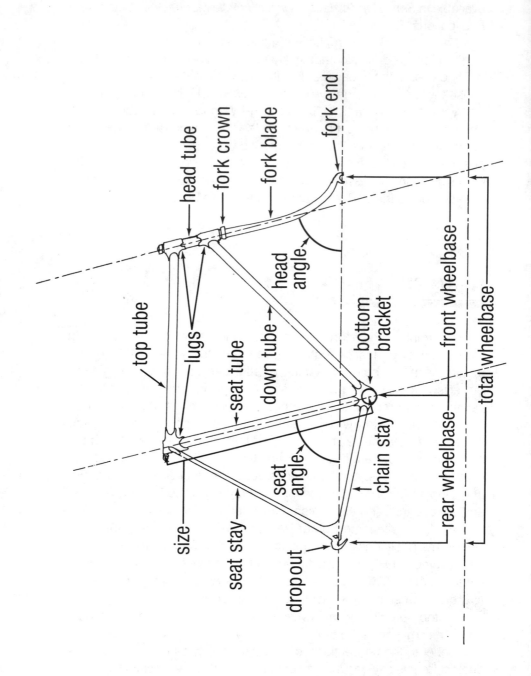

THE FRAME

HOW GEOMETRY RELATES TO USE

As mentioned in Chapter 2, wheelbase, frame angles, and fork design have a direct connection with how a bicycle handles and responds. A short bike with a "tight rear triangle" (distance from bottom bracket to rear axle) makes for super response; a high bottom bracket raises the pedals and lets you pedal through corners; shallow angles make for stability, etc. Thus, bicycles can be categorized by geometry: the track-sprint bike is one end of the spectrum, very tight and hot; next comes the road racer, followed by the smooth, stable touring bike, which is also the approximate pattern for many mass-production bicycles.

FRAME ANGLES

Frames are often described in terms of the head and seat tube angles, as indicated in the illustration. These have definite significance, and dropped-bar bikes follow clear patterns. Current competition road bikes are generally built with angles in the 73–75 degree range; tourers usually use angles from 70–72. A typical tourer is described as "72 parallel"; 73 parallel is a common choice for noncustom long-distance road racing. With custom bikes, the angles and tube lengths are set up for your particular body.

RAKE AND TRAIL

Rake is the forward offset of a fork, which is easily visible in its curve; it is the difference between the centerline of the fork and the centerline of the front axle, measured in inches or centimeters. Trail is another measurement of forward offset, expressed as the relationship between head angle and rake; if you drop a plumb line from the middle of the headset (or head tube) to where it touches the ground, and do the same from the centerline of the front axle, the distance between them is the amount of trail. Interestingly, some builders "work with" rake, others are very concerned about trail.

RAISED-BAR BICYCLES

Bikes ridden in the upright position created by raised handlebars have a different geometry. Adult three-speeds, cruisers, and off-road

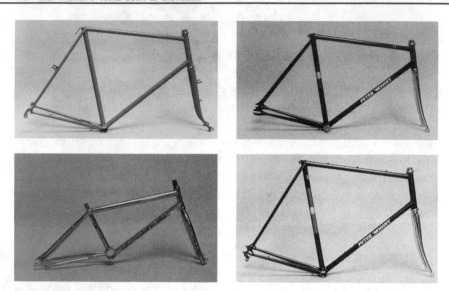

FOUR FRAMES
Subtle and not so subtle differences are apparent among different frames. Clockwise from upper left: tourer, track, road racer, and BMX.

bikes tend to have head and seat tube angles in the 68–72 degree range. Some efficiency is lost, but since the upright position restricts speed to begin with, you don't opt for these bikes if you are planning to go superfast. These are stable bicycles that feel good and handle well even on poor roads, not unlike those faced by 19th-century riders, whose bikes had similar geometry. Shallow angles, long wheelbase, and more fork rake create an inherently stable frame that soaks up road shock. These are basic truths most authorities agree on, but an endless debate on the fine points of frame design has been going on more or less forever in bike shops and magazines. As ever, the best builders are not the best arguers.

TUBING AND CONSTRUCTION

There is more agreement on tubing, which falls into several basic categories. At the bottom is thick, heavy, low-quality soft steel, usually with a seam that weakens it. Bikes made of this tubing are often welded (a high-temperature process that is not used with better tubing) and rarely of good quality. "Bicycle-grade" tubing is a step up from this, being thinner, lighter, and stronger. Better yet is high-carbon steel, which can be trusted in most applications. The next step up is "chromoly" (chrome-molybdenum steel), which is stronger and lighter yet, and available on many mid-priced bikes. All of these tubings are stronger if seamless, but the seam may be well concealed, so look closely or ask about this.

Except in low-price and special-purpose bicycles, tubing is usually joined by brazing (a low-temperature process), with lugs at the joints. The lugs may be omitted, but lugless bikes, while elegant, are "labor-intensive" and pricey. Recently another method of joining has been added to welding and brazing. In this new method, all tubes and lugs are joined simultaneously at a very high temperature. The result looks like a conventional lugged, brazed bicycle, but it is a mass-produced item. Faster and less expensive than individual brazing, this process can turn out a solid frame, but cannot be used with higher-quality tubing, which is damaged by extreme heat and must be skillfully brazed.

AEROSPACE QUALITY TUBING

Upper-middle and top-of-the-line bikes are built with expensive, name-brand tubing, usually chrome-molybdenum or manganese alloys. Some of it is so tough and thin that while you can dimple it with a strong finger, it can take the hammering of professional road racing. The English Reynolds brand has the widest selection of gauges and diameters, but somehow the Italians prefer Columbus, the French tend to like Vitus, and the Japanese favor Tange or Ishiwata. There is surprisingly little difference; they are all excellent, state-of-the-art, aerospace quality materials, often made by manufacturers who pioneered that field.

Tubing of this high quality is available in a wide range of gauges, and in most applications, it is "butted"—thickened at the ends—where it is brazed, and thinner in the middle, to save weight and distribute stress more evenly. Brand name is less important than gauge (thickness), mitering (fitting), and the builder's skill. Even at the butted portion, these tubes are thin and must be joined carefully; too much or too little heat weakens the joint. But a properly made diamond frame is a pretty miraculous thing; weighing as little as four pounds, it can carry 50 times its own weight and resist the formidable torque of hard pedaling by superfit athletes.

Does this mean that a good bicycle must carry the sticker of some famous manufacturer? Not anymore. A remarkably high grade of Japanese butted chrome-molybdenum tubing has been working its way down

FRAME BUILDER PETER MOONEY

Right up there with frame geometry and wheel design as matters for debate is the question of which tubing is best. The problem is even more confusing because while Reynolds measures tubing in gauges, Columbus does so in millimeters. Butted tubing is described in two figures; one for the middle section, another for the butted end. One thing most builders would agree on is that anything lighter than .6 mm is hard to work with. (This is the thickness of Columbus PL, a special-purpose straight-gauge tube.) And it's also true that a superlight frame often can't be rebuilt. Crash it, and it may be gone forever, which is not usually true of standard-gauge frames.

Frame builder Peter Mooney observes that, "Columbus PL is suited basically to (track) pursuit frames, and Reynolds 19–22 gauge or Columbus PS are often used in (track) pursuit or criterium bikes, but it is hard to generalize. Rider weight and frame size are very important factors in choosing materials. Small, light riders pose one design problem; very tall riders pose another, requiring heavy tubing. Columbus SL (.6–.9 mm) and SP (.7–1.0) are basic tubings for both touring and road-racing bikes, and so is the Reynolds 'Club Set,' which uses 21–24 gauge for top and seat tubes, and a slightly heavier 20–23 gauge for the down tube.

"The truth is, I often mix and match to meet the situation, and many builders do this; I think you often get a better bicycle for a given rider this way. People come up with flat statements about what is appropriate, but I've been doing this ten years and I'm still learning."

to the better mass-market bicycles. This tubing is so close to name-brand standards that the difference is marginal in most applications.

BRAZED LUG AND FORK CROWN
Neat brazing is a necessity, filed-down lugs a luxury.

BUTTED TUBING
High-quality tubing is thin in the middle and thick at the ends, where it is brazed; this allows a lighter, stronger, smoother bike.

ALUMINUM FRAMES

Aluminum does seem to be a viable alternate construction material, but there are no mid-price aluminum bikes. European aluminum racing frames like the Vitus, Alan, and Torpado have been accepted since the late 1970s, and there were several teams using the Vitus frame in the 1984 Tour de France. Built with more or less standard tube diameters and assembled with aircraft-type epoxy resins, they are light and strong, but they do flex more than some riders prefer, especially big, powerful riders. For many riders, though, they are a good buy.

The very expensive Klein bicycles use welded aluminum and larger tubes to make up for the softness of the material, and have gained respect; some reviewers have raved about them. The new $600 Cannondale tourer is similarly constructed. Bicycling's reviewers liked the prototype they tested, partly because aluminum has a different feel and seems to damp road shock differently. Welded aluminum frames can be even lighter than those made of the very thin Reynolds 753, and apparently somewhat stronger under certain kinds of loads. Klein has been making these unique bikes for some time, and has unquestionably matured the technology; how low the price can come without quality loss is yet to be seen.

THE DERAILLEUR

FRONT AND REAR DERAILLEUR
Reliable equipment from Shimano (rear derailleur, left), and SunTour (front derailleur, right).

Until recently this gear-changing device has probably turned off more would-be cyclists than any other component; it took half a century to perfect a smooth system of lifting a chain from one cog or chainring to another, and another 20 years to make a good one affordable. Not until the mid-seventies, largely through Japanese initiative, were inexpensive quality derailleurs that could handle all kinds of gears made available.

A derailleur may be made of steel, alloy, plastic, titanium, or a combination, and it is adapted to either racing (narrow range), touring (wide range), or an intermediate range (best for most riders). Derailleur options, functions, and maintenance are treated in detail in Chapter 8.

BRAKES

Most people immediately grasp the importance of brakes to a motor vehicle, but a lot of the same people are pretty casual about whether they can actually stop their bicycles. The problem has less to do with equipment than bike owners; genuinely poor brakes tend to come on genuinely poor bikes, and the rest can be made to work. Most current adult bicycles come with caliper brakes, which divide into side-pull and center-pull types, so named because of where the control cable joins brake arms, or calipers.

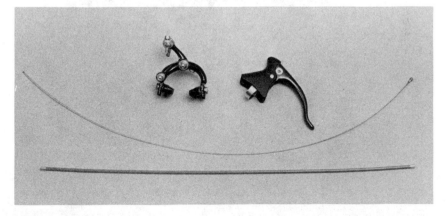

BRAKE PARTS
All caliper brakes have calipers (brake arms) and control levers (top) plus cables and housings (below). These Gallis are neat, simple, easily adjusted racing brakes of the side-pull type; the cable passes through one caliper and pulls up on the other.

CENTER-PULL BRAKES
Center-pulls also work fine, and Jacques Anquetil won five Tours de France on
Mafacs much like these. Cable goes down through a hanger and pulls up on the yoke
cable connecting the calipers.

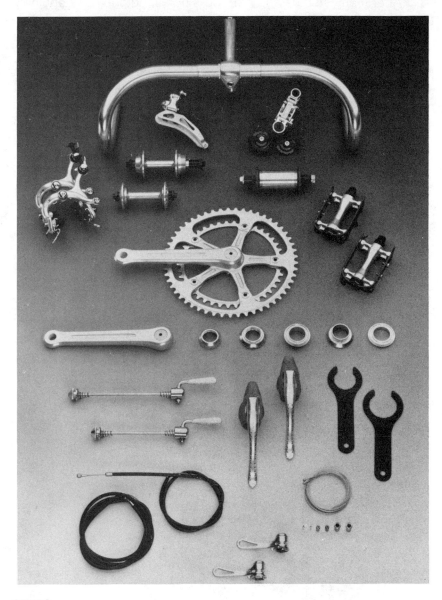

GRUPO
This race-proven group of components by Mavic is essentially everything but the frame. Innovations include sealed bearings, variable-cage derailleur, and easy-off stem.

After many studies and pseudo-studies, no one has genuinely proved one better than the other. Alignment and stiffness (created by good design and construction) are the real secrets. Center-pulls have a slight theoretical advantage, but the side-pull brake has an elegant simplicity that is appealing, and it is still the favorite on competition bikes. Cantilever brakes, which mount on special fittings, are the firmest of center-pulls and are found on many quality bikes, especially tandems. There are also hand-operated hub brakes, typically found on tandem bicycles, and rod brakes, an early version of calipers still found on some rugged, old-style three-speeds.

OPERATION

Caliper brakes work by the movement of levers on the bars; you squeeze the lever, which pulls a cable, which tightens the calipers (brake arms), squeezing blocks against the rims, and stopping the bike by friction. The blocks are held by metal shoes and are replaceable. Rubber is the standard material for brake blocks, but it is dangerously ineffective in the rain, especially with the chromed steel rims found on

BRAKE BLOCKS
Finned Mathauser block is designed to dissipate heat on long descents; oversized pad helps too. Their standard block to right is easy replacement for most original equipment. Very good for all but out-of-true or textured rims; especially good in the rain.

three-speeds and low-price bikes. Chrome-leather blocks work best on wet chrome rims; the Mathauser composition pad is better for alloy rims, wet or dry, so long as the rims are smooth and true.

For the brake system to be effective, levers, cables, and calipers must move freely; it's easy to lose braking power in a neglected system which corrodes and loses adjustment. Poor assembly also reduces braking effectiveness; cables travel inside a housing, which must follow a smooth course, free of sharp corners and kinks. Rear brakes have longer cables, which make them less responsive, but they are necessary for control. Chapter 9 explains brake adjustment and repairs.

THE AUXILIARY LEVER

The very common auxiliary or "safety" lever also reduces braking power, which is why it is called the "suicide lever" by many mechanics. It is a bastardized version of the old French Guidonnet touring lever, and is used because it allows braking from an upright position, but at a price. Inherently lacking rigidity, it also has the added disadvantage of

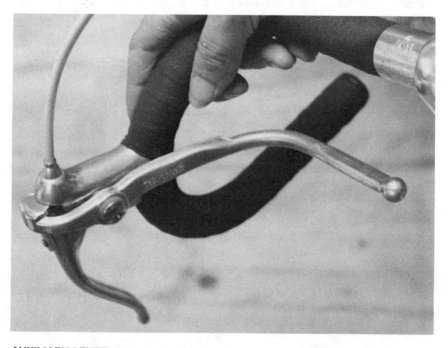

AUXILIARY LEVER
The long lever bends, and this is only one of its problems. Some mechanics call it the "suicide lever" because of its limited stopping power.

reducing full movement of the primary levers. The high-forward position it creates can throw you over the bars in an emergency stop. When these auxiliary levers are removed, brakes perform better, which is one reason they are never seen on quality bicycles. Make sure to have a rubber hood fitted if you remove them; as explained in Chapter 7, you will be able to rest your hands here, and also operate the brakes from this position.

THE STEM

When Major Taylor came up with the idea of extending the handlebars forward on an adjustable stem back in the 1890s, he gave the bicycle an indispensable component. The dropped-bar stem is very important in terms of establishing a comfortable position on the bike, and can be anywhere from a mere stub to 140 millimeters in length, though something between 90 and 120 is best in terms of handling. Except on three-speeds, cruisers, and sprint bikes, steel has largely been replaced by alloy. Whatever the material, make sure that you do not raise the stem beyond the manufacturer's safety mark; if there is no

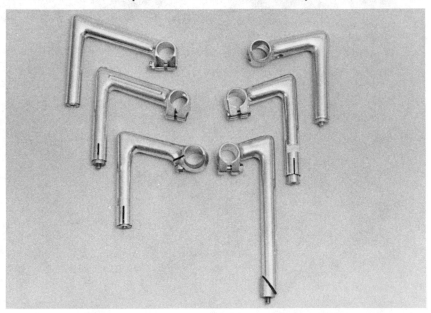

ASSORTED STEMS
Varying forward extension is no problem, but extra-high stems like Technomic (lower right center) are hard to find; the SR Swan is similar.

mark, at least 2½" should remain inside the head tube; less than this and you may snap the stem, leaving you with no control. If you replace a stem, bear in mind that it must match both steerer tube and bar diameters.

HANDLEBARS

Handlebars (just plain "bars" in the vernacular) attach to the bike via the stem, and like the stem they have special significance because they directly affect riding position. They are divisible into raised and dropped types, but there are many other important differences.

Except for track sprinting, where the stresses are way beyond normal, aluminum alloy bars are preferable, and steel bars on a modern road bike indicate that price has been the major factor in its design. (Steel is standard on a sprint bike, three-speed, or cruiser.) Good alloy bars are engineered for strength where it is needed, and some are sleeved at the middle for additional strength where bars meet stem.

RAISED BARS

Raised bars come in several styles: the classic North Road bend seen on Raleigh three-speed products over the decades, a flatter Continental bend, and the Bullmoose ballooner style designed by Tom Ritchie, which is reinforced for use on high-performance off-road bikes. Where the North Road and Bull Moose sit you quite upright, the flat or Continental bend, often found in alloy, allows a lower, more forward position, better in terms of leverage and aerodynamics. This is the bend most used when converting a dropped-bar bike to upright position.

DROPPED BARS

Dropped bars are more critical because the riding position is more demanding. There are two general bend patterns, each modified by manufacturers. For many years the Maes bend has been the basic road bar; it allows several different riding positions, which is useful because these different positions allow you to relieve stress over the miles. The Randonneur is a touring bend which allows a more upright position. It is a general rule that broad shoulders demand wider bars for free breathing, and Chapter 7 explains the relation of bends and measurements to body dimensions.

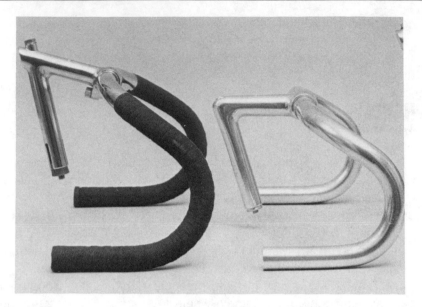

DROPPED TRACK AND ROAD BARS; RAISED BARS
Dropped track and road bars (above) are one end of the spectrum; wide, stable, raised Ritchie Bullmoose (below) is at the other. Even minor differences in handlebar design can have major effects on comfort.

THE HEADSET

The headset resides in the head tube, and consists of two sets of bearings, held by cups and cones, which allow the fork to turn inside the tube. Cheap, nonstandard headsets wear quickly, are difficult to adjust and sometimes impossible to repair. But even a good quality headset correctly adjusted and lubricated will wear faster than other components, especially with a heavy rider. If the crown race is not machined correctly or the adjustment is off, it will wear faster yet. When the steering seems to click into a straight ahead position, the cups are "brinneled"—the bearings have hammered themselves into the cups. But manufacturers are coming out with new headset designs every year, and this is one case where a big-name brand is not necessarily superior to the competition.

HEADSET IN HEAD TUBE
The headset tends to wear faster than most components. A clunking sound indicates looseness.

PEDALS

Pedals range from disposables that cannot be adjusted to extremely expensive alloy-and-titanium works of art that last forever. Three-speeds often have inexpensive rubber-tread pedals, but metal pedals are standard for all other types. Most are constructed around a spindle that runs the length of the pedal, with a set of ball bearings at each end. The really good ones will take amazing abuse because they are race-developed equipment designed to take steady punishment. Alloy is lighter, more expensive, and more delicate; steel weighs a little more and lasts forever. Titanium confers bragging rights and costs a fortune.

Because pedals take tremendous stress, heavy use can blow out a pair of cheap ones in months. Sometimes they loosen up because of poor factory assembly, and at least one careful adjustment is worth trying, but this doesn't always work. Quality pedals are a good investment, especially for the strong or frequent rider.

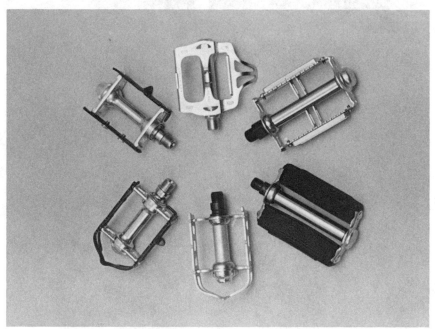

PEDALS
Clockwise from the top: (1) Lyotard Berthet model platform, (2) Union Steel rat-trap, (3) Union rubber, (4 + 5) KKt and Campagnolo quill-type, (6) SunTour Superbe track pedals. In mechanical terms, the bottom line is access to adjustable parts; disposables are strictly for around town.

The rubber-tread pedal is handy in urban traffic, and is less slippery with leather soles than a metal pedal without toe clips, but for riding more than a few miles, metal pedals with toe clips (Chapter 7) are safer and more efficient.

Finally, consider the size of your foot and what shoes you'll wear. "Quill" type racing pedals offer the best quality, but a big foot in a wide shoe won't fit. The wider "rat trap" will handle big feet, and so will the new, wide, off-road pedals like the Shimano Deore.

THE CRANKSET

Today's crankset is no different in principle from that of Starley's Rover; it connects foot-power at the pedals to a pair of levers (the crank-arms), which convert it to circular energy at the front sprocket

COTTERED STEEL CRANKS
This three-speed crank is at least ten years old, still working fine. The (corroded) cotter pin goes into the right side just above the axle; removing one is no fun.

COTTERLESS CRANKS
Clockwise from upper left: Sugino Tourney and Maxi (both with triple rings), SunTour Superbe and Sugino Mighty (both double rings). Center is blue-anodized Galli. A little cap at the center of the crank unscrews, giving access to a bolt that threads into the axle. It is a better system than cotter pins if the aluminum is forged, but be sure the bolt holding crank to axle is tight; if not, you are destroying some expensive hardware.

(chainring). The standard arrangement is to have two chainrings, but triples are available for heavy touring loads. Steel cranks are still found on some low-price bicycles, and they come in three types: one piece (Ashtabula style), cotterless (often brushed to resemble alloy), and cottered. All tend to have problems, and cotter pins can be particularly troublesome, often giving out at the wrong time. They can also be difficult to replace because there are so many different sizes.

The contemporary mid-price bicycle has largely replaced steel with cotterless alloy cranks, which are attached by a bolt threading directly into the axle. It is an excellent system, but the bolts should be checked for tightness after the first rides until the alloy forms to the axle; otherwise the crankset can be ruined. It can also be ruined by overtorquing: No more than 30 foot-pounds should be applied in tightening the bolt, or the steel axle may spread the alloy cranks, fatiguing them and changing clearances.

As with many components, type and intensity of use are major considerations. Strong riders occasionally break cranks, and the serious rider needs beefy equipment. Finally there is the question of crank-arm length, covered in Chapter 8.

THE BOTTOM BRACKET

This is where the crankset fits into the frame, and it is the site of very high stresses. There are two sets of bearings which support the axle, the left set fitting into a removable cup, the right into a fixed cup. The left cup should be correctly adjusted (the axle must turn freely) and tightly fitted; it is fairly common and very aggravating to have a cup come loose on the road. Equally important, the bracket itself must be

BOTTOM BRACKET WITH CRANK AND AXLE ASSEMBLY
Once adjusted correctly, cups should be torqued down very solidly. Trouble down here is serious.

correctly threaded and faced; poor quality here can cause a chronic problem, and repair is costly.

THE SADDLE

The saddle, or seat, is an enormously important piece of equipment, second to none as cause for irritation. Cyclists who ride long miles experience various aches and pains, but it is where you are sitting that you feel it most. And just as every human body is framed and muscled differently, bottoms are different too. Saddle design, especially for women, has improved vastly since the middle seventies, and is covered in Chapter 7 as part of the fitting process.

SADDLE
This Arius Imperator is built along racing lines, narrow and firm; touring saddles are wider and softer.

SEATPOST

For generations saddles were secured by a post-and-clamp method, and this was all right as long as the clamp worked. Since the sixties, cheap clamps have been more and more common—clamps that don't allow fine adjustment and fail under stress. The alternative is the microadjust seatpost, and it is a good investment. Reliable, inexpensive ones have been on the market for some years; the modern ones adjust from the bottom, and this is very handy. Note that diameter (marked on the post) must match seat tube diameter.

SEATPOST
The microadjust is a better deal than separate clamp and post. This Laprade is inexpensive, reliable, and conveniently adjustable from the bottom. Quick-release seatpost is typical off-road setup.

WHEELS

Wheels have been a preoccupation with cyclists from von Drais forward, and learned debates about The Best Wheel go on and on. The big breakthroughs were tangential wire spoking and the pneumatic tire, but the bad wheel is still with us, mainly because manufacturers know that most people don't look at them closely. Wobbly wheels, cheap hubs, popped spokes, and flat tires are all very bad experiences. Light, tight wheels with high-performance tires are a decidedly good experience, worth looking into. Current equipment is pretty amazing in terms of lightness and strength, which is why bicycle wheels were used on the lunar hauling cart. In fact there are so many kinds of tires and rims available today that making choices is no longer simple. Tires, rims, hubs, and spoking are the variables; the trick is to fit wheel and tire to rider and application. Wheel building being one of the higher arts of bicycle mechanics it cannot be explained well in few words. By all means spoke up a wheel for fun, but don't true it without the advice of an expert unless you are really a natural mechanic.

HUB AND QUICK-RELEASE
Throwing the lever (center) allows you to get wheels off and on quickly, without tools. Developed by the Tullio Campagnolo, this item was a cornerstone of his well-known empire. His product is pricey, but now everyone makes them.

HUBS

There are high- low- and medium-flange hubs, free- and sealed-bearing hubs, and hubs of steel or alloy. Cheap three-piece steel hubs can loosen up, and some sealed-bearing hubs are impossible to repair with common tools—or without replacement bearings. Medium flange hubs sometimes require odd spoke lengths, which can be very annoying. Rugged sealed-bearing hubs are standard for off-road use (notably the Phil Wood), and Mavics are being raced in the Tour de France by major teams. But the easily serviced free-bearing, one-piece alloy hub continues to be adequate for most riders. It is classic design at its best, the axle (often hollowed out to accept a handy quick release mechanism) carries two cones, with the bearings riding between the cones and the hardened races of the hub itself.

The low-flange hub favored by long-distance racing cyclists gives a slightly smoother ride appropriate to European roads, while the high-flange hub transmits forces somewhat more efficiently. But basic quality and who builds the wheel are more important than flange design, because good wheels can be built on both. Circa 1984, low

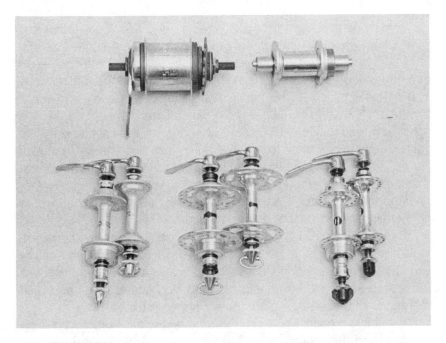

HUB SELECTION
Hubs can vary in many ways. They can also house gearboxes, generators and brakes. Good ones last a very long time.

flange is the "in" hub, but the most responsive clincher wheels can be built on the high flange, which counteracts the greater "give" in most of these tires. Campagnolo hubs have legendary durability, but there is plenty of adequate equipment at much lower prices that will last tens of thousands of miles if properly maintained.

REAR HUBS

The rear hub for a road bicycle is threaded on one side to accept a freewheel; threads must be compatible. Rear hubs also come in two standard spacings, and the spacing must match the width of the rear fork. Until the mid-seventies, 120 mm was standard, and accommodated a five-speed freewheel. Around that time race-developed custom frames began to appear with a 126 mm rear fork, which takes an Italian-standard six-speed freewheel; this 126 mm width is becoming the new standard for quality bicycles. As explained in Chapter 8, this is preferable, because it allows better and simpler gearing.

DISH

If you look at a pair of bicycle wheels edgewise you'll notice that while a front wheel is symmetrical (spoked the same on both sides), a rear wheel is "off center," to make room for the freewheel; the spokes go from rim to hub at different angles on each side, and the difference is visible. This is called "dish," and it is the subject of much controversy. All other things being equal, the more extreme the dish, the weaker the wheel—and rear wheels, of course, absorb torque transmitted by the chain. On the basis of all this, some authorities feel that the narrower five-speed wheel is significantly stronger than the wider six-speed, which has slightly more dish. Critics of six-speed spacing usually recommend that to get extra gears on your bike, you are better off with a triple chainring and a nice, strong five-speed.

This is a critical point affecting both frame design and gearing possibilities. The rebuttal from those favoring the wider, more sharply dished 126 mm wheel is much less theoretical: If a big bike-bender like Eddy Merckx used 126 mm sixes on the long, steep mountains and poor roads of European racing, the six-speed must be okay.

They have a point. Many professional racers have unthinkable leg strength, and they climb very hard for long periods in very torquey gears. Even allowing for smooth pedaling technique, three hundred hilly kilometers of hard racing probably do more to a wheel than most riders can imagine. Ergo, it's clearly possible to build very strong wheels on the 126 mm six-speed spacing. It's also possible to get more gears as explained in Chapter 7.

SPOKES AND SPOKING

Spokes come in heavy and light gauges, straight and butted, in plain, plated, or stainless steel. Name brand is the name of the spoke game, with DT and Robergel being among the best in recent years. Most women benefit from light, butted spokes, but big, strong, heavy pedalers are better off with heavy, straight-gauge spokes.

For the true bikie, debate about spoking patterns is a sacred rite. Since Starley worked out tangential spoking, spoke pattern has been defined in terms of how many times the spokes cross each other. Radial spoking, where the spokes do not cross at all, is still used for some front wheels in races against the clock. There are also one- and two-cross patterns (rare), followed by the most popular three-cross design, long accepted not only by manufacturers but most cyclists. The four-cross wheel yields a smoother ride, but the difference is marginal, and more depends on who built the wheel. A tight wheel (one with tight spoking) reduces breakage by limiting flex, which in turn reduces metal fatigue. Anodized rims allow tighter spoking, but there is a point of no return, which good builders come to know.

Those curious to learn more about this and other aspects of wheel design should read Jobst Brandt's *The Bicycle Wheel* (Avocet Inc.: Menlo Park, CA, $7.95) It's not a manual for wheel building but it is definitely worth reading if you're technical-minded; if you're not, it's pretty formidable. Brandt debunks the supposedly crucial importance of flange-height and suggests that the difference between three- and four- cross-spoke patterns is not significant; he also says that rider weight is more significant than torque, and that tightly laced wheels are stronger, so long as the rim is not deformed by spoke tension. His computer modelings and general expertise are very impressive, but he doesn't evaluate spokes or the infinity of current rim/tire variations.

TIRES AND RIMS

TUBULARS

For generations, cyclists had a simple choice: tubular or clincher tires, two very different items. The tubular is a traditional race-bred creation, also called a sewup, because the extremely light tube is actually sewn into the casing. Tubulars come with a lightweight European Presta valve and mount to a special rim with special glue. (European Clement is popular, and 3M Fastack is becoming so; track racers often use shellac.)

If all this sounds like alchemy, the reasoning turns out to be very

TUBULAR TIRES
This collection runs the gamut from board track to cyclo-cross (off-road). For normal road use try a 250–290 gram narrow profile, herringbone, or mixed tread cotton tire and run it around 95–105 psi. Anything much lighter is vulnerable, and heavier ones are less responsive.

clear: Combined tire and rim weight is the most important weight on a bicycle, and the tubular reduces it dramatically. With its capacity for high pressure (over 110 pounds per square inch on the road) and its narrow profile, the tubular has less rolling resistance, and the greater flexibility of good ones allows them to hold the road extremely well even at these pressures. Until the late-seventies, if you wanted to feel what a bicycle was really about, only sewups would show you. Handmade of high quality rubbers and specially selected long-staple cotton or silk, tubulars for track events can weigh less than 180 grams; 250–275 grams is about average for road racing. Light weight and minimal rolling resistance make tubulars very satisfying at the purely sensual level, and very hard to give up, even at $20–$40 a throw. Alas, the tubular is also difficult to repair, and most cheap ones are heavy (300–400 grams) and unreliable.

PRESTA AND SCHRAEDER VALVES
The lighter European Presta valve (top) takes a different pump-head; it's growing popular here too. Circa 1984 some Oriental manufacturers are still having problems with it. Schraeder valve (bottom) is still found on many mass-market bikes.

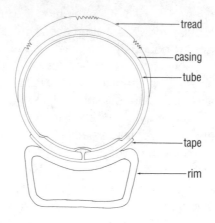

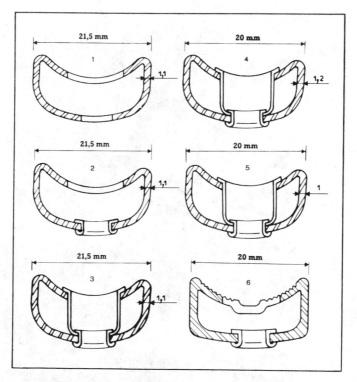

TUBULAR DESIGN

Bugatti must have loved this early example of monocoque design, in which a thin, light (200–400 gram) shell gives optimum strength for weight. Drawing at top shows glued-on tire and tube; variations by Mavic (bottom) show major differences in construction. Track rim (lower right) has extra-firm grip on tire to resist stress of banked turns. On the road, rims below 300 grams are too light for general use; anything over 400 starts to lose responsiveness.

CLINCHER TIRES

Clinchers are like old-fashioned (pretubeless) automobile tires. Inside is a tube, and outside there is a casing that is held on by air pressure clinched into place by a wire or "bead" which locks under the edge of the rim. Clinchers for dropped-bar derailleur bikes traditionally came in two sizes: 700C (European), and the slightly larger 27", long a U.S. standard. The 700C is preferable, and growing in popularity here, because it is compatible with quality frames designed for tubulars; the 27" is a hair larger. But until the mid-seventies, clinchers stood for slow and soggy. The clincher experience was like driving the family sedan; cheap, reliable, easy to repair, and pretty unexciting if you were into the feel of a good bike. Rims were heavier and weaker, tubes and casings formidable. Running at 70 psi, they were soft—more comparable with three-speed or balloon tires than good tubulars.

The rim and tire revolution of the late seventies widened options greatly. First came the French Michelin Elan. The Elan had a light tube with a Presta valve, a light, narrow casing, and an operating pressure of 90 psi. Early models were not reliable, but Oriental manufacturers saw the future of this idea, and in a few years you could get clinchers from East or West as narrow as ¹⁵⁄₁₆", weighing as little as 195 grams and running at 85–100 psi (light latex tubes add another 100 grams). Equally important, there are now reliable fold-up "skinwall" clincher tires like the Specialized Turbo, which can be stowed under the seat, so that a blown-out casing doesn't mean a long walk to the nearest bike shop.

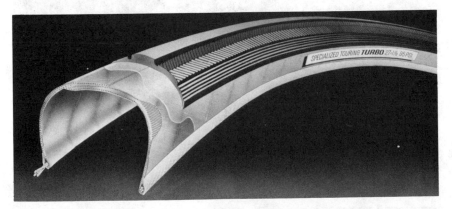

CLINCHER CROSS-SECTION
Low cost and easy access to the tube (not shown) with simple tools are the clincher advantages. This foldable Specialized Turbo has a bead (lower left) of flexible Kevlar (rather than metal wire) which allows it to be stowed under the seat like a tubular.

STANDARD CLINCHERS

For trouble-free touring (or just an extra-stable, comfortable ride) Schwinn's Le Tour and Michelin's Chevron 50 (both 1¼″) are standards for comparison. These are updated traditional-type clinchers that fit medium to wide rims and put some rubber on the road without feeling

CLINCHER TIRES

There's more variety each year. Picking Tires and rims to match your needs is what you're after. Rim and tire selection should be guided by the combined bike, load, and rider weights and modified to suit road surfaces, and distances.

dead; Specialized makes a 1⅜" tire that adds traction and cushion but fits a 1¼" rim. For a combination of responsiveness and enough durability for light touring, try a 1⅛", 90–100 psi tire on a medium-width, medium-light rim like the Mavic E-2 or Super Champion Gentleman, which will leave you plenty of other tire options.

THE FOLDING SKINWALL CLINCHER

With people who ride enough to become attuned to differences in tire performance, there's a general consensus that the lighter folding "skinwalls" have the most responsive road feel of any clinchers. Most would also agree that they are also quite secure on good roads, and that they are actually preferable to cheap, heavy tubulars on heavy training rims. This is quite an achievement, but these tires are not for everyone; they require the narrow-to-medium rim designed for them, and compared to medium-weight clinchers they are vulnerable to punctures. And they can, with a heavy rider, allow rim damage. The narrow (1") tire does not provide much of an air pad, and heavy riders should definitely avoid potholes; bent rims are difficult to repair, and expensive to replace.

Light riders will love 1" skinwalls but for most the slightly heavier 1⅛" version is preferable. It wears better, the rim is protected by a thicker air pad, and it mates with wider, more versatile rims. Specialized is the leader in this field, and their rim-and-tire chart (see illustration) goes a long way to solving the mix and match problems created by new options. Mount these tires carefully according to directions, and if you want light, narrow, long-lived wheels, try the new hardened rims like those from Mavic and Ambrosio.

TIRE GUIDELINES FOR DERAILLEUR BIKES

Weight is the most critical factor in selecting wheels and tires. These guidelines assume average paved roads in the USA and are based on combined weight of *rider, bike* and *load*. Lighter equipment will cost you in the long run because of higher failure and wear rates. Big riders can and do use skinwalls and tubulars, but they pay for it, especially on bad roads, and where there is glass.

COMBINED WEIGHT	SUGGESTED RANGES			
	TUB'S	1"	1⅛"	1¼"
135	OK	OK	OK	?!
150	??	OK	OK	??
165	??	OK	OK	OK
180	?!	??	OK	OK
195	?!	??	OK	OK
210	!!	!!	OK	OK

?? = questionable
?! = avoid
!! = very expensive

CLINCHER RIMS

To go with this wide range of clincher tires (as many as seven models from one manufacturer) there is a new generation of alloy rims: lighter, stronger, and available in different widths. The wider (known as 16–22 mm) take wide to medium tires; the narrower (aka 13–19 mm) fit the new, thin 90–100 psi tires. (Check with your dealer about borderline cases.)

These new rims are structurally different from their predecessors. The old-fashioned unbraced "U" cross-section rim had a tendency to spring out of shape when spokes were pulled really tight, because it had less inherent strength than that of a tubular rim, which derives rigidity from thin material through its hollow design. Super Champion strengthens its excellent standard rims with box sections, and Weinmann varies this with a unique concave design. Ambrosio's specially hardened, reinforced half-oval Model 19 Elite is a high-performance work of art, well suited to those running high-performance tires, so is Mavic's 640. Most of these manufacturers make both wide and narrow versions.

What it all comes down to is that you can now buy low-priced, easily repaired clincher tires that perform as well as many tubulars—or much improved heavier ones for touring and commuting.

Rim	Cross Section	Constr.	Cross Section (mm)	Weight (grams)	RECOMMENDED		TIRE USE RECOMMENDATION**		
					Rim Tape	Tube Size	Turbo/S 700 x 25cc 27 x 1	Touring Turbo 700 x 28cc 27 x 1-1/8	Touring Turbo 700 x 32cc 27 x 1-1/4
Rigida 1320		M	19.2	435	#51	700 x 25c	Recommended	Recommended	Not Recommended
Araya 20A		M	19.6	410	#51	700 x 25c	Recommended	Recommended	Not Recommended
Araya Aero ADX-1W		M	19.6	500	#51	700 x 25c	Recommended	Recommended	Not Recommended
Mavic Mod E-2		M	19.8	415	#51	700 x 25c	Recommended	Recommended	Not Recommended
Super Champion Gentleman		M	20.3	480	#51	700 x 25c	Recommended	Recommended	Not Recommended
Weinman Concave A-124		C	20.4	540	#56*	700 x 25c	Recommended	Recommended	Not Recommended
Mavic Mod-3		M	22.0	500	#51	700 x 28	Not Recommended	Recommended	Recommended
Araya Aero ADX-2W		M	22.0	600	#51	700 x 28	Not Recommended	Recommended	Recommended
Araya 16A		C	22.0	490	#56*	700 x 28	Not Recommended	Recommended	Recommended
Weinman Concave A-129		C	22.2	580	#56*	700 x 28	Not Recommended	Recommended	Recommended
Super Champion Mod. #58		C	22.8	490	#56*	700 x 28	Not Recommended	Recommended	Recommended

* OR rim rope.
** SPECIALIZED TURBO Tires will work with *any* compatibly sized rims. However, for best performance we recommend the combinations listed here.

M = Modular   C = Channel

CLINCHER RIM DESIGN
The range of weights and designs categorized here for tire compatibility by the Specialized Company shows how much variation there is. All these are sound designs; the simple unreinforced U-section is not. You can get clincher rims as light as 410 grams, and you can also get hardened ones like the Ambrosio Elite—a wise precaution with narrow rims.

BALLOONERS AND THREE-SPEEDS

The choices are relatively simple for a three-speed or ballooner. Most three-speeds come with a steel-rimmed wheel that weighs a great deal and lasts forever, and the heavy-duty, 26″ × 1⅜″ tire does not vary much. It usually rides on 55–65 pounds pressure, and puts plenty of rubber on the road, also creating plenty of rolling resistance. Upgrading is possible, as described in Chapter 7.

Ballooners normally use 26″ × 2.125″ or 26″ × 1. 75″ rims and tires. Wheels are usually built on a beefy, sealed-bearing hub, with heavy, straight-gauge spokes. While inexpensive cruisers use steel rims and routine tires, the good off-roaders come with a very well built alloy wheel that is light-years ahead of what you find on a clunker. It is

SHIMANO A/X SERIES

As always, competition spawns innovation. The Japanese Shimano company has sometimes taken a scattershot approach to the market, offering almost too many innovations, but Shimano's A/X and similar E/X lines are impressive. Criticized at first because of advertising emphasis on largely irrelevant aerodynamics, the A/X series turns out to have other, more significant differences—so many, in fact, that it seems to represent a new and influential school. Imitations are already on the market.

SHIMANO INNOVATIONS

very strong, for obvious reasons, and it is surprisingly light. It is also more versatile than some owners realize, because there are two distinct types of tires offered as well as two rim types: One is knobby, intended for grass, dirt, mud, and gravel; its rolling resistance is high. The other is smooth, intended for road use, and has less rolling resistance. It can run at medium-high pressures, and improves road-feel considerably.

Close examination shows good quality, but more important, it reveals pedal, crank, hub, derailleur, freewheel, and brake innovations that are genuinely new, and not just for racing. By shortening the axle, the A/X pedal drops the rider's center of gravity about ¾"; in addition, the pedal is shaped to maximize cornering clearance; the result is better adhesion. Another result is that you can ride a smaller frame, or make a frame that is a bit small fit better. Alas, the A/X pedal fits only the A/X crankset, and poor seals on early models led to fast wear in some cases. But the crankset also has interesting features, accepting chainrings with as few as 39 teeth, where many cannot go below 42 teeth; this gives more gearing versatility. The "parapull" brakes are distinguished by cables buried neatly out of the way under the bar tape, and an original, compact, quite rigid approach to center-pull caliper design. The derailleur is very different and very positive in its shifting, though some riders have said it wears rather quickly if run while full of grit.

Finally, the "freehub" has a few things to be said for it. Designed to accept seven cogs, it too contributes to gearing flexibility. It is also a "cassette" system, which means that the nasty business of cog-changing is much easier—remove the small cog, and the others simply lift off. The payoff is that the combination of 39-tooth chainring to 26-tooth cog (the current listed A/X maximum) yields a 40" gear, making it useful to the general cyclist, not just the racer. (Larger cogs from others of this manufacturer's systems can be used to obtain lower gears.) This equipment, if backed up by ongoing developments (and replacement parts), represents a potentially serious challenge to European racing components.

FREEWHEEL AND CHAIN

The conventional freewheel, also known as a block or cluster, screws onto the rear hub and provides cogs for the chain to drive. It also allows freewheeling or coasting by way of an internal arrangement of springs and pawls successfully penetrated by only the best mechanics. Its threads must match those of the hub, and its cog selection is worth thinking about, as this is one place where gears can be varied. It's possible to buy freewheels with alloy cogs (which more or less melt away within weeks) or titanium cogs, and you can spend as much as $200 for a freewheel, but it's overkill; stick with steel.

As mentioned earlier, freewheels come in two widths: 120 mm for the standard five-speed, 126 mm for the standard six. With the use of a narrower Japanese standard freewheel (SunTour Ultra series, etc.) the standard five converts to a narrow six and the standard six becomes a narrow seven. These narrow freewheels have less spacing between cogs and require use of a narrow chain, but they are becoming very popular.

Other recent developments include "cassette" freewheels, which disassemble much more easily when cogs are being changed, and the "freehub," which integrates freewheel and hub. These innovations are genuinely valuable because they offer more convenient and precise gearing, as explained in Chapter 8.

The chain transmits power from chainring to cog, and on a derailleur bike it also moves laterally, bending in the process, as it shifts from gear to gear. From chain to chain there are significant differences in both design and durability, not to mention the old compatibility problem. Regina has been a long-wearing standard for years and works well with Italian freewheels, but with the advent of narrow freewheels, the Sedisport chain has become extremely popular. It is accepted in both touring and racing circles because it seems to handle more or less any freewheel and wears well.

5.
DEALING WITH BIKE SHOPS

Today's bicycle is a highly evolved piece of machinery, but engineering logic is not the only thing that influences mass-market design. Manufacturers build bicycles the way they think people want them. The $1000 bicycle is (or used to be) aimed at an expert market, but the features of mass-produced bicycles are strongly influenced by sales reports and market research. Input from both these sources confirms that trendy features sell bikes, and that color coordination is more important to many buyers than the tubing underneath. Thus we have the 30-pound, flamingo-pink bicycle complete with oval tubing, steel rims, kickstand, giant pie-plate spoke protector, stem-shifters, and auxiliary brake levers. Super-wide-range gears are another common feature; great for heavy touring, they require a vulnerable long-cage derailleur, create awkward gaps between gears, and tend to shift slowly (though, it must be said, reliably).

But while no mass-produced bicycle is perfect as purchased, the mid-price ($200–$300) bicycle is a generally good deal, and most component problems can be solved. Under the clutter is a much-improved bicycle compared to that of ten years ago and it is no problem to strip the junk.

LOWER-PRICE BICYCLES

The low-price ($170–$200) bicycle is by and large the mid-price bicycle in softer tubing, with steel rather than alloy components, and without the refinements. Being practically all steel, these bikes are heavier and less responsive, but they can be adequate. Less-powerful riders will notice the weight of the steel rims, and heavy riders who hit bad potholes may find the soft steel fork vulnerable to bending—though rarely actually breaking. (For some reason, three-speeds, though usually low priced, seem to avoid this particular problem.) If the weight doesn't bother you, these bikes can provide good reliable transportation, but don't expect the impossible. Upgrading is expensive, too.

In the low $200 range, frames are often similar, but more components will be made of alloy. These bikes can often be upgraded at a reasonable price.

This legitimate economy bike is very different from the class of bike that sells for $100 or less, almost always through some kind of outlet store. Bike shops will not handle such merchandise because it is shot through with bad engineering, cheap components, nonstandard parts, etc. This is the so-called supermarket bike, and it has done the ten-speed, in particular, a lot of harm; seeing one of these disintegrate, observers often assume all derailleur bikes are basically unworkable.

THE WHEELWORKS
This Belmont, Massachusetts, shop is a clean, well-lighted place, which is in its favor. On the other hand, some very good shops are somewhat messy. Personnel are as important as anything, but a big selection of bikes is also a good sign.

BETTER BIKES

Around $300 you begin to find bicycles made of butted chromoly tubing. These bikes often have better-chosen gears and a better finish. The auxiliary levers and stem-shifters are gone, and the bike is a pound or two lighter.

Equally important, you will have more choice in geometry. You can find bikes in this range that lean more definitely toward competition or touring. If you find exactly what you want in this range, think about buying it, because upgrading an inferior bike will cost more than you'd expect. But try not to fall in love with some elegant $1100 fantasy. For most uses, the differences between a $375 bike and one that costs three times as much are marginal. These really expensive bikes, often custom-built, are for people who have real experience and know exactly what they want. Buy the wrong one, and you'll be pretty annoyed with yourself.

THE SHOP

You can tell something about a shop by how requests for minor component changes are handled. If the personnel seem in any way bothered or confused, they are either naive or lazy. They won't be much help later on if you decide to switch gear clusters or derailleurs. Bear in mind that unlike a component problem, the shop itself is not correctable. As with automobiles, there are places to buy and places to avoid; look around. A good bike shop is worth finding. It's your best bet as far as getting the right bike, having warranties honored, and generally avoiding problems. If it's been there long enough to establish a reputation, it's an even better bet. Discount and mail order houses seldom provide service, and it is the rare bike that doesn't need this from time to time. The 10–15 percent you save in bypassing a dealer can be quickly eaten up in repairs and adjustments, and dealers naturally tend to favor their own customers.

Service can be an intangible too; it may consist of honest, informed advice given even when it would be easier for the salesman to go along with your prejudices. At a good shop they take the time to listen to your complaints after purchase; they're interested in working out problems and keeping you as a customer. Unless you happen to be mechanically and technically talented, this kind of service is extremely important. Finally, good shops are less amenable to bargaining than poor ones because they figure in the cost of service, and understand that their reputation is built on this.

As implied, some shops are pretty poor, and it's up to you to avoid them. There are racing shops that won't give you the time of day, and there are shops that just can't do basic service. Owners can be surprisingly narrow-minded. There are shops with an attitude you could cut with a knife, and there are shop owners who just don't want to know about your problem, even if they helped create it. Definitely visit a few shops before buying. Do *not* carry and quote a consumer magazine; these tend to be poorly regarded in bikie circles, not without reason. Also, don't expect to be flattered. At its best, this is a cottage industry peopled with artisans who deal with a unique item. It's not a get-rich-quick business. Expertise does tend to breed eccentricity, so don't be quick to judge. You may come to find the absence of slickness pleasant.

Whichever shop you deal with, it should have an attitude you can live with, good repair facilities, and a wide range of bicycles to choose from. If the shop doesn't stock ballooners, for example, they may not know much about an off-road bike. If they don't have three-speeds, they may knock them—and so forth. Dealers tend to sell what they have in stock.

THE WEST HILL SHOP
Southern Vermont is a haven in more ways than one; West Hill is a bike shop in summer, a ski shop in winter. Note plentiful tools, space, solid workstand, quantities of replacement parts; they can back up a warranty. Cog-board along right wall indicates capacity to build up custom freewheel clusters (also called blocks).

REPAIRS
Technical consultant and Wheelworks manager John Allis doubling as mechanic; his
knowledge of bicycle construction and repair is not superficial. At least one person in
a shop must have this expertise; a shop full of sales types is not a good sign.

KNOWING WHAT YOU WANT

It's essential to be clear in your own mind about why you are buying a bike and how you will use it. If you have a hilly 12-mile commute in
mind, a dérailleur bike makes sense; a shorter, flatter urban commute
suggests a three-speed, cruiser, or folder. If you must arrive looking like
Mr. Clean, you might want something with a chain-case. It looks
square, weighs a pound or two, reduces maintenance and eliminates
grease spots.

Think your purchase through. The inexpensive raised-bar bike is
no great temptation to bike thieves, and the upright riding-position bike
fits into urban traffic well. If you are athletic and competitive, you may
want to go the dropped-bar dérailleur route so you can keep up with
your athletic and competitive friends; in this case, look for tight geome-

try combined with light wheels and tires. If you are hard on equipment, go for quality; a powerful rider who stretches out on his rides can stress his equipment on the order of five to ten times as much as the casual day rider. He might be better off with an expensive pair of Campagnolo pedals simply because they last forever. If you are thinking about touring, don't assume you want a dropped-bar bike; your real desire may be to get away from traffic and paved roads, in which case a fat-tired mountain bike is the answer.

Knowing what you want is not simply a practical consideration; it sets the tone of your dialogue with shop personnel. Lack of sophistication is one thing, total ignorance something else. You will get more respect if you know your own mind. Bicycle people do have an attitude about dilettantes; if you can offset this, you get more serious responses to your queries.

How important is it to know what you're looking for? Very. Sal Corso of New York's Stuyvesant Bicycles tells a story about a couple in their late fifties who planned to retire to Florida and were looking for a pair of bikes. They chose a pair of three-speeds and placed a deposit, but failed to reappear. When they finally showed up some weeks later, they

STUYVESANT BICYCLES
Stuyvesant is b-i-g, and the sheer volume of goods can be confusing; but this lower Manhattan shop stocks (and can fix) almost everything. Where else can you find a chrome-plated Raleigh three-speed? Sal Corso, proprietor, says this model was intended for British distribution, "but we got a few."

explained that another shop ("Which Shall Remain Nameless") had talked them into a pair of track bikes—expensive, 18-pound hair-trigger racing machines, tricky to the point of being dangerous. Definitely not street bikes except for alert, adroit competitive riders.

"Well, he did install a brake on the front as I recall," says Corso, "but those people did not belong on those bikes."

THE FIT KIT

There are many theories about how to interface bodies with bicycles, and they often yield contradictory results. Many of them are simply antiquated, and ignored in the very countries where they originated. The ultimate fit comes from having an experienced coach work with you, but this is impossible for most people. The closest thing to this is Bill Farrel's Fit Kit, which was derived from Farrel's photographing a nearly infinite number of top riders in action over a period of years. Its one great advantage is that Farrel—a math teacher, former national-class competitive rider, and cycling coach—proceeded from no fixed assumptions. His approach was purely inductive: See how the best riders ride, measure them, and measure their bikes. He is firm on one point though—frames and components should be adapted to bodies, not the opposite.

The Fit Kit notion was one of those simple ideas, like Columbus deciding to get some boats and sail west to get to the mysterious East. Farrel seems to have measured everything, including whether your feet toe in or out, and how much. Out of the Fit Kit measurements come recommendations for frame size and components that can be followed with confidence. They yield what he calls a "developmental position"—one in which body alignment is basically sound and neutral—easily adaptable to any kind of racing and touring. The kit is seen in the lower left corner of the photograph; a plumb-bob is being dropped from the tibial bump just below the girl's knee to set seat position in relation to pedal.

"The surprising thing is that you find a close similarity between a good road-racing position and that of an experi-
(continued)

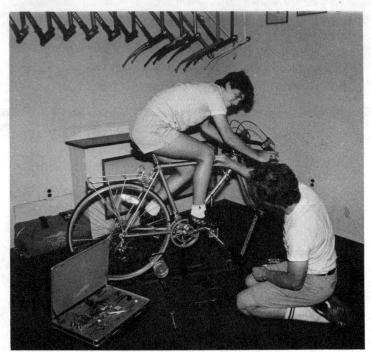

MERCEDES GALLUP BUYS A BIKE

enced tourist with lots of mileage. Often the only difference is a slightly higher stem or a slight change in seat position."

The Fit Kit is professional equipment, too expensive ($795 for the kit, $35 for the instructional videotape) for a rider to purchase, but it is finding its way into many clubs and bike shops because it does a difficult job as well or better than anything else available. One place it has been used is the Olympic Training Center at Colorado Springs, where Farrel has worked with the Elite Athlete program.

It's a good sign when a shop owns a Fit Kit. They usually charge $15–$25 for its use, and it's money well spent. Women will benefit especially, since the system makes no assumptions about body typology, but works only with the measurements of a given person. For further information, write Farrel at the New England Cycling Academy, Box 140, Danbury, NH 03230.

BASIC FITTING

The first thing to check on any bicycle is whether it fits, or can be made to fit. Don't buy the biggest horse in the corral unless you have the longest legs in town; unlike a pair of shoes, the frame of a bicycle does not break in. An oversized bike brings your groin too close to the top tube, and, because tall bikes are also longer, they place the handlebars too far forward. You find yourself reaching for brake levers that are always too far away. Compensating through radical changes in seat adjustment and stem length will distort your riding position, and good position is essential to smooth, comfortable pedaling. This in turn has a lot to do with whether the bike is comfortable on long rides.

Frame fit is important in all bikes, but especially so with the dropped-bar dérailleur, the usual choice for long-distance road riding.

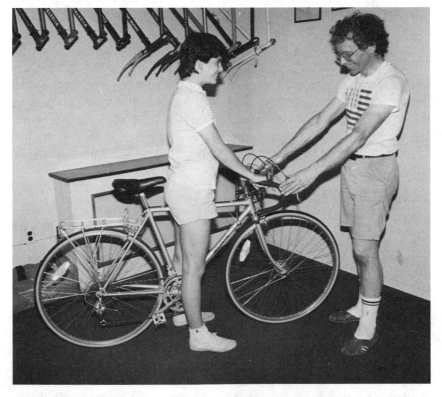

STAND-OVER TEST
A bit of clearance over the top tube is basic, and don't let anyone talk you out of it.

The basic "stand-over" test is the same with any bike, though; you must be able to stand flat-footed over the top tube in stocking feet, preferably with about an inch of clearance. Bottom-bracket height varies on stock bikes, but this is how you get your best idea of how the bike will fit. Subtracting 10 inches from your full inseam (measured to the floor) is another method; both methods will almost always come to similar (and workable) conclusions.

The most foolproof method of finding the right bike is through use of the Fit Kit, and there are also adjustable "stationary bicycles" that are useful for this when used by experienced people. Whatever method you use, just make sure you have that inch of clearance when standing flat-footed over the bike.

RAISED-BAR BIKES

With a three-speed, you have little choice; these usually come in two triangulated ("men's") sizes, 21" and 23", and in a drop-frame ("women's") model. (There are also 19" and 25" three-speeds from some makers, but they are hard to find.) Ballooners come in more variety, and the rule with off-roaders is to buy a little smaller than usual, for more clearance and better handling. Directions for fitting the Gary Fisher MountainBike clearly state that the bike is designed for an extra-length seatpost to allow for a smaller frame—one that can give as much as 2½" clearance when you stand over the bike. It's also customary to change seat position often with off-road bikes, lowering it for fast descents, raising it for climbs—hence the quick-release seatpost.

SEAT-TO-BARS LENGTH

With a dropped-bar bike, the next step used to be the seat-to-bars measurement. As it turns out, this works best with medium-sized men of average proportions and is not applicable to women, who are proportioned differently. The procedure is to make sure the seat is properly mounted, then place your elbow at the nose of the saddle, with your fingers stretched toward the bars. If they come within ½" of touching and don't overlap by more than ¾", the bike can usually be made to fit pretty well, but this test works only for those of average proportions.

A better approach to this lengthwise measure (the length of top tube plus stem) is to have an experienced rider watch you pedal the bicycle on a stationary training device like the Turbo-trainer. If the fit is

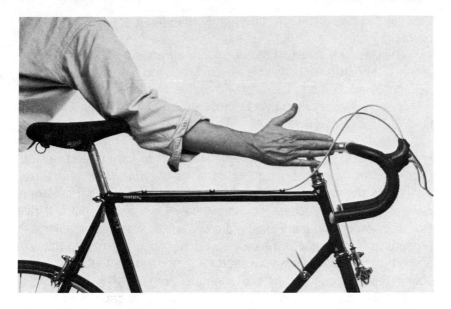

SEAT-TO-BARS MEASUREMENT
The idea here is that with your elbow at the tip of the saddle, your fingers should just graze the bars. This doesn't work reliably, but if you miss by as much as two inches it should make you thoughtful.

fairly close, a change in stem length will make up the difference; Chapter 7 goes into detail. If one bike is way off, try another brand; some have longer top tubes, some shorter. You may not like some of the components on the alternate bike, but these can be changed; the frame can't. Given two bikes that fit, though, there may be differences in geometry and tubing. Take your time, and try to draw the salesman out. If you are a high-torque type that goes as hard as the traffic will bear, you don't want a thin, mild-steel frame and long wheelbase. If you're into comfort, you may want just exactly that.

WOMEN'S BICYCLES

This is as good a time as any to point out that many women have special problems buying bicycles and setting them up. In the past, mass-market bikes were generally built in 19″, 21″, 23″, and 25″ frames, of which the smallest was often "phony," i.e., built with a high bottom bracket that raises the top tube higher than it ought to be, creating a problem for the short rider.

There is little question that for years bicycles were designed primarily with men in mind; this created bicycles too big for many women, who could not find a stock diamond-frame bike small enough. This is no longer the case, though you must shop carefully to find the right bike.

Wheel size is definitely part of the problem: The height of traditional 700C and 27" wheels, combined with the angles created by standard lugs, make it cheaper to build frames of about 19½" and larger. These are simply too big for many women. An additional problem is created by the Consumer Products Safety Commission (CPSC) rule that the toe must clear the turning arc of the front wheel, a meaningless precaution that lengthens the bicycle; a long bicycle forces a rider with a short upper body into a very stretched-out position, though this can sometimes be corrected by changing the stem.

Experienced builders, who are usually experienced riders as well, tend to ignore CPSC nonsense. People have been riding bicycles on which the wheel doesn't clear the toe clip for years, because by the time you've got the wheel turned that far you're already in trouble; only in a very tight U-turn is the wheel turned that far, never in normal riding. The shorter bike is extremely advantageous to most women riders because the female body tends to be proportioned longer in the leg, shorter in upper body and arms.

SOLUTIONS

Where there are problems, people come up with solutions. In this case the solutions are (a) a patient search for the right diamond-frame bike, (b) a drop frame, of which the mixte is your best bet. It's hard to find light mixte frames of quality butted tubing, but they are worthwhile, weighing only a little more than similar diamond frames. The mixte is a bit flexible, but this is perfectly okay if you are not into heavy torquing, which most small riders are not. Solution (c) is a custom frame, which is pricey but which opens up new possibilities, because it is possible to build a frame as small as 18½" on standard (27" or 700C) wheels. Bertin makes one, though it's hard to find.

SMALL BIKES

The search for small (under 19″) frames compatible with standard wheels has produced curved top tubes (Panasonic Sport, $185, Nishiki Custom Sport, $235), tilted top tubes (Rodriguez, $759, Zebrakenko Thunder, $250), and mixed wheel sizes (24″ front wheel, 27″ rear, as on the custom Bill Boston bicycles, which are light but expensive). There are also relatively conventional designs on 26″ alloy wheels (Univega Nuovo Sport, $250) and 27″ alloy wheels (Sekai 2700, $540). As with folders, small bikes differ enormously in dimensions and geometry— and therefore in handling. Ride at least two before you make a purchase. If you find one that feels right but don't like the wheels or components, ask the dealer to switch them and give you some credit on the unused originals. It will cost you, but you will then have a bike you can enjoy, rather than struggle with.

SMALL TEN-SPEED
Built by Luis Arroyo of Paris Sport, this is a well-designed small bicycle with standard wheels. Set up with Campagnolo components, it cost $1200, but it's light and it really fits, largely owing to the unusually short head tube made possible by modified lugs. "Worth the money," says owner Abby Cohen, "stock bikes just didn't fit." Neither did some other custom bikes, owing to weird geometry.

WHAT REALLY MATTERS

When you've found a bike that fits, check components carefully. For most women, light equipment is very advantageous. The less powerful the rider, the more important such factors as weight and gearing become, and these are not only of concern to women who ride small-frame bicycles. Many women become smooth, light pedalers who can benefit from lower gearing (Chapter 8) and light equipment that a big man would soon destroy. A 120-pound woman is only ⅔ the weight of a 180-pound man, and her strength is usually on the same order or less, though her endurance may be equal or superior. To ride comfortably with men, women must ride appropriate bikes. Most important are the wheels and tires. While the new, high-pressure, narrow rims and tires are questionable for the heavy riders, they are just fine for most women.

MODIFICATIONS

Women as a group may need to make more modifications to stock derailleur bikes than men, but any rider may want to change a few things on a new bike. The typical problem for inexperienced buyers of expensive bicycles is discovering that they can't live with the expense of tubular tires. This problem is complicated by the fact that these tires mount on a rim that won't accept clinchers. Unless you are willing to pay the price ($20–$40 a pop) the tubular wheels and tires should be exchanged for clinchers at time of purchase; it won't be free, but for most riders it will be worth it. Women riders are the exception: Light riders suffer fewer punctures and some gain vastly by the lightness of tubulars; in areas with clean roads, the cost of tubulars is often justified by improved performance. (See chart page 104.)

At the other end of the price scale, the classic deletions for low-price and mid-price bikes are auxiliary levers, stem-shifters and "pie-plate" (spoke protector). It should be said though, that if you're a total klutz, you may want some kind of spoke protector. Without one, the chain can get jammed between spokes and freewheel. A small spoke protector does the job without looking ugly.

DECIDING WHAT TO REPLACE

One reason for a Fit Kit session before you buy is that you will not only have a bike that fits, but you'll know what needs changing when making your purchase. This is helpful, because it may not just be a matter of removing junk. The ideal time to negotiate these or any modifications is before you have made your purchase. Saddle and stem are common changes, and a microadjust seatpost is another standard upgrade.

You might also want a good derailleur bike, but not the dropped bars. This requires changing brake levers and cables as well as bars, and once the original equipment has been used, the dealer can't sell it as new. Work it out before buying; the change will cost much more after you've bought the bike.

Before making major decisions, it's wise to discuss the matter with someone who really knows bikes. If you do switch components be prepared to pay some labor costs. If the dealer just doesn't want to be bothered or seems confused by the idea, say good-bye, because you aren't into a good shop. On the other hand, if he suggests that your ideas may be a little farfetched, listen. He might save you some time and money.

RULES FOR BUYING

The first rule, and it is really important, is to time your visits away from sunny spring weekends when shops are knee-deep in repairs and impatient customers. You have a right to a certain amount of undistracted attention, but during the peak season a bike shop resembles the floor of the stock exchange during a rally. It's really too crazed for any kind of extended communication. You get better dialogue going in late fall and winter (except before Christmas). And weekdays are always better than weekends. Here are some other pointers:

1. *Don't buy on a whim.*
2. *Buy a bike that fits.*
3. *Don't nickel-and-dime the dealer.*
4. *Avoid exotic, hard-to-replace components.*
5. *Check frame size and construction carefully.*
6. *Get experienced advice if possible.*
7. *Buy a bike that is usable for the kinds of terrain and distances you will encounter.*
8. *Make sure the bike does not pull or wobble.*
9. *Test the bike methodically every possible way.*
10. *Don't buy a bike you don't like.*

GETTING THE MOST FOR YOUR MONEY

It's been suggested that recreational cyclists simply buy the cheapest derailleur bike with alloy rims made by a reputable manufacturer. This is not a bad approach, but there are other things to consider. Assuming a bicycle fits, the factors below should strongly influence your decision; sometimes spending a little more buys you a lot more bicycle.

CONSTRUCTION

Brazed and lugged construction is preferable in the stock bike, and look for the best tubing: seamless is better than seamed, and high-quality butted chromoly is very good stuff in a mid-price bike. Welded joints are a no-no at this level. Lugwork is not superclean on stock bikes, but avoid a bike with sloppy work; you can spot such if you look carefully.

STRING TEST
If a bike pulls to one side or shimmies, try this simple alignment test: Tie one end of the string to a rear dropout, run it around the head tube, and tie the other end to the other dropout. The string should be equidistant from seat tube on both sides; if it's off more than 1/16" you may be buying a dangerous problem that shows up only at high speeds.

FORK: Make sure there is a separate, brazed-in fork end rather than flattened tubing with a notch cut into it to accept an axle. Check for visible deformity, and be sure the wheel goes on and off without a struggle, seats properly, and lines up at the center. (Careful filing of the fork end will often cure this common flaw, but road testing is necessary to make sure the problem is really solved.)

FRAME: This should have a separate, brazed-in dropout to accept the rear wheel. Most bicycles are fractionally out of alignment, but this is not necessarily a fatal flaw. The String Test will check front-to-rear straightness: Run a piece of string from the dropout around the head tube, and back to the other dropout. The string should be very close to equidistant from the seat tube on both sides. Make sure the wheel goes on and off easily.

COMPONENTS

What you are looking for, generally, is name-brand alloy (i.e., aluminum) components, not so much because of the weight saving but because in today's market less and less good equipment is made from steel. Generally, you will find that while European equipment evolves slowly, some Japanese manufacturers make major revisions very frequently. The upside of this approach is that improvements can be made quickly, but the downside is that totally redesigned equipment is not road-proven, and you may have difficulty finding replacement parts. Very irritating. If you are uncertain about some item, ask the dealer if he stocks the parts.

Some names that appear frequently on mass-market bike components can be counted on. Mavic, Ambrosio, Super Champion, Araya, and Weinmann rims hold up well. Campagnolo and Shimano conventional hubs are very good, as are Mavic and Phil Wood sealed-bearing models. Sugino, T.A., and Stronglight cranks are good value; SunTour, and recent Huret derailleurs likewise. Most one-piece alloy hubs are reliable. The SR Laprade seatpost is an exceptional value, and Avocet seats represent comfort and quality. Maillard, Regina, and SunTour freewheels are well proven. Shimano offers a wide range of reliable mid-price and low-price components. SR equipment has a well-earned, dollar-value reputation. Everyone likes Campagnolo brakes, if not the price; the same is true for Cinelli stems and bars. We might add that this is very far from an exhaustive list of reputable manufacturers. These are just a few names that have been around long enough to establish themselves.

WHEELS AND TIRES: Except on low-price bicycles, you can expect alloy rims and hubs. The 36-spoke wheel is standard and it's the best choice. Alloy rims are important because they strongly affect the feel of the bike; equally important, they allow more effective braking, especially in the rain. All alloy wheels are not equal though. One-piece alloy hubs are preferable. Wheels should be laced tight (check by squeezing a pair of spokes), and they should run free and true when you spin them.

As per Chapter 4, consider your weight and the roads you expect to ride when deciding on standard or narrow rims. Rims dictate what kind of tires you can use. Think twice before buying a bike with tubular (sewup) racing-type rims and tires. If cost is no object, they're great; otherwise, go with clinchers. If your dealer won't arrange a switch from sewups to clinchers, switch dealers. If you can afford it, consider owning a pair of each; as you gain skill, you will notice and appreciate the response of good tubulars, but knocking around on them on city streets is very expensive. Again we repeat, the exception to all this is the very light rider, for whom rim and tire weight may be critical.

STEM, BARS, HEADSET: Stem and bars should be tight, and the "safety line" on the stem should be inside the head tube, or it can snap, leaving you with no steering. The fork should turn freely but have no play in the headset. Dropped-bar road bikes should have alloy bars; raised bars are usually steel.

SADDLE ASSEMBLY: Good saddles have dense (rather than soft) padding. Check this. Women generally need a widish saddle that is not usually standard. If you suspect you can't live with the saddle, trade now. (See Chapter 7 on saddles first, though.) Whatever saddle you end up with, make sure it's firmly attached, as level as possible. A microadjust seatpost is gravy; some mid-price bikes have them, some don't. It's a basic and inexpensive upgrade that pays off in comfort.

BRAKES: Side-pull versus center-pull is not the issue. What matters is that brakes are solid, and correctly installed, preferably a known brand. Dia-Compe, Shimano, Universal, and Weinmann have wide acceptance in the mid-price market. Levers should not quite touch the bars when squeezed hard by the average hand, and should release quickly. New brakes often have too much cable housing or kinks in the housing, either of which can make them sticky, but this can be worked out through adjustments. Squeeze the brakes on a few other bikes to get a feeling for how much freedom is normal, and allow for breaking-in. Make sure the brake blocks are lined up parallel with the rims and are secure. If you remove auxiliary levers, have rubber hoods installed, so you can rest your hands here comfortably.

QUICK RELEASES: These come on wheels, brakes, and sometimes seats; they are a boon. Quick-release wheels can be removed without tools, and quick-release brakes can be adjusted more easily. Better bikes have both of these, and some bikes also have them at the seat-lug. (You can always have one added later if you want.)

CRANKSET: Cotterless alloy is the mid-price standard, typically with 52- and 40-tooth rings. As per Chapter 8, a crankset that accepts smaller rings is generally preferable, as this allows wider choice of gears. Avoid steel on a derailleur bike; it can be a good construction material, but not as used in today's market.

Better alloy cranksets allow you to replace both chainrings, which is very handy when they wear out; on some low-price cranks you can't switch the outer ring. Crank length has long been 170 or 171 mm on most road bikes, but some small riders prefer (and can sometimes find) 165 mm cranks. (Big riders should definitely *avoid* these shorter cranks.) If you plan hard-core, heavy touring or off-road riding you may want a triple-ring crankset, but make sure you can live with it before going those extra bucks. It can be a tinkerer's delight, not necessarily a nifty upgrade.

PEDALS: Get pedals that can be adjusted rather than cheap disposable ones, and make sure they will accept toe clips if you plan to ride any real distances. Avoid counterweighted, self-balancing pedals if you ride hard, because they hang low enough to dig in on corners. Quill (racing style) pedals come on better bikes, but make sure they aren't too narrow for your feet. *Don't* remove the pedal reflectors; their movement really catches the motorist's eye at night.

DERAILLEURS: These are rarely a problem when correctly installed and adjusted. Practically all low- and mid-priced bikes have long-cage, wide-range derailleurs of good quality. If you haven't mastered shifting, have the dealer check out the gears for you while the bike is on a stand; all should work smoothly except the extreme combinations—large ring to large cog, small ring to small cog.

FREEWHEEL: Wide-range freewheels are the typical mass-market component; live with this until you have some experience. Given the choice of a five- or six-speed freewheel, go with the six; it has advantages explained in Chapter 8.

THE TEST RIDE

One thing that helps enormously in making decisions is a test ride, preferably in the company of a knowledgeable acquaintance. This can be difficult to arrange, though—it's just too easy for people to ride away and not return. Be prepared to sign a waiver of responsibility and leave a sizable chunk of cash and/or credit cards; the dealer will want to be protected. Ask him to set the seat correctly, and tell him you'll be gone no more than fifteen minutes. Check the brakes thoroughly, then really ride the bike. If you haven't mastered the dérailleur, find a good middle gear and stick with it. If you know about shifting, check out the gears. If you don't feel qualified to test the bike thoroughly, enlist your friend who knows about bikes.

Don't ride no-hands if you're out of practice, but try to sense whether the bike pulls consistently to one side on an unbanked road. This is important: If you have to lean to hold the bike straight, you'll be leaning with the thing as long as you own it. Take the bike through some turns and see if it gets squirrelly. After you have the feel of the bike, get it rolling fast enough to check for shimmy or "flutter." (If this happens on a downhill, get it under control by grabbing the top tube very firmly with your knees or hand before braking, and don't buy the bike.) Finally, try to figure out if you can live with the seat. Seat design, especially for women, has improved a lot recently. Listen to your expert acquaintance, and don't hold him or her responsible if the bike is imperfect. Except for very good ones, bikes tend to resemble the human species in this; they're somewhat perfectable if you know how to go about it.

USED BIKES

A used bike can be a good deal, but it needs to be checked out even more carefully than a new one. An inexperienced purchaser should not buy a used bike without both a test ride and the advice of an experienced cyclist. The key to this situation lies in the warranty, which will be strictly between you and whomever you buy it from. If you buy from a private party, try to arrange at least a one-day grace period during which the bike can be returned. A shop will usually allow credit toward the purchase of another bike. Whatever the arrangement, get it in writing.

There is little rhyme or reason to the used-bike market; a bike may be sold simply because it did not fit, or because of a real problem such as a bent frame or poorly threaded bottom bracket that keeps coming apart. Along with pitfalls, there are bargains to be found in used bikes. Often it's possible to pick one up with butted tubing and quality components for the same price as a stock bike. Just make sure it passes inspection by someone who really knows. Cycling seer John Krausz says the only fixed rule is never to buy a used track bike.

UPSCALE BUYING

If you find yourself strongly inclined to spend 20–30 percent more than you planned because a particular bike seems just right, go for it, especially if you're athletic and know you'll spend time on it. Most bicycles are not just transportation; it's more like owning a saddle horse. People who ride horses are very definite about which ones they prefer, and once you get into the bicycle it's pretty much the same thing. Most people ride more for fun than anything else, and the fact that a bike gets you where you want to go is often secondary. If you buy a bike the same way you buy a tennis racket or fly rod, that's not wrong. But if you find yourself convinced you need something that costs three times what you planned to pay, you're probably fooling yourself; it's like buying a Ferrari when you don't really know what it's about.

WARRANTIES

Bicycle warranties are closely related to the ability and inclination of the seller to honor them, which is one reason why a reputable shop is so important. Unlike automobile dealers, who handle few lines and are more closely allied with their manufacturers, bike shops typically handle many brands. Ultimately, it comes down to the shop owner's willingness to take responsibility, and it is useful to be on good, realistic terms with the person who owns the shop. Service on a bike sold at no profit can be very different from service on a bike sold at a reasonable price. You should ask about warranty twice: the first time you speak with the owner, and again when you are at the point of making a decision. Eye contact is a good sign.

Keeping some options open on any purchase is a very good idea, but bike exchanges are ticklish. If you've damaged the bike, you'll definitely have problems; "newness" is important to most inexperienced buyers (mainly because they don't know what else to look for), and every dealer knows this. To protect yourself, check the bike carefully for defects before buying. If you want to maintain the option of moving up to a better bike in a day or two, say so clearly, and take it as the favor it is.

STAYING WITHIN THE CODE

Finally, there's a certain way to behave in a bike shop. Most shop owners want you to be happy with your bicycle, but if you're unreasonable in your demands, you will be just another irritation and will be treated as such. Make your tests and requests quickly and politely, and a good shop will accept you; wasting people's time and patience is something else, especially during the peak sales season.

THE PACKAGE

One way to get off on the right foot with a bike dealer is to give him a chance to at least break even, especially if you've taken a lot of his time. Buying your basic accessories when you buy the bike gives him some margin, and it leaves an impression.

Certain accessories are virtual necessities for anything but neighborhood runs. Buying them as a package with the bike, you do yourself a favor as well as the dealer, because you'll have what you need when you need it. It's a foregone conclusion that you'll need some of the items below in a matter of months if not weeks. Trifling things like loose cables or seatposts just can't be fixed if you don't have a few tools, and you will find a flat tire much easier to deal with if you have a spare tube. New bikes are theft-bait, of course, so you need a lock. And if you manage to spill during the learning process, or get caught out at dusk, helmet and taillight suddenly change from extras to necessities.

The collection below runs below $100—not enough to drive your dealer wild with joy, but enough to make him like you a little. Strictly in bicycle terms, you are making sense by having these things:

Frame pump	$12
Tools (as per Chapter 9)	$25–$30
Tube	$4
Patch kit	$3
Lock	$10–$30
Taillight	$10–$20
Toe clips and straps	$8

6.
CONFIDENCE AND CONTROL

Some people say that the automobile is the enemy, others favor the dog, but the real enemy is within. Everyone understands that people don't just get into automobiles and drive away without instruction, but they do this with bicycles, thinking that riding a bike is something you learn as a child and never forget. This idea is pure fantasy, and presumes skills that were never learned in the first place. When those skills are called for and aren't there, the rider can get in trouble.

The problem is even more insidious because at age 11 (the age most people regress to) a child has certain things in his or her favor that have nothing to do with skill. These include superquick reflexes, coordination sharpened by plenty of physical activity, and a fearlessness based largely on ignorance. Kids often luck out because an agile 90-pound body can somehow get itself out of a situation that would freeze many an adult. The downside of this approach comes around in the daily papers from time to time. Lack of peripheral vision and failure to anticipate have sent many young riders to the pavement.

SOME BASICS

Most people who think of themselves as knowing how to ride a bike have actually learned to balance on a bicycle. It's roughly equivalent to being able to steer a car, which is not enough to get you a license.

Starting fresh can actually be an advantage, as any driving instructor will tell you, because you don't have any bad habits and don't think you already know it all. If you are at this stage, there are a few things you need to consider:

1) People have learned to ride by themselves, but in the process one tends to fall down a lot and pick up scrapes known to the cognoscenti as road rash. It helps to have someone along who knows what he or she is doing.

2) The easiest learning position is very different from the most efficient—the seat should be low enough that your feet reach the ground easily. A small frame with upright bars makes it easier yet.

3) A bicycle is easiest to ride at about 10–15 mph. Like an airplane, it is unstable at lower, or stalling speeds.

4) The sidewalk or street is not a good place to learn. You want a big open space that will allow for your meanderings. The best place is a deserted parking lot.

5) *Confidence and control are the basics of road technique.*

FIRST MOVES

To get your bike rolling, put one foot at the two o'clock position and the other on the ground. It doesn't really matter which foot goes where, but most right-handed riders seem to start with the left foot on the ground. Try to have an assistant who is (a) experienced with bicycles and (b) calm and patient. First have him take hold of your belt firmly. When you're ready to roll, say so, and press down on the right pedal, while lifting your left foot and getting it onto the other pedal. You're not trying to actually ride, but to get the feel of pedaling while your friend jogs alongside. If you have to do this quite a few times, it makes no difference—just give your assistant a chance to rest. As you go through this routine, try to control the bike yourself as much as possible. You will notice that overcorrecting with handlebars and body weight is the main problem. At some point you will begin to relax.

When you have yourself balancing and pedaling at the same time, get the feel of the brakes. With your assistant still jogging alongside, gently test the brakes and get the feel of how they work. If you grab them hard while turning, you can spill. Apply both brakes at the same time, and make this a habit.

SOLOING

Next, try riding alone, starting in one corner of your parking lot (or wherever gives you the longest, clearest run). Start out as before, and

PIXTON'S RULES

John Pixton, a history teacher at Penn State, also teaches an eight-session course called Phys-Ed. 5, which trains cyclists to be "competent (and) independent on existing roadways." He has boiled down much wisdom into five rules:

1. Ride right with traffic.
2. Obey traffic laws.
3. Use hand signals.
4. Be visible.
5. Keep your bike roadworthy.

That doesn't say it all, but it comes as close as you can get in sixteen words. The final element is establishing a relationship with motor traffic whenever possible via eye contact and road technique. If any of this bothers you, it's time to check your attitude; you will create problems on the road for yourself and others. If you ignore these rules you won't be popular on the road, and you're much more likely to get hurt.

LEARNING POSITION
Lowering the seat (left) makes beginners more stable and less nervous; it can go low enough that feet are flat on the ground when you're seated. Starting off (right), make sure upper foot and pedal are at the two o'clock position, which allows a strong pedal stroke and better take-off control.

have your belt released after getting up as much speed as possible. Pedal hard during takeoff, and try to accelerate in a smooth power curve until your assistant releases you. When you are on your own, keep up the same rhythm and increase it slightly. You'll feel the bike become more stable as it picks up speed.

The three classic beginner's mistakes are (a) slowing down (which makes the bike unstable), (b) overcorrecting, and (c) freezing. Just keep pedaling and try to stay loose; your arms should be relaxed, not locked. Lean your body gently into corrective movements, and don't jerk. If there's nothing in your way, precise control does not matter. What matters is to keep going; time on the bike brings confidence.

When you are about 50 feet from the end of your run, gently squeeze both brake levers and stop pedaling. As the brakes begin to take hold, remove both feet from the pedals, and continue to squeeze gently. You may spill, but it's unlikely, and at this speed, with the saddle set low, you aren't going to get hurt. Stop for a minute or two after the first run, and then do it again. Do this enough times so that you relax; then concentrate on riding as straight a line as possible. This is the first sign of real control. With a bicycle, turning is easier than riding a straight line.

SOLO STARTS

The next step is starting up under your own power, which you do from that same position—one foot at two o'clock, the other on the ground. The secret is not to hesitate. You already know you can control the bike once it gets going, and you know you can stop. Push off with the foot on the ground and press down on the pedal hard enough to get rolling. Then get the other foot on its pedal quickly, and keep your feet going around. If you can't seem to make this solo start, your assistant can help the first time, releasing you as soon as you are under way. Practice the start until it's smooth and strong. Some people just fumble their way into traffic like idiots, and it's a bad habit.

TURNS

When you can start off on your own with confidence and ride with some control, try some turns. The trick in turning, as the Wright brothers observed, lies in banking (leaning slightly) into the turn. For whatever reason, some people turn more easily to one side than the other. Plot your course beforehand and practice until you can turn either way.

When you have this under control, learn (and use) the legally required arm signals. You'll find that signaling requires thinking ahead and it's sometimes irritating. It's also a good habit, because it keeps you in contact with traffic.

CHECKING YOURSELF OUT

Sooner or later you will find yourself riding the bike—balancing and pedaling well enough to meander around the parking lot without having to stop. This is satisfying, but it's only step one. When you're bored with this, take another break and make things a little tougher. One of the classic horseback riding disciplines is the gymkhana, which amounts to riding a preset course with some problems thrown in. This makes sense with the bicycle too, and it lets you know just how much you've really learned.

Set up a course marked out with whatever miscellaneous items you can lay hands on—discarded milk containers, cola cans, rocks, sheets of paper, or anything big enough to be seen. You need four objects, and they should be placed about 20 feet apart, in a line. You will now do a slalom. Try it a few times, then move your makeshift pylons closer by about five feet. When they are 10 feet apart, you can assume you have some degree of low-speed control. This is vital.

Now put your pylons in a small square about thirty feet apart and ride around it; then ride around inside it. It's useful to see just how much room you need to make a U-turn. Test yourself by moving them closer.

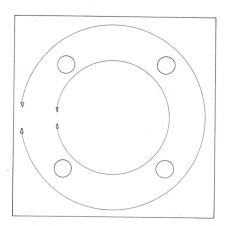
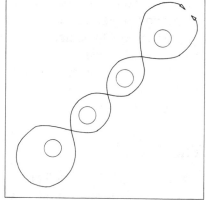

LEARNER'S COURSES
Riding around these home-made pylons in both directions will test your control at low speeds; it's easy to wander along on a bike, but that's not *riding*.

By now you will be developing the essential skill of riding a straight line at low speeds. The next step is learning to do this while looking back over either shoulder. The trick is to turn your head with relatively little body movement. Practice this crucial skill: *Until you can look behind you without losing control, don't go into traffic.*

BRAKING

If you ride a dropped-bar bike, learn to brake from both the drops and the hoods. Smooth, controlled stops from both positions are step one; step two is the abrupt, unexpected or panic stop, which can be done only from the drops. Front and rear brakes are both used in a panic stop, and body weight is shifted back and down. The wheels should be straight when you practice this; a turned front wheel and/or weight too far forward equals road rash or worse. Practice braking until you have the feel of it.

 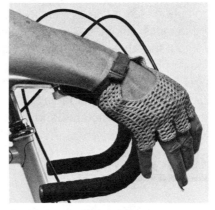

BRAKING FROM DROPS AND HOODS
You get maximum braking from the drops (left), but if you're cruising with hands over the hoods you can slow down by dropping forward and squeezing the levers from the top (right).

If your bike has auxiliary brake levers, be careful. These make panic stops more dangerous in two ways: (1) the bike can simply fail to stop in time, and (2) if it does, and you are in the semi-upright position they create, you may find yourself flying over the front wheel because your weight is too far forward and too high.

Finally, learn how to get off the road quickly without being nervous about it. Try riding off the pavement and into the rough, and do it a few times. It is just another skill, and one worth mastering. It's not really difficult to go off the pavement onto the shoulder, or even into a ditch, but you have to try it. Knowing you can do this gives you a confidence that you can't get any other way.

FURTHER STEPS

If you have a dropped-bar dérailleur, your next step is installing toe clips (Chapter 7) and learning to get your feet in and out of them. Start with one foot in the clip, and don't try to get the other foot in until you are rolling along fast enough to coast for a while. Then stop pedaling, tip the loose pedal with your toe, and slip the foot in. It's a skill that takes quite a few attempts to master, but it's not really difficult unless your control of the bicycle is still shaky, in which case you need more practice. Finally, raise the seat as described in Chapter 7, and get used to this higher position.

Few people can really get all this together in one session, and it is easy to forget. Coming back a second day, or even a third, before you go out on the road is an excellent idea, because you are trying to make these skills automatic. Until they are, you don't belong on the road. Without the ability to start, signal, turn, shift, brake and ride a straight line, you are a menace to yourself and anyone in your vicinity. The dislike many drivers and pedestrians feel for the bicycle is rooted in a very justified fear that the rider is not fully under control, and is liable to do something unpredictable and dangerous.

ROAD TECHNIQUE

Before even thinking about going on the road, you should be sure your bicycle is working properly. If your brakes are sticky or out of adjustment, you are asking for trouble; likewise, the shift mechanism. The same holds true if the bike is loose in any way, or if you have clothes flapping around near the spokes. You should also consider other safety-connected elements such as helmet, reflectors, lighting, and your fitness (which will affect your speed, balance, and reaction time as you tire). All this is simply common sense, but there are specific techniques you need to learn. No book can substitute for a good teacher, and the L.A.W.'s Effective Cycling program is the equivalent of driver training. Information on this is available through The League of American Wheelmen, P.O. Box 988, Baltimore, MD 21203.

The remainder of this chapter presents a basic approach and ways to handle the most common traffic situations, but an experienced instructor is better.

STREET LEGAL VS. GUERRILLA-STYLE

When riding on public roads, remember two things: (a) almost everywhere the bicycle is regarded by the law as a vehicle, and is subject to the same laws as a motor vehicle, and (b) bending those laws is justifiable only in terms of safety, not convenience. If you happen to cause an accident by violating the law, you are responsible. If you only come near to causing accidents, you are still an irritant, making your contribution toward antibicycle sentiment and possible legislation, as appears imminent in New York City in 1984.

This may seem obvious, but we mention it because there is definitely a fast-and-loose or guerrilla-style approach to the bicycle. Lots of riders think they are above or beyond the law, of course. In fact there is a whole school of guerrilla-style cycling of which the members are very proud. They feel free to talk it up and write letters to cycling magazines. They are a hassle for everyone.

These are the riders who come at you head on, riding against traffic, use the sidewalk, run red lights, and freak drivers out by weaving through traffic. In urban traffic where road space is at a premium, these people are dangerous and much disliked. As a group, they also jeopardize the bicycle's right to the road. They exist largely because the law is often vague, and the police are reluctant to deal with them. Many of them are unaware that the pedestrian can strike back: A jogger knocked the very experienced racing cyclist Jock Boyer from his bike during the 1983 Mengoni Gran Prix race, sending this Tour de France cyclist to the hospital with a broken collarbone and concussion.

What happens when a lot of guerrilla-style riders start acting out in public? Big problems for everyone. During the New York City transit strike of 1979, the bicycle was king; the mayor was being photographed with leaders of cycling groups, and it was generally felt that the city might have been paralyzed without pedal power. Out of this came bikeways and generally increased bicycle use in this very congested city. A very important corner was turned in terms of acceptance and respect. A year or so later came an incident in which then-Governor Carey was nearly struck by a wrong-way rider, and reacted with clear, definite anger. Not long after came a sequence of three pedestrian deaths-by-bicycle within a year, noted by the press.

Increased numbers of riders (whose road technique was usually unpredictable) then brought on a general irritation with cyclists, and the increasing presence of quick, nervy and aggressive bicycle messengers eventually resulted in a campaign to license these couriers. This then escalated into a general reaction against the bicycle which was dealt with by, among others, prize-winning *New York Times* columnist Russell Baker, *New York* magazine, and the *New York Post.* Letters to the editor were heated and numerous—so much so that the *Post* carried them as kind of a running debate, with headlines like THE GREAT BICYCLE UPROAR: PROTESTS KEEP POURING IN ON RED-LIGHT RUNNER, and BICYCLE RIDERS FIGHT BACK. One letter in *New York* magazine suggested that since the automobile was being subjected to "tough new laws," there ought to be similar laws for the "reckless and fearless generation of bicyclers." Most letters tended to agree with this point of view, and ran strongly against the bicycle and those using it.

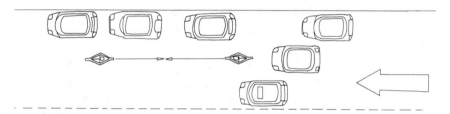

WRONG-WAY RIDER HASSLING STREET-LEGAL RIDER
This is a nasty situation that sets rider against rider. Wrong-way (left) creates real danger for street-legal (right), who may be forced further out into traffic. This can be dangerous. Street-legal should cut toward the curb and let the troublemaker face the problem. The driver of the car would probably like to shove a broomstick into somebody's spokes. Wrong-way is a dangerous jerk, and he's also very likely to blind-side pedestrians who look for traffic where it belongs.

ROADS AND BIKE PATHS

Being legally defined as a vehicle is an enormous practical advantage, because it allows you the use of the road rather than restricting you to sidewalks, bikeways, or bike paths—none of which is a real alternative in terms of getting where you want to go. This is why people who use their bikes frequently are wary of bikeways and bike paths. It is possible to design and maintain such systems, but more often makeshift arrangements are set up without the advice and consent of those expected to use them. Often bicycles are denied access to roads in the vicinity, as has happened in Holland, so that the bikeway/

path brings an effective de facto restriction on bicycle use. Basically, bike paths and bikeways are of interest only to neighborhood riders who want a little exercise. To get real use out of your bike you need access to roads.

LIVING WITH THE LAW

Sometimes it is almost obligatory to bend the law, but it can become a very bad habit; eventually you will cause trouble and/or get hurt. As a vehicle operator, you are expected to ride a reasonably straight line, stop for red lights, turn from the proper lane, signal for turns, and obey traffic signs.

You are also required to ride with the traffic, rather than against it. Some riders choose to ignore this, feeling safer dealing with what they can see. These "wrong-way riders" are wrong not only legally but practically. For one thing, the "closing-speed" of vehicles approaching head-on is much greater: a car moving at 55 mph toward a bicycle moving in the same direction at 15 mph closes at 40 mph; with a head-on approach, they close at *70* mph. Also, drivers do not expect head-on traffic slipping by on the right, and do not know how to react. The combination is lethal. Statistics indicate that the untrained rider's fear of being hit from behind is unfounded; relatively few accidents occur this way. Drivers hate the wrong-way rider, and so do other cyclists, for whom they create even worse problems.

PREDICTABILITY

One of the basic principles of road safety is to be consistent and predictable. Your skills and how you apply them make you comprehensible to motor traffic. Drivers sense your relatively constant "line" and speed in a very basic way. They intuit that you know what you are doing, and they feel less confusion, annoyance, and aggression. Changes in your line should be definite, accompanied by a signal, so they will not be perceived as random or challenging behavior.

OPTIMAL LINE

Predictability dictates your optimal traffic line. Experienced cyclists usually ride in the right (not parking) lane. Avoid riding on the *extreme* right, which is dangerous for several reasons: (a) you can't ride

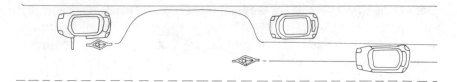

PASSING PARKED CARS: SAFE AND UNSAFE
Each time you move into the empty space between parked cars you create your own "dead-end" from which you must emerge. A following car may hit you as you do. Riding this way you're all over the road. The straight path a little further out is safer, and less likely to run into an opening car door. (A glance through the car's rear window doesn't hurt, either.)

a reasonably straight line while weaving in and out of parked cars; (b) drivers can't keep track of you as you pop in and out of their field of vision; (c) you have no space to yield in case of emergency; (d) it is more difficult to maintain steady speed, and (e) the gravel thrown to the shoulder of the road does not provide a solid footing. Many riders feel that under normal circumstances the cyclist should take two or more feet of his lane, simply to establish visible presence, but Doughty, George, and Pavelka (*The Complete Book of Long-Distance and Competitive Cycling,* Simon and Schuster: N.Y., 1982) suggest riding six inches to the left of the white line that separates road from shoulder. Actually, your optimal line varies with circumstances and road design.

Wherever you ride, your right-to-a-lane is not written in stone. Road design, shoulders and surfaces, traffic density and speed, weather, visibility, the presence of storm drains, and common sense all should affect your decisions. When it's time to move over—something your ears will tell you in most cases—don't press the point. If you don't trust your ears, look back, or try the Mirrycle mirror that attaches to a brake hood. Shatterproof glasses are also a good idea; they protect your eyes from dust, bugs, and glare (if they're tinted). Bear in mind that your general effectiveness in traffic correlates highly with where you position yourself, and that timidity can be dangerous.

ANTICIPATION

Another basic safety principle is to think ahead. You need to know not only where you are going, but how you want to get there. Thinking ahead also involves going beyond alertness into anticipation. It's important to keep track of the traffic around you, and other things as well. A parked car with someone in the driver's seat may open its door; a car stopped at an intersection will probably move in the direction the wheels are turned. Pedestrians at the curb are usually waiting to cross, driveways emit cars, and so on. Really good riders are analytical; they are alert to more than the immediate situation. They see patterns, and ride less by habit. Like good drivers, they understand a wide variety of traffic situations and how to handle them. They break laws only when forced to.

THE UNWRITTEN LAWS

Wisdom says that you must command enough road space to allow yourself room to ride a safe line. It also says that if you plan to command road space, you must keep moving at a fair pace. If town traffic moves at something like 30 mph, you want to get up to somewhere around 12–15 mph. If and when moving that fast becomes a problem, you should think about getting off the road, because you are dropping out of the flow. Cars are closing on you faster from the rear, and you are probably getting tired and losing your sharpness. Like physical strength, attention tends to ebb and flow; if you sense it's not there, get off the road, take a break and think about getting your blood sugar up with food and/or drink. If this happens at dusk, think about buying at least a taillight.

LOCAL REALITIES

Beginning cyclists tend to jump right into traffic wherever they happen to live. Often they get by through familiarity with neighborhood traffic, and become guerrilla-style riders. City dwellers with minimum

STORM DRAINS
The one to the left is *extremely* dangerous! Drop a wheel into one of those slots and you can be very badly hurt. Getting rid of these is a high priority for cycling groups. Good riders notice things like this. Diagonal slot drain (right) is safe, but don't try riding over it no-hands, especially in the rain.

skills and amazing arrogance do survive this way if they have natural aptitude.

Whatever your local reality, it is bound to be very different elsewhere. City streets, the suburbs, hilly winding roads, and the wide open spaces pose very different problems and have to be dealt with in their own terms. Forester (see page 146) suggests that in traffic it does not hurt to make eye contact with drivers around you—not to stare at them, but look for the flicker of recognition. Often it becomes obvious what they're going to do. Likewise the sound of an approaching vehicle yields useful information to the experienced ear; on the open road your ears are the first line of defense. The Walkman-type cassette or radio is dangerous on a bike.

ENTERING TRAFFIC

Any move into traffic should be clean and sharp, not casual, not hesitant. Wait for a safe gap between cars and enter with the flow. Do it with a physical effort that gets the bike rolling quickly. On a three-speed, use the middle gear; on a derailleur bike, use the small chainring to a middle cog—something between 17 and 20 teeth, which will let you get rolling easily. Work out the derailleur system (discussed in Chapter 8) before trying it in traffic. If your starts are unsure, practice. This move should be a definite, organized action with the kind of body language that conveys clear purpose.

STOPPING

Signal first; your bike does not have brake lights. Even if you've signaled, don't stop abruptly in front of following traffic. After your signal, use both brakes at the same time. Be especially careful when traveling in a group of bicycles. For a panic stop, drop your body, slide back on the seat, and brake from the drops (if you have dropped bars).

RIGHT TURN

This is a relatively easy maneuver most of the time, made from the right lane. In urban traffic, keep toward the middle of the lane, and avoid turning inside a car's line of motion, where you can't be easily seen; this can get you into a squeeze play. Also keep an eye on traffic coming from the left.

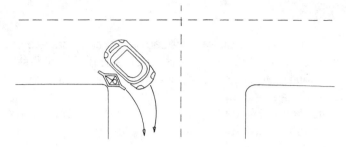

GETTING SQUEEZED

This is why you don't turn "inside" a car in the right lane. For openers, you're in a blind spot—even if the driver is willing to concede the point, he may not even know you're there.

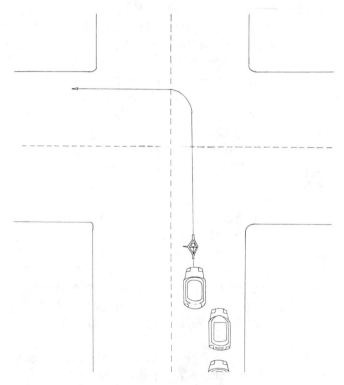

CONVENTIONAL LEFT TURN

Working your way into the left lane beforehand is the key. Bear in mind that cars in the left lane usually have the option of going straight; if you haven't claimed space in the middle of that lane, you can find yourself blocked by a stream of traffic that isn't turning left. On a left turn, move fast enough that you're not perceived as stationary, but don't race cars through the turn. Try to fit into the flow of traffic.

LEFT TURN

The left turn is more difficult, because you often have to cross traffic to get into the left lane before making the turn. Signal first, and get into the left lane well before the intersection, as you would in a car. If it's a left-turn-only lane, keep to the right of the turn lane; if traffic is also going straight ahead, keep to the left; this avoids the problem of having a car trying to pass you on the left as you're trying to turn.

JOHN FORESTER

The best recent in-depth book on sharing the road with motor traffic is John Forester's Effective Cycling, on which the League of American Wheelmen bases its training program. Written in 1975, this book put the bike boom of the early seventies on course. The heart of the book lies in its realization that the automobile must sometimes be forced, somewhat unwillingly, to share the road, and that the cyclist is safer claiming lane-space than dodging along at the edge of the road. From this realization Forester constructs a positive attitude and a variety of specific techniques. He dissects the fearfulness of the untrained, unskilled rider and points out the dangers it creates. The book describes more or less every traffic situation, and how to handle it. Equally important, it is compatible with the Uniform Vehicle Code, including this crucial paragraph:

Except when preparing to make a turn, bicyclists shall operate as close as practicable to the unobstructed traveled edge of the roadway. (Author's emphasis)

Forester, the L.A.W. (of which he has been president), and experienced cyclists everywhere follow this rule, claim their road space, and ride more safely by doing so. Anyone who doubts this approach should read the book and Forester's statistical analysis. If anyone in this country has really explored the nature of safely interfacing pedal and motor traffic, it's Forester. His book is available through Custom Cycle Fitments, 726 Madrone, Sunnyvale, CA 94806.

Another way of making this turn is what the Europeans call the Big Left turn, made from the right lane. What you are doing here is skirting the outside of the traffic, then picking up the flow of traffic from your right—it is slower, but if the traffic flow suggests this move, use it.

As a beginner, you can feel justified in doing this at times. Four-lane rush-hour traffic can be handled, but not without the skill that comes with road experience. It is not a sin to stop at the light and cross with pedestrian traffic; it depends on your experience, skill, and familiarity with the traffic.

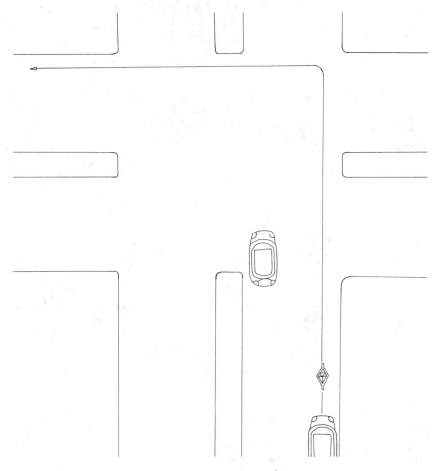

BIG LEFT TURN
In heavy traffic you may feel safer doing this; it's slower, but takes less skill. Stop at the far corner if necessary until you can proceed safely.

ARM SIGNALS

Clockwise from upper left: Left Turn, Stop, Conventional Right Turn, Natural (Bikie) Right Turn signals. The natural thing is to use your right hand for a right turn but it's not legally accepted in areas where the automobile system is the model; a right arm signal wouldn't work in a car but it is totally clear when used on a bike. Another useful signal is waving the following car past when the road is clear; you want them past you as much as they want to get past. Get used to using your arms as directional signals—the movement draws attention to the fact that you're about to do something different.

RIDING ENVIRONMENTS

THE SUBURBS

The suburbs can lull you into sloppy riding, but the frequent street crossings, parked cars, driveways, and unpredictable kids actually require more attention than you might think. Some relatively isolated suburbs are designed to protect children and pedestrians by slowing traffic; others are not much different from the city. The former are good places to build up early mileage because speeds are low, and there is enough traffic to practice with. You meet situations similar to city traffic, but have more time to react less frequently at lower speeds.

RURAL

Country roads are a very different proposition from city streets—and from each other. There are fewer cars, but traffic is usually heavier in early morning and late afternoon. Surfaces and shoulders are different, as are driver attitudes; in some areas drivers are more accommodating, in others more aggressive. Be prepared for a different kind of stress. While the air is generally a lot better than in the city, the miles are longer, too, and so are the hills, in most cases. Fatigue becomes a factor.

Equally important is the shape of the road, which affects the way you ride. Cities may be chopped up into handy rectangles, but a country road has the contour and complexity of nature as it shapes itself to the countryside. Riding in the country is fun, and this may distract you from some elementary precautions. As always, it is important to be visible and predictable.

HILLS

Hills rattle many beginners because they create a special and sometimes sustained stress. You are at a disadvantage in relation to other traffic because you are moving slowly and can't accelerate; accept this and ride closer to the shoulder. Climbing a hill, you want to concentrate on finding the best natural rhythm for sustained effort, but always reserving enough attention to listen for traffic and notice the shoulder, which is where you will go if a great beastly roaring sound comes up from behind. Look behind you before it seems necessary, and wave following traffic on; your arm movement increases visibility. Hold enough of your lane to allow some room to maneuver, but be prepared to yield that lane. You're definitely slow-moving traffic on a climb.

Riding hills well is partly a mental thing; concentrate on your pedaling. Don't let the bike wander, which can happen under prolonged stress; good basic fitness, good shifting, and gears that let you maintain pedal cadence (Chapter 8) all help. The bottom line is not to blow up (suddenly run out of energy) by going too hard, and then struggle

THE DOG

One of the odd facts of cycling is that certain people communicate well with dogs and rarely have a problem. For others, dogs can be really irritating, but only occasionally are they actually dangerous. The real danger (and it is very real) lies in cutting blindly out into traffic to avoid one. One noted woman cyclist of the 1890s carried a revolver, and used it to shoot a dog that had "attached itself to her leg," but this was an extreme case.

Ultimately, anything but a pack of wild dogs can be held off by dismounting and putting your bike between yourself and the offending animal. This too is an extreme case. Most of the time a decent rider on a dérailleur bike can outrun a dog if it's spotted in time, because dogs are sprinters. They are also very territorial; usually, they don't go on chasing forever.

The worst situation is a sneak attack when you are going uphill. The best weapon is a plastic squirt bottle full of ammonia solution. Damn his eyes anyway; he's after you, and you're defending yourself. If you're forced to get off the bike, you may be able to calm the dog and walk away; an aggressive one may be vulnerable to a snout-clout with your pump (a dangerous trick while riding). But revolvers are out; the owner probably has a deer rifle.

blindly up, oblivious to what's going on. If you have to walk—well, so what? Just keep your bike to your left and breathe deeply. And if it's raining, take the downhills S-L-O-W, with your brakes half on. This keeps water from loading up on the rims; the brakes work better when you need them.

The final thing to remember about hills is that just after you go over the top, you become invisible to following traffic for a brief period; don't let your feelings of exultation lure you out toward the center line as you chase your faster friends.

WORST-CASE DOG
A really skillful rider can take a more aggressive approach to The Dog. This Doberman used to get a snootful of Silca pump from Olympic and professional racer Mike Neel every morning during Neel's training ride. The move requires considerable skill, though, and you can go down. A pump is always helpful, but dismounting may be necessary from time to time. Keep your bike between you and the dog.

CURVES

Curves also modify the lane-claim rules because they constantly change both the driver's viewing range and the path of the car. On inside curves, the driver sees what is ahead in the curve; on an outside curve, his view is restricted. As a cyclist, you must be prepared to give ground when overtaken on a curve. Obviously, this is not a good place for riding two-up (abreast). If traffic is heavy, use your ears to the full. In the ebb and flow of concentration and relaxation, this is a time to be alert. As on hills, yield space when required.

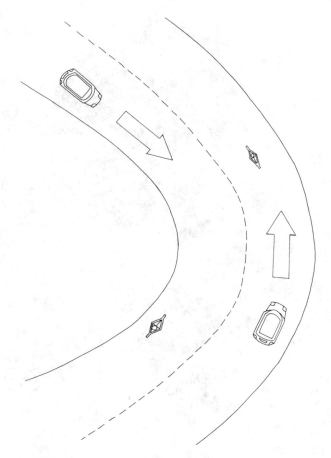

EFFECT OF CURVES ON LINE OF SIGHT
Rider ahead of car on "outside" curve (left) is often invisible to driver of following car. If the curve is on a climb and/or the bike is moving slowly, this is a good time to concede the point and stay at the shoulder. Rider on inside curve (right) does not have this problem.

COMMUTING

There's a lot to be said for commuting on your bike, and a few things against it, too, one being that if it's just no fun, it can spoil the bike for you. Method can become madness. Drudgery may be part of your job, but the real reason for bike commuting is that feeling of copious oxygen pouring through your sleepy brain and bored muscles. It feels good.

Contrary to some authorities, there are few hard and fast commuting rules: Northern commutes are cold and wet and dark much of the year, requiring good lights (Chapter 10) in the winter. In the Sunbelt, commuting can be consistently pleasant. A few miles is nothing at all, but you may find that you just don't really want to haul a hilly fifteen miles every day, because it makes you sweat a little too much. (Easing into it is the secret; after a while your body adapts, and you sweat less.)

Practical aspects of commuting include things other than the ride itself. Unless you are into long miles and big hills, an inexpensive three-speed or cruiser makes sense; bike thieves generally disdain them. A detailed map is very useful for figuring urban/suburban routes, and a place to lock your bike (preferably inside) is your first priority. You can often leave the lock itself wherever you park the bike, which saves you hauling the extra 2–3 pounds of a good one. A washroom and a place to hang extra clothes at work are great. You also need to think about the possibility of road repairs, although a good bike doesn't often need these. A spare tube, tire irons, crescent wrench, and screwdriver are usually enough; Chapter 9 tells how to use them.

The route itself is the heart of the matter. On some commutes there may be half-a-dozen ways to get from here to there, and the shortest isn't necessarily the best on a bike. When you work out the best route, you will find the ride smoother and safer; you'll know where the potholes are, how traffic lights are timed, and how the traffic behaves.

It takes a while, but commuting really does get you healthy and fit, even as little as half an hour a day. How fit can you get? Well, Martha Stafford of Sausalito, California trains for the Coors International bike race almost entirely by commuting twenty five hilly miles a day to San Francisco—less than an hour each way. She never rides when it rains, and she usually finishes The Coors in the top fifteen—against world class competition.

RIDING IN GROUPS

This is a real test of character and personal flexibility, because very few groups match up in terms of physical ability and expertise. But almost every group has its natural tempo—a speed that can be comfortably sustained in flat to rolling terrain. Almost every group will break up on a long climb, too, but can usually get back together or form smaller groups afterward—if the people involved really want to.

Similarly, there is a kind of general agreement, accepted by most experienced riders, whereby the strongest riders are expected to take the most turns into the wind at the front of the group. These turns are called *pulls;* following riders *draft*—shelter from the wind and save their strength. There is also a more complex set of rules by which sheltering (wheelsucking is the racing term) is kept within reasonable limits. Make sure you pick this up. If you're strong, ease up a little; if you're not, make the effort to ride efficiently and stay with the group rather than drifting off the back.

DRAFTING TECHNIQUE

How close do you draft? Under normal conditions racing cyclists routinely stay less than a foot away from each other, even in training. However, their reflexes are honed as close as an Indy car driver's; most people are much better off allowing about 2–3 feet. Contrary to popular opinion, the draft effect falls off gradually. And there is a particularly nasty situation known as wheel-overlap that can develop from following too close: when a front wheel touches a rear wheel, the chances of a spill are about 98% for the rider in back, and almost nil for the one in front. You can ride your way out of this, but it's one of the rarer skills.

ECHELONS

The most efficient way to deal with sidewinds is with overlapping *echelons,* as per the illustration. This requires more skill and experience than staying in a line. If traffic is light, the road is broad and straight, and the speed is up around 20 mph, echelons of three can be safe for experienced riders. Narrow, winding roads and heavier traffic completely change that. It's all common sense, and until you know your

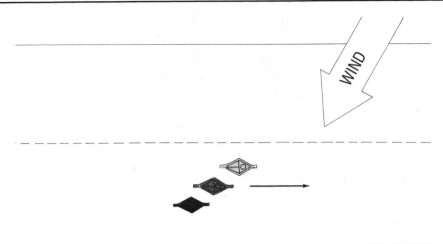

GROUP RIDING IN ECHELON
Former Olympic coach Oliver Martin observed that in the seventies, even competitive riders in the U.S. did not understand how to ride efficiently in a crosswind. Overlapping echelons protect darkly shadowed riders from the wind. But don't even think about trying this when visibility is questionable, as on winding roads.

way around a bike, the smart thing is to defer to experience. Try to get a feel for what the good riders are doing, and why.

Most important of all, when riding in a group, always spread out on descents and in wet weather; the speeds you reach going downhill require better handling skills, and wet rims reduce braking efficiency greatly. If you're carrying anything but yourself on the bike, allow for its effect on handling and braking. Many first-time tourists find out about this the hard way.

NIGHT FLYING

Riding at night without special equipment is extremely dangerous. There are those who will tell you that reflectors and plenty of experience are enough, and they are wrong. Statistics show that most serious accidents occur at night. In its less than infinite wisdom, the federal government has mandated that American bikes be sold with reflectors fore and aft and on the wheels, but this is inadequate. At dusk you can get by with a good strobe-type taillight, but after that you need a serious headlight. *You must be seen*. Lighting options are detailed in Chapter 10.

All of which is not to deny the definite pleasures of a summer night's ride if you're equipped to handle it. Europeans frequently do extended after-dark runs, usually in groups, but it is worth thinking about that: (a) these are well-planned rides by experienced riders; (b) European drivers, while seemingly mad, understand bike traffic—they spot bicycles faster and react more consistently—and finally (c) the bicycles are well lit. You need a lot more than a little flashlight.

Absolutely avoid riding at night in rain or fog. Seeing and stopping are more difficult both for you and those driving cars. Also consider that you're likely to tire more quickly at night, particularly if you're extending a day ride. If you're in strange country, plan ahead; the last thing you want is to get lost. If you do get lost, you'll wish you'd brought extra batteries. You'll also need extra clothes; night riding raises adrenaline levels, but after the initial rush, you'll probably be colder than anticipated, so be prepared. If you don't use a helmet (and there's no better time than now), bring something to cover your head; much body heat is lost here.

Finally, don't overdrive your lights. It's easy to do on a long descent, especially if you're in a hurry. You're taking your life in your hands to ignore the obvious possibility of defects in road surface, loose gravel, or something in the road that doesn't belong there.

SUMMING UP

Just how tricky is all this? Not very, as long as you give yourself time to learn. When road skills become second nature, you stay out of trouble, which is why the safety record of trained, experienced riders (like that of trained, experienced drivers) is so good. Using a bike to act out your problems—playing games in traffic—is a dangerous trip. Take your problems somewhere else. Letters to the editors of cycling journals notwithstanding, the rule-breakers that survive are generally those who "live on the bike"—racers, bike-messengers, or fit, agile athletes. Strength, experience, speed, and coordination bail them out. If you add judgment, you're that much ahead.

7.
GETTING COMFORTABLE

The magic of the bicycle definitely lies in using it well. The goal is smooth, relaxed, efficient pedaling, which creates a flow that eats up the miles. None of this occurs if the bike doesn't fit. For muscles to work freely, arms, legs, feet, and knees all have to be in the right places. Discovering how to set up a bike for your particular body is known as finding your *position.* There are formulas, but these are only approximate; finding your position usually takes some time. It is made more difficult because position is a kinetic reality—it is defined in terms of motion—and because it gradually changes as your body adapts. It can be elusive, but it's worth working out; when you have your weight where it belongs, you are more relaxed, breathe better, and get energy to the pedals more easily.

No bicycle fits when you buy it unless it was custom-built, but if measurements follow the recommendations in Chapter 5, the bike can be made to fit. It may take time to work out, but good position is the difference between pleasure and pain. The longer you ride, the better you know this. The Fit Kit (Chapter 5) not only helps you evaluate bicycles; it also provides the best means of finding a good position quickly and reliably. You start with definite, detailed knowledge that will let you bypass much of this chapter.

THE SACRED TRIANGLE

If you look at someone on a bike, you will notice that they are in physical contact with the bike at three points: bars, pedals, and seat.

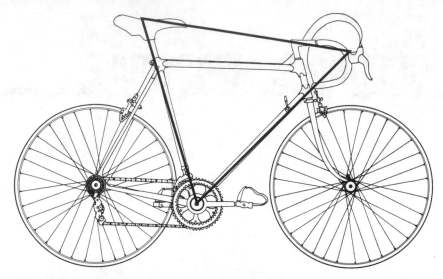

THE SACRED TRIANGLE
This triangle is constructed around the three places where the body touches the
bicycle. Foot position is averaged at bottom bracket (i.e., crank axle); hand position is
that most used by experienced dropped-bar riders, slightly above brake hoods.

These three points form a very significant triangle, sacred in the sense
that if it isn't right, you won't ride comfortably or well. The triangle
formed by a racing cyclist is low, stretched out, and forward; the tourist
is somewhat higher and further back, while a three-speed or ballooner
pilot is upright, forming yet a different triangle. The principles are much
the same, though. The upright rider is not concerned with wind resistance, but he still wants to get power to the pedals without undue pain.
     Ignore the sacred triangle, and you will feel a progressive discom-
fort caused by a badly used body. The longer the ride, the more obvious the problem. This is when you know for sure that your foot is not
where it belongs on the pedal, that your hands are numb, or that your
seat was designed by the Marquis de Sade. After twenty miles there's
no doubt. At thirty or forty you may be in real pain.

ADJUSTMENTS

     Adjustment means reshaping the triangle, moving it back and
forth, or tilting it; this is how a rider finds a comfortable position. Adjustments shift weight from seat to bars, get the legs advantageously posi-

tioned over the cranks, and move stress away from vulnerable areas. Seat angle and height, bars, stem, brake levers, and toe clips are the components involved. Bear in mind that adjustments interact; changing one leg of the triangle affects the others.

Basic adjustments fall into three areas. At the front end, you can raise, lower, or replace stem, bars, and brake levers; at the back end, you can raise or lower the seatpost, slide the seat forward and back, and adjust its angle; at the bottom, you fit toe clips to position the foot correctly, and, just perhaps, change crank length. Adjustments are less critical on three-speeds and ballooners, more so on dropped-bar bikes. Go as far as you can with original equipment; ride for at least several hundred miles, and only then consider changes in equipment.

SADDLES AND SEATPOSTS

The saddle (or seat) has been an object of abuse from cycling antiquity, and with good reason. The chances of a given person buying a bike with the right saddle are fairly slim. In the mid-seventies the Avocet company began improvements, described later, and today there are more options. These options work in relation to several principles:

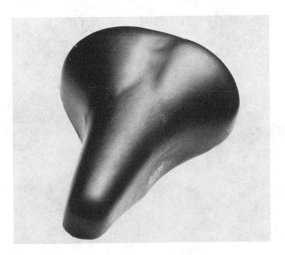

TOURING SADDLE
The wider design favors a slightly more upright position. Avocet's innovative raised pads are visible; equally important changes in shape and resilience of the "anatomic" plastic body underneath are less obvious but equally important.

1) A rider truly sits *on* the saddle of a raised-bar bike, and because of this, these bikes require a wider (and usually softer) saddle.

2) By contrast, less weight rests on the saddle of a dropped-bar bike; it is more of a fulcrum. The problem is in allowing the leg levers to work freely, because as the body drops forward, the thighs need more clearance. The narrower seat of a dropped-bar bicycle minimizes friction.

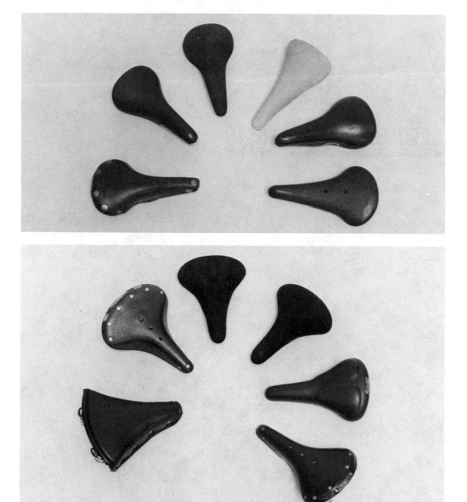

WHOLE LOT OF SADDLES
The range of shapes and widths is clear from these shots, but don't expect one shop to have them all. The narrowest are for racing, the widest for raised-bar bikes; the ones in the middle are for touring and "flat" bars, which give an in-between position.

3) Loose springs and heavy padding are signs of a cheap, poorly designed saddle that will waste energy bouncing you around; they also tend to chafe on longer rides.

4) There are definite anatomical differences between men and women, and a comfortable saddle is designed with this in mind. The ischial tuberosities ("perch bones") which bear a rider's weight are farther apart for most women, and usually require a slightly wider saddle.

OLD AND NEW

For about a hundred years you could get a saddle made of anything you wanted as long as it was leather. It was cut wide for uprights, narrow for dropped bars, and narrower yet for track racing. State of the art for decades was a Brooks Professional or Ideale 90; women often opted for the slightly wider Brooks B–17 if they could find one. You bought whichever seemed to fit better, and either suffered in silence or went at the thing with ball peen hammer, neat's-foot oil, or spell-casting. Unknown to most people this side of the Atlantic, those heroes of the Tour de France and Giro d'Italia were not riding stock leather saddles off the shelf; they had been disassembled and reworked by craftsmen who knew how to do it. Getting a leather saddle comfortable is secret lore, and a leather saddle that fits is to be treasured. A coat of wax on the bottom will help protect it from water thrown up by the wheels when you're caught in the rain, but the thing is vulnerable.

In the 1960s, plastic-shell saddles began to appear, usually covered with a layer of dense foam and topped with a thin sheet of leather. Early ones were not easy to live with, but Unicanitor became the competition (and café-racer) standard.

It came in one basic shape, though, in contrast to the endless variety of human design in this area. Not only was it chauvinist in assuming an average male pelvis width, it was only comfortable in a true racing position, and only for some people.

RECENT DESIGN

The next revolution came about ten years later, when Avocet modified both the plastic shell and the padding for greater comfort, and extended this type of construction beyond racing seats. Avocet not only offered several different basic shapes, they also made the plastic shell thinner and more flexible at contact points with the perch bones, and put some extra padding there. Their specially designed women's models were the first generally available plastic-shell saddles of this type, and were quickly accepted. These saddles have been copied by other manufacturers, though sometimes not very well.

CHANGING SADDLES

Bad position can make any saddle uncomfortable; try adjustments first. If you just can't live with your saddle, buy carefully. Some shops will let you try a saddle for a day and accept it back in trade if it's not damaged. Try to go for a long ride before passing judgment.

SEATPOST

As mentioned elsewhere, the microadjust seatpost is stronger and more reliable than the old post-and-clamp found on cheaper bikes. In terms of position, its great advantage is that you can get the saddle *exactly* where you want it, and make almost invisible adjustments that make all the difference in comfort. The SR Laprade is a low-price favorite, and is also offered in a special model (SR MTE 100) with extended fore-aft adjustment, handy for off-road bikes and people with very long femurs (thigh bones).

THE UPRIGHT POSITION

The upright position created by raised bars is not very aerodynamic, but it continues to be popular. It is easier to learn, partly because vision is similar to that when walking or driving, partly because many people don't like to bend any more than necessary. But it can definitely be done wrong. There are several approaches to doing it right, one of which is English. An Englishman on a three-speed looks as if he's seated at a desk. He manages to have good posture, move reasonably fast, and look ready to meet the Queen only moments after dismounting from a twelve-mile commute. The flat "continental" bar brings your body down and forward, which improves efficiency, and the off-road bike is much more of an athletic event with rules of its own.

Whatever your style, the first thing is to get the long front thigh muscles (quadriceps) set up well, and this alone can increase efficiency as much as 10–20 percent. Saddle height is the first adjust-

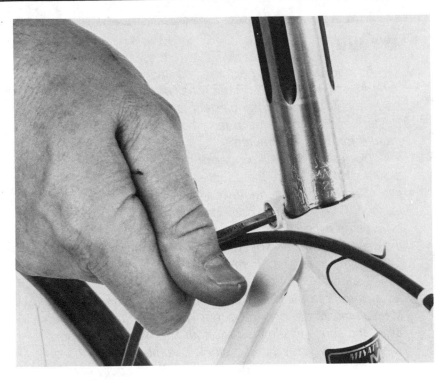

RAISING THE SEAT
An Allen (hex) bolt works best here; it's neat and easy to adjust, and the little hex wrench weighs next to nothing. Saddle height is the first step; angle and fore-aft position are adjusted at the seat clamp.

ment, and it is figured on several formulas, none of them sacred, because the human body varies so much. (109 percent of inseam leg-length is one formula, but it ignores foot size.) Luckily, it is possible to ignore the formulas.

POSITIONING THE SADDLE

For starters, loosen the clamp and set the saddle as level as possi-ble, at the middle of its forward-backward adjustment. Then set it high enough that your heel (in a flat-soled, heelless, cycling-type shoe) rests on the pedal at the bottom of its stroke, with just a slight bend at the knee. If you don't have a flat shoe, allow for the thickness of the heel.

The next step is to balance on the bike with one hand against a wall and pedal backward with your heels on the pedals: if you can just barely pedal, you're about right. (A training stand is better yet.) You can forget the old formulas if you have exceptionally large or small feet. If you rock from side to side, in *normal* pedaling, you're too high.

JOHN ALLIS

As part owner of an active shop, technical consultant John Allis now feels that "probably half our customers would be better off with raised handlebars." Belmont is just outside Boston, and limited miles in fairly heavy traffic is the basic pattern for many commuters.

"You sense the skillful rider, or the one that will become skillful, and you sense the people that just want to ride that five miles to work when the weather is good to maintain a little physical tone. You don't sell them the same bike, or even fit them the same way; and the guy who's going out in the country on his ten-speed for fifty or sixty miles whenever he has time is different from both.

"I spend a lot of time fitting people. I try to sell people an appropriate bike and make sure they're comfortable. Measurements are one thing, but I try to see them on the bike, and sense where their strength and balance are, how they are likely to pedal. We stock a number of brands of bikes here, and this is helpful in fitting. If the rider needs a short top tube and sporty frame geometry for example, we can find a bike like that, and we can change it around if necessary, so it will fit. People come back, and we try to help. Often the mistakes are very obvious; they will have their knee an inch behind the bottom bracket, or the brakes set wrong, or just a bad saddle. When they get comfortable, they are grateful. I think we hold customers this way."

Short distances, frequent stops, and pedals without clips suggest dropping the saddle about ¼"–¾". Longer miles suggest adding toe clips and staying with the higher position, both of which will improve your pedaling. If you have a long foot, you may want to raise the seat just a hair. But don't get so high you lose smoothness; this can lead to hyperextension of the leg and possible knee problems.

Next, slide the saddle to the spot that places your knee directly over the pedal axle with the pedal at the 3 o'clock position. A plumb bob dropped from the bump in front of your knee should come pretty close to drawing a line through the pedal axle. (See pages 116 and

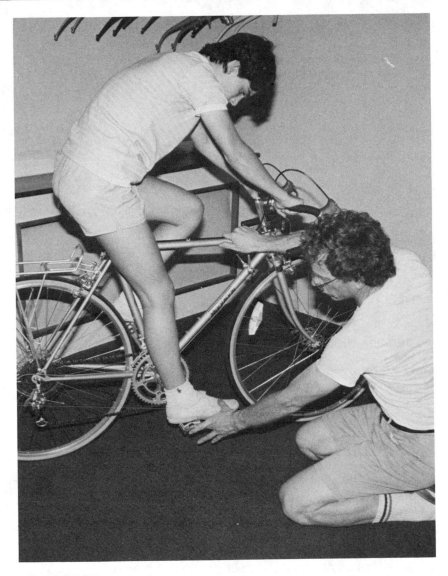

LEG POSITION

For most people, the leg should be not quite fully extended with the heel of a flat shoe on the pedal at the bottom of the stroke. You should be just barely able to pedal backward with your heels. Extending the leg fully (without hyperextending the knee) is important on long rides and will help you climb hills better while seated.

166.) You are now set up for basically good ergonomics, balance and control. Note that this knee-over-pedal-axle position also holds for the dropped-bar bicycle, discussed later.

POSITION OF KNEE OVER PEDAL AXLE
Under the pants, just beneath the knee is a little bump called the *tibial tuberosity*. With the pedal at three o'clock, a weighted string dropped from that bump should bisect the pedal axle. Like everything else this can vary, but not by much.

BARS AND STEM

Raised bars on most stock bikes tend toward the high, wide, Ritchie Bullmoose found on ballooners and the smaller North Road found on most three-speeds.

The flat "continental" bar mentioned elsewhere is wrong for off-road use, but fine for everything else, and the alloy version has become an accepted urban commuter's substitution for a dropped-bar bike. In combination with thumb shifters and off-road-type brake levers, it makes a quality bike easier to handle in traffic.

Stem replacement is rare on low-price upright bicycles, but raising and lowering the stem and tilting the bars are important adjustments. Dropping the stem and/or replacing high bars with flat ones is advantageous for those who ride longer distances.

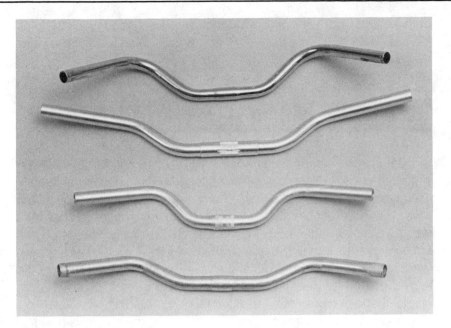

VARIATION IN RAISED BARS
The steel bars on top are a typical three-speed design; others are alloy. The third set from the top has more forward extension—better for rider with long trunk and arms; bottom set would be better for rider with short upper body.

SADDLES

The leather Brooks B-72 is a three-speed classic, but for something that won't suffer in the rain, try a wide, padded plastic-shell model; some Avocet touring models are just about right. If the seat is the only thing worth stealing on your clunker, use a quick-release seatpost and take it with you to work.

OFF-ROAD

The mountain bike can be ridden with or without toe clips, and it can also be ridden on or off the road. On the road, clips and a slightly higher seat position give better efficiency, but in its favored territory the rules are different. Balance and control rather than perfect pedaling and aerodynamic efficiency are what matter on the dirt roads, turf, and gravel it is designed for.

These bikes are fitted small, as mentioned in Chapter 5, and this allows a lower, more stable seat position on tricky descents. Use the quick-release seatpost to get the seat down at these times. Off-roaders perform wild and hairy descents in relative safety because dropping the seat also drops the center of gravity. You raise it back up when rolling the flats or climbing.

THE DROPPED-BAR BICYCLE: GENERAL

Setting up a dropped-bar road bike is a fine art. The thing is designed to cruise for long distances at speeds where aerodynamics are the major factor, and the bars are designed to take you down out of the wind. It can be uncomfortable at first, partly because it is a learned technique that uses the body in unfamiliar ways. Mostly though, people are uncomfortable mainly because the bike doesn't fit. On a dropped-bar bike, you want weight distributed with roughly 60 percent on the rear wheel, 40 percent on the front. But bear in mind that there are different kinds of positions for different kinds of riding, and total efficiency is not necessarily what you want. You can move surprisingly fast perched butt-high over the cranks of a racing bicycle, but the rest of you had better be ready for the stress.

PSEUDO DROPPED-BAR POSITION

Earlier, we commented negatively on stem-shifters and auxiliary brake levers. These exist because, while people like the dropped-bar image, many really prefer to sit more or less upright. Stem-shifters and auxiliary levers let you ride a dropped-bar bicycle in an almost upright position, but it's a basically unstable and inefficient position, too. It's not a good way to ride a bicycle. For one thing, the auxiliary levers interfere with the very basic hand position on top of the brake hood. There are mechanical disadvantages, too. Stem-shifters take very long cables, which can cause sloppy shifting, and auxiliary levers can be treacherous when you really need to stop. This is why we suggest removal of auxiliary levers and replacement of stem-shifters. Riding upright on a derailleur bike is no sin, but the way to do it is to switch to flat alloy bars and thumb shifters; you lose some efficiency, but not so much that your friends immediately ride away from you.

SPECIALIZED POSITIONS

Forget generalizations; even the cognoscenti can't agree. Bodies vary too much. It's true that racing demands a flat, stretched-out aerodynamic position, and it's also true that many tourists ride with their bars high, stems short, and saddles further back. But many people find themselves falling into a near-racing position with little or no problem; they have appropriate bodies and a feel for this approach to the bicycle. It's also true that some very tough racers seem to do it the hard way, with the chest catching a lot of wind. Think about "finding yourself" on the bike rather than copying an illustration out of a book. Riding smoothly without undue stress is basic, and this comes from breathing and pedaling freely. For many people, the goal is to be able to ride a painless forty miles. For them, the good position is the one that allows this. Other people enjoy pushing themselves more.

RACING AND TOURING POSITIONS
Only a handful of Americans can match the efficient position of California's Tour de France rider Jock Boyer (left). Saddle is high, bars are low, stem is long. Boyer is in an attacking/climbing position where the grip on the brake hoods is very important. This kind of efficiency is for purists, not tourists (right). Touring is supposed to be fun, and if you can't see anything but the road it's less fun. Slightly taller frame and shorter, higher stem, higher brake-lever position allow this.

STEPS IN ADJUSTMENT

TOE CLIPS

Fitting a dropped-bar bike begins by attaching the toe clips. These come in three sizes; buy the ones that put the balls of your feet over the pedal axles. This may not be quite an absolute rule, but it's very widely accepted, and you won't go wrong following it. If necessary, you can shim the toe clip out for a long foot, as in the illustration. Be patient. If this is wrong, it throws everything else off. Cheap clips bend, and alloy clips are delicate; name-brand spring steel are best, and Christophe is the classic.

LONG SHOE, SHIMMED-OUT CLIP
A very common U.S. problem: Getting the ball of a long foot over the pedal axle sometimes requires a washer or two between pedal and clip. The deeper position is more relaxed, and you'll feel the difference on longer rides.

TOE STRAPS

You need straps for your clips too; it feels good having them tight on the open road, but loosen them in town so you can get your feet out quickly. Contrary to popular opinion, there's no real problem getting your feet out of the clips when you want to, unless you've cinched the straps down very tight. If your toes are irritated by contact with the clips, try padding them with cloth bar tape. Nervous urban riders can use strapless "half-clips," which keep the feet from slipping off the pedals but don't actually hold them. Once mastered, toe clips are addictive. It's not just the added control and efficiency; they make you feel like part of the bike.

CLEATS

Cleats further improve foot-and-pedal interface. The improvement in energy-transfer is substantial, because cleats enable you to pedal a fuller stroke. On the other hand, Lou Maltese of the Century Road Club Association remarked once that he had set records in the old days without cleats; he obviously knew how to pedal.

True racing shoes (see Chapter 10) have slick soles, and don't work well without the stabilizing effect of cleats. They also have thick, stiff soles, which make them more comfortable. If you're not ready for cleats, try riding the shoes as is (with clips) until they are scored; then cut a shallow (1/8"–3/16") notch in the sole, not where it is scored, but just in front. The notches will stabilize your foot on the pedal, though less efficiently than cleats.

This will work with leather soles, but more and more shoes are coming with nylon soles and integral, adjustable cleats. This is good in that you don't have to buy and nail on separate cleats; the bad side is that nylon is very slippery; these shoes don't work well at all without cleats. Finally, given a choice, go for nylon cleats; they won't destroy floors, or costly alloy pedals.

INSTALLATION

In theory, the cleat must point the foot straight ahead, with the ankle as close to the crank-arm as possible, and with the toe not quite touching the clip. In practice, anatomy makes compromise necessary, and cleat installation should be supervised. Farrel's Fit Kit (page 115) solves this problem elegantly, by measuring toe-in (or out) through the entire pedal stroke, and averaging to find the angle of least overall stress. Riding your shoes without cleats and working from the score mark made by the pedal is much the same thing, but be sure to mount the cleat so the slot is slightly in front of the mark, or your toes will be jammed against the clip.

Nailing (or bolting) on non-integral cleats is a fair job of work; it used to be an informal test of whether you really knew what you were doing. Do it wrong and your knees hurt, as happened with Olympian David Boll early in his career. Exasperating as this installation can be, people rarely give up cleats once they have it together. Properly adjusted, they make a big difference.

SADDLE ADJUSTMENT

Begin as described earlier for raised-bar bicycles (page 163). The next step is some cautious experimentation. These adjustments are very critical on the dropped-bar bicycle, so proceed slowly. You will find that very small vertical and horizontal adjustments make quite a bit of difference. Work in increments of ¼"–⅜" inch, and check each adjustment with a fairly long ride.

SADDLE ANGLE

The classic recommendation is that the seat should be level, and there are people who will stand the bike up and use a level to make sure this is achieved. This is generally correct for upright-position bicycles, but with dropped-bars it's not quite this simple. In practice, many women riders will prefer a level or slightly down-tilted saddle, while men will often tilt the nose of the saddle slightly up. In any case, this variation should be very small, or you will find yourself sliding forward or aft, putting a strain on the arms and/or back, and interfering with smooth pedaling.

BARS AND STEM

Begin by setting the stem at its highest safe position. Loosen binder bolt two turns, shield the head with a block of wood, tap it with a hammer, and set the stem so that an absolute minimum of 2½" remains within the head tube; breaking this rule can crack the stem, which can mean complete loss of control. Before completely retightening, make sure the stem aligns with the front wheel, then tighten it slowly and carefully; if working alone, lock the front wheel between your knees. The stem must be tight enough that the front wheel can't move semi-independently, but don't freeze the binder bolt either.

There are extra-height stems on the market for those who don't like

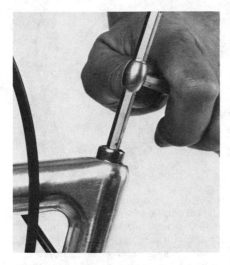 

LOOSENING THE BINDER BOLT
Unscrew the bolt about two turns, protect the head with a block of wood, then tap. The plug at the bottom of the stem will loosen, and so will the stem, if it's not corroded. Tighten carefully; unnecessary torque can deform the tube.

to bend over, but if your bike is the right size, you should be able to live with a standard one. If not, you might actually be happier with flat-style raised bars with different brake levers and thumb shifters, as suggested earlier. (If you do switch, save the old bars, cables, and levers as a unit that can go back on the bike if you change your mind.)

Set the bars within the parameters in the illustration on the top of the next page, by loosening the bolt that holds them in the stem. (There are several systems). Make sure they're solidly torqued down after adjustment; loose bars are very annoying.

BRAKES

Lever position is important because it affects body position. If you have small hands, check the distance between lever and bar. Different companies make levers with different clearances; a really good shop will know which is which. Short-fingered people can also loosen the brake mechanism from the bar and place a shim under the upper part of the hoods to bring the levers closer. The adjustable-clearance Shimano A/X lever assembly solves the problem neatly.

Set brake levers within parameters in the illustrations. Beginners usually like brakes very high on the bars, but this makes it hard to

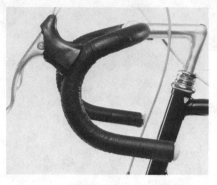

BAR AND BRAKE-LEVER POSITIONS
These two shots relate to several basic adjustments and equipment options. The Cinelli bars (left) are tilted up about as far as they can be; having the drops parallel to the ground would be the other end of the scale. Their Campagnolo levers are just about as high on the bars as they should go. Most tourists like them here; they're easy to reach from the top. The SR bars (right) are tilted up less, and their Dia Compe levers are mounted a little lower. The result is closer to a racing position.
Finally, note the considerable difference in lever clearance. A short-fingered rider who could handle the Dia Compes easily would have problems reaching and pulling back the Campagnolo levers; this is definitely a race-bred design for the male hand. State of the art in lever-clearance is the adjustable Shimano A/X; (Chapter 2).

brake from the drops when you really need to stop. Moving the lever assembly involves unwrapping the bar tape and loosening the brake cables to get at the adjustment bolt, as explained in Chapter 9—tedious but worth it. Lever position strongly affects body position, and getting it right is essential.

HAND POSITIONS

There are four basic hand positions for dropped bars, and contrary to popular opinion, you don't often ride with the hands on the lower section of the bars, or *drops* as they are called. The best combination of efficiency and comfort comes with the hands just behind, or on top of, the brake hoods; tests also show that this position can be quite aerodynamic. You can also reach the levers for braking from the tops; brake hoods are always padded with rubber on good bicycles to make this position comfortable.

But the real key to comfort on dropped-bar bicycles is to vary hand position. Your bike should be set up so that you can use all the posi-

HAND POSITIONS

Clockwise from upper left: (1) Skilled riders spend more time in this position than any other because it's efficient and comfortable on both hills and flats. Dropping forward onto the hoods (2) streamlines the position somewhat and gives instant access to brake levers. The hoods also come into play in hard climbing as in the earlier photo of racer Jock Boyer (p. 169, left). Holding the straight upper portion of the bars (3) is good on long climbs if you keep your hands well apart, but balance and access to brakes suffer; don't go down hills in this position. Riding on the drops (4) means you're either taking things pretty seriously or there's a headwind. But *do* go to the drops during descents; it lowers your center of gravity and maximizes braking effect.

tions shown. They shift stress on hands, wrist, back, and neck enough to make all-day rides comfortable. This is not to say you should be constantly shifting around. In a given situation, you may stay with a position anywhere from a few minutes to half an hour. But if you lock into one more or less forever, you may find that while you can move right along, the body complains.

MISCELLANEOUS TIPS

The above adjustments will get you close enough to ride without feeling all wrong. Any adjustments from this point forward should be tested on longish rides. Especially in the beginning, you are better off putting some miles on the bike rather than tinkering with it, unless there is some very obvious problem. Riding will gradually adapt your body; as you become stronger and more flexible you may find yourself getting comfortable on the bike without extensive change.

If you feel cramped, slide the seat back just a bit. If your knees bother you, come down ¼″, and check cleat alignment. If necessary, give the cleats up for a while and see if the pain goes away. If you move your seat back, consider lowering it slightly; moving the seat back lengthens both horizontal and vertical legs of the triangle. If you drop the stem and/or switch to bars with a longer reach or drop (below), the seat may want to come forward slightly—you've tilted the triangle forward a bit.

As a general guide, these factors tend to raise seat height: clips, cleats, a long foot, and the desire to move fast. Long femurs (thigh bones) suggest moving the seat back, but there is too much variation in human design for ironclad rules.

When you find comfortable settings, mark them clearly; it's really annoying to make changes and find you can't locate the previous settings which you preferred. And always consider saddle adjustments in terms of how they affect breathing and pedaling; these are important to comfort on longer rides.

FINAL STEPS

Good position may ultimately involve a change in components, but unless you have genuinely qualified advice, don't rush to do this; it can be expensive. When you've done everything above and still feel need for change after half a dozen rides, consider the components below, in order:

STEM AND BARS:

Somewhere between 90 mm–120 mm is the most desirable stem length, but with a stock bike this may not be possible. What you're doing in replacing the stem is compensating for the length of the top tube, and this is your first consideration. When your body is at its flattest (bent forward, with hands on the drops), your nose should be about ½"–2" behind the place where the bars pass through the stem. If you must replace the stem, buy for size first, aesthetics second. Stem length is not easy for beginners to figure, so don't lay out the money until a knowledgeable rider (or the Fit Kit) has confirmed your choice.

Stem height determines bar height, hence it is a very important adjustment. In touring ("civilian") setups, bars are usually about level with the seat, but in road racing they will usually be a couple of inches lower, for aerodynamic reasons. Most beginners automatically set the bars as high as possible, but there's no reason to stick with this; if you're a café racer at heart, you'll find yourself dropping down and stretching forward. Doing it little by little helps avoid pulling muscles. When you begin to loosen up and find your way into the bike you will get a different sense of what you can do with it.

BARS:

Dropped bars on most mid- and high-price bikes are slight variations on the Maes and Randonneur bends; the Maes is better-looking to most eyes, and Cinelli sets the standard. The Randonneur is often preferred by tourists because it allows a slightly higher position. Avoid oddball and track bends for road riding.

Bars of a given bend also vary in *width, reach,* and *drop.* Broad-shouldered riders use wide bars, slight riders small ones. The typical six-footer feels good with the so-called Merckx bend (Cinelli 66), which comes in an extra-wide 42cm width; most bars are 38cm–40cm wide; Eddy Merckx was big for a bike racer.

Reach (forward extension of the bar) can be especially important to small riders. By switching to small bars (and a short stem), many women can make a borderline-size bike much more comfortable.

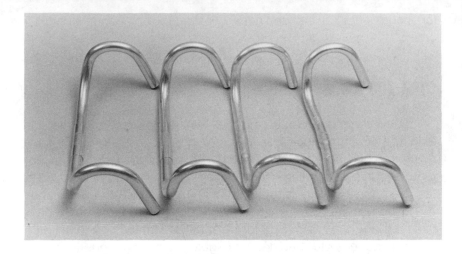

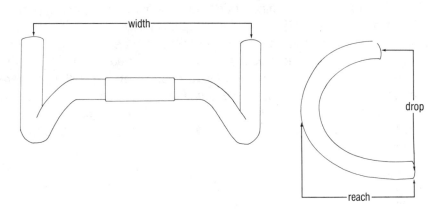

DROPPED-BAR VARIATIONS
Four bars (top) appear similar but are not; even this basic Maes (a.k.a. "square")
bend varies quite a bit in width, reach, and drop. Illustration (bottom) shows how
these are measured.

Equally important, this change also brings the brakes closer. Drop is
less critical, except to racers, because much less time is spent on the
drops.

When replacing stem and/or bars, check compatibility. No shop
wants to take back scarred parts even if they're unused. When making
a substitution, be sure that bars, stem, and frame (headset) are compatible. The dealer should know; if not, bring the bike in and have the
mechanic check it out.

BAR TAPE AND PADDING:

Another consideration is bar tape, or its equivalent. Circa 1984, plastic tape is very in; it's colorful, long-lasting, and easy to clean, but it's slippery, and its shock-absorbency is nil.

Cloth tape also gives a hard ride, but it feels different, partly because your hands don't slide around as much. Both are much more comfortable if you wear cycling gloves. There are also several kinds of foam rubber grips marketed by Grab-On, Kryptonite and others. These can be a boon to those whose hands go numb because of pressure on the ulnar nerve. Thick foam absorbs the most shock, but many prefer the feel of thin foam covered with cloth tape. Leather-wrapped bars are expensive and quite comfortable, but not easy to change once installed.

GEAR CLUSTER AND CRANKS:

Gearing and crank-arm length are both hot topics of the eighties, with pseudo-scientists all over the place telling you what to do. Both are treated as part of the drive-train in Chapter 8.

DISSATISFACTION AND PROGRESS

After a certain number of miles, every bike rider discovers the complexities of position: any alteration interacts with other adjustments. If you tilt the seat, your wrists feel it; slide the seat back, and the stem seems too long, and so forth. It's all part of a learning process, and dissatisfaction indicates you are becoming more aware of how your body wants to operate. When you are really fed up, try to remember that there is a position for almost anyone. Michel Pollentier was a childhood polio victim working with an imperfect body, but he learned to operate it smoothly enough to become one of the top European professionals, good enough to win major events and hold the leader's jersey in the Tour de France.

VARIETIES OF DROPPED-BAR POSITION

ROAD RACING

Even in the racing fraternity there is always a bit of disagreement among experts as to what exactly constitutes good position. Today's road racers are positioned like trackies of ten or fifteen years ago—well forward, on a smallish frame, with the legs very extended and bars 1½"– 3" inches below seat level. Unless you're pretty serious about going fast, this isn't for you. But oddly enough, long-distance racing cyclists are a better guide than most researchers, whose lack of practical knowledge has led them to strange conclusions. Simply riding hard and long tells the sensitive rider the basics about force and leverage, just as serious auto racing tells drivers about handling cars as nothing else could. In both cases, the physics of the situation becomes body knowledge.

From the pure racing style (achieved mainly by riders logging 300–600 weekly miles) comes the *cyclo-sportif/*or café racer approach, just as the sports-car pilot usually patterns himself on the competition driver. Raising the bars and moving the seat down and back just a little gives a position many athletic part-time cyclists can enjoy. Ride a bike frequently and fast, and you'll find yourself digging in and tucking down, evolving toward better position.

TOURING POSITION

While these racing folks can be very helpful as to leg extension, toe clips, and cleats, bear in mind that most tourists ride with bar and seat more or less level with each other. To achieve this, they often ride with a slightly taller frame and randonneur bars. In addition, most tourists have just a little less leg extension than racers, and ride with the saddle further back. Be careful about this if you travel American-style with heavy rear panniers; the front wheel can get precariously light, especially with a short-wheelbase bike.

Riding with heavy loads, there is also a tendency to pedal more slowly, and in a high-shouldered, short-coupled position. Moving more slowly, the tourist rightly allows leg position and comfort to take priority over aerodynamics. Most riders sense a definite threshold created by adding weight. Twelve or fifteen pounds tightly fastened exactly where it belongs is one thing; you feel it, but it doesn't completely change the bike. Twenty-five or thirty pounds is something else again; it definitely changes the way you ride; so does the wide-range gearing it requires. As one converted racer observed, "It's one thing to go like hell for a few hours, then get off, have a shower and massage. You can't approach it that way if you're riding with friends and camping out. Your pedaling and position and psychology have to adjust."

CLASSIC PROBLEMS

KNEE PAIN

There are two classic problems encountered by cyclists the world over, and both of them have to do with bodily alignment, or position on the bike. Where runners tend to have shin splints and an assortment of foot, ankle, knee, and hip problems, long-distance cyclists sometimes develop *chrondomalacia,* which manifests itself as pain under the kneecap. It derives from a combination of hereditary factors, poor pedaling technique and being generally oblivious to warning signs. As you get stronger, the knee takes more torque, and it can also change alignment ever so slightly as you develop more muscle.

Smooth, light pedaling goes a long way to eliminating knee problems, but while some knees can take just about anything, others definitely cannot. Under-the-kneecap pain is often the result. Most riders first notice it after unusually long, hard riding. The thing to do is to pull your horns in at all levels, because you are probably doing something basic incorrectly. Don't try to "ride through it" or you may have to stop riding altogether. Wrong seat height, incorrect gearing and poor foot position (caused by wrongly mounted cleats) all have been implicated. Relax, calm down and get off the bike for a few days. When the knee feels better, try a really easy little ride—no more than a third of your usual, whatever that is. Try riding without cleats for a while.

"Stay away from the big gears," says Dr. Robert Arnot, who puts in plenty of miles. "When I feel something there, I back off the big gears and pedal faster; I think forcing the gears at low rpms is often the problem." So do a lot of other cyclists and doctors. If the pain persists, try to get access to a Fit Kit, or an experienced coach. Absolutely avoid hard rides for several weeks, and gradually ease back to higher levels of effort. If pain continues and you consult a doctor, pick one carefully. A knee specialist who works with athletes is preferable; if he rides a bike so much the better. There are exercises that can help, and he'll know about them.

ULNAR NERVE

It's not uncommon for riders to experience numbness in hands and fingers when they ride for long periods. Usually this is restricted to those riding dropped handlebars, and is due to compression of the ulnar nerve. As with chrondomalacia, the first thing to check is your position on the bicycle.

Basically, you want to get some weight off your arms, which means a more upright position. Often just raising the stem and brake levers a bit and switching to foam padding on the bars will solve the problem. Randonneur handlebars will get you higher yet. If the problem persists, and if you don't mind giving up some aerodynamic efficiency, you'll find that substituting raised handlebars will almost invariably do the trick. But don't ignore the problem completely; continued compression of the nerve can affect its ability to recuperate, and the numbness can actually become chronic; it's rare, but it happens.

HARDCORE URBAN TRANSPORTATION
Owner Nick Peck says that a street bike "only has to work. That's all that matters; but it should look like it doesn't, especially in New York."

MODIFYING A THREE-SPEED

It's been said that three-speed owners as a group would feel a lot better about riding a bicycle if they had air in their tires. Those half-filled tires exist because most people accept the all-steel, 40-pound three-speed as a basic zero-maintenance clunker. This "commuter bike" is not so phlegmatic if you tinker with it, though, and the best place to start is with the pedals, which are usually cheap, heavy rubber ones. These can be inexpensively replaced with metal ones, which will allow you to add toe clips, giving you better control and allowing a slightly higher position.

Another simple change that improves this kind of bike is lowering the gear ratio (explained in Chapter 8) by changing the rear cog. Many three-speeds come with a 46-tooth chainring and a 16- or 17-tooth cog, which yields absurdly high gears for such a heavy and wind-resistant bike. Try a 19- or 20-tooth cog. Three-speed guru Nick Peck suggests that two sprockets be fitted on the hub, which can usually be done if the inner one is reversed: "Then you have two ranges—a low one for hilly country and urban riding, and a high one for open country. Switching over takes about 50 seconds and a crescent wrench."

Except for a few recent European and Oriental imports, three-speeds have come equipped with formidable 26 × 1⅜ chromed-steel wheels that weigh a lot and don't respond to brakes in the rain; get chrome-leather brake blocks or Mathausers. Standard tires are heavy and soft even at the full 50–55 pounds. Many people don't know that three-speed wheels can be built up in alloy. These rims are becoming more and more available. Mounted with lighter tires they make a big difference. Some three-speeds will also accept the narrower 700C wheel, which is better yet, because of the much wider selection of tires and rims.

You can also change bars and stem to create a more efficient position. Thirty years ago the British would turn the North Road raised bars upside down, achieving something like the racing position prior to Major Taylor's invention of the bar extension. It still works; and it works more smoothly with a slightly narrower saddle.

8.
GEARS AND SHIFTING

The art of riding the bicycle is largely in how you pedal. Doing it the right way in the right gear puts you onto a sweet spot where everything feels a little easier. As you learn how to hold that spot, you ride well for longer periods. *Cadence* (how fast you pedal, expressed in *rpm*, revolutions per minute) should be fairly steady; you shift gears to maintain cadence, yielding the basic rhythm only for hard climbing, when your pedaling slows down. The result is free, supple muscles, and this is the basis of smooth, efficient riding over long periods of time.

THE DRIVE TRAIN
These are the things that move when you pedal and shift. If they don't work smoothly you won't enjoy your bike, especially on climbs.

RHYTHM AND CADENCE

The rhythm of a talented, specialized athlete is different from that of an ordinary mortal, but not all that different. There is a certain way to ride a bicycle well, and along with it, a recognizable bodily sensation that tells you you're spending energy effectively at the right cadence, extending your stamina over longer periods of time. It is a learned thing, requiring a mix of technical understanding (learning when and how to shift), combined with practice and an open mind.

Beginners are always inclined to pedal slowly because it seems easier, but a few hundred miles can change this if you work at it. The bonus is superior body-awareness. As you stop fighting the bike, you learn to coordinate rather than force your pedaling, and your energy flows more efficiently.

RPM

What is the right cadence? Early studies seemed to indicate somewhere around 60 rpm was the most efficient pedaling speed. Unfortunately, these studies used off-the-street subjects poorly positioned on exercise bicycles with no toe clips, and did not deal with long durations of effort. Unskilled subjects under such awkward conditions tend to simply stomp on the pedals, a sure way to reduce rpm. A more recent study with experienced competitive cyclists indicates that these riders are most efficient around 90 rpm and above—the pedaling speed they are used to.

But really high rpm are a special skill; about 80 rpm is the best range for the recreational cyclist. Very few recreational riders pedal smoothly outside this range for long periods. Count the strokes of one foot for 15 seconds and multiply by 4; try to stay in the 76–84 rpm range (19–21 rpm every 15 seconds). It's surprising how quickly you get a sense of cadence.

Learn to shift to a higher gear when you "spin out" (can't keep up with the pedals), and to a lower one when your pedaling slows down. If you consciously try to do this, it will become automatic; it will also smooth out your pedal stroke and ultimately save you from the pain created by the stress of high-torque, low-rpm pedaling. The French use the word *souplesse* to describe the smooth, efficient muscle action of a good pedaler. This is what you're after.

PEDALING

Good position is the first requirement for smooth pedaling, and the second is appropriate gearing, explained later in this chapter. The third is best expressed by John Krausz, who said that good pedaling "is making perfect little circles with your feet." That is definitely the Zen of It. Some find it in a few months, most during their second season; a few go on pedaling squares and triangles forever.

For openers, try to follow the downstroke by pulling back at the bottom, then lifting (not jerking) on the upstroke. This won't add a lot of power, but at least you won't be forcing one foot around with the other. On the downstroke, try to apply energy in a long, smooth arc rather than with a choppy motion. Let yourself feel the relation of pedal and foot. What you want to avoid is square pedaling—brief, choppy surges in the pedal stroke. If you can keep your feet feeling light, you're probably in the right gear, pedaling at the right cadence. When this is all happening, the pedal action smooths out into a spin. If you're pedaling too fast for your skill and coordination, you will bounce up and down; if too slow, you will be awkwardly muscling the pedals around; between these extremes is where you can spin.

Learning to spin is important. Among bikies of long standing there is a very definite feeling that getting this together is a first priority, and that anything that interferes with this (like radical position, wrong gearing, or extra-long cranks) is bad. For those who want to go really hard, John Allis remarks, "Lifting the foot is part of it, but getting extra power is largely a matter of bringing the foot over the top of the stroke quickly, and starting the downstroke earlier. Coming 'over the top' harder will make you go faster, but of course it also sets up additional stress. It's harder to stay smooth; you have to be aware and concentrate."

GEARING

From an engineering viewpoint, gearing is the relationship of pedal rpm to the speed of the bike. For the cyclist, it's simple and physical: If your legs are spinning away and you're not going very fast, that's a low ("small") gear; if your legs are grinding slowly and the bike is moving pretty fast, that's a high ("big") gear. When pedal and road speed are in balance, you've found the right gear for the situation. In a derailleur system, high/big gears are created by the big chainring driving to the small cogs and are used on flat terrain and on downhills. Low/small gears come from using the small ring to drive the big cogs, and these are used for climbing.

BIG GEARS

Speaking about developing strength and the ability to use big gears (almost an obsession with some riders), California-born Tour de France rider Jock Boyer remarked, "It's not wise to force; I really try to avoid it. In the spring I keep training my usual ways, and then one day it's just there. I find I have the strength to turn the higher gear, so I do. But I won't sacrifice technique and just force the pedals around if I can possibly avoid it. In terms of racing, it can shorten your career; in general, it is a wrong approach."

Perhaps the most eloquent testimony about the matter of pushing too big a gear comes from the words of triathlete and Hawaii Ironman winner Dave Hornung. Hornung is a big, powerful man of the type very likely to favor big gears and use them effectively. Talking to rank-and-file participants at the '83 Mighty Hamptons Triathlon, he described doing this early in his bike training, staying in very big gears on the theory that a higher work level would be beneficial. Then he described the disastrous effect on his knees, and finished by saying that whenever he felt pedal pressure getting up into that range, he would downshift and "just keep on spinning. It's something I learned to do. You don't really need that 108-inch gear very often."

DESCRIPTIVE SYSTEMS

In this country and Great Britain, gearing is figured in inches (see next page) through a formula said to have been invented by Druids. Naturally, there is a Continental formula that yields meters. Both of these systems offer a useful way of describing gear ratios, but for some reason derailleur operators always seem to talk about gearing in terms of ring-and-cog combinations; the number of teeth on the chainring comes first, as in "I made it on 42 by 26 [44 inches by the British system], but, God, I was suffering." This is universally understood.

THE INCHES SYSTEM AND GEAR CHART

The gear chart below is based on the English "inches" system, and the figures show the size of wheel an old Ordinary would have had to move an equivalent distance with each pedal revolution. In other words, if you are in a 100-inch gear, you would havc to bc riding a 100-inch high Ordinary.

(The formula is $\frac{\text{\# teeth on ring}}{\text{\# teeth on cog}} \times$ *wheel diameter).*

If this seems somewhat silly, it is; the Brits were in love with the Ordinary. But this makes no difference; the system's use lies in providing handy reference in figuring gears. If someone tells you the European "meters progressed" system is more logical, they are right too, but the inches system is the one people use in this country and Great Britain. When your body learns the feel of certain gears, you leave the inches system behind; you're in "53 × 17" or "40 × 26," and that says it in any language.

GEAR CHART FOR 27″ WHEEL

CHAINRING

COG	36	38	40	42	43	44	45	46	47	48	49	50	51	52
13	74.8	78.9	83.1	87.2	89.3	91.4	93.5	95.5	97.6	99.7	101.8	103.8	105.9	108.0
14	69.4	73.3	77.1	81.0	82.9	84.9	86.8	87.7	90.6	92.6	94.5	96.4	98.4	100.3
15	64.8	68.4	72.0	75.6	77.4	79.2	81.0	82.8	84.6	86.4	88.2	90.0	91.8	93.6
16	60.8	64.1	67.5	70.9	72.6	74.3	75.9	77.6	79.3	81.0	82.7	84.4	86.1	87.8
17	57.2	60.4	63.5	66.7	68.3	69.9	71.5	73.1	74.6	76.2	77.8	79.4	81.0	82.6
18	54.0	57.0	60.0	63.0	64.5	66.0	67.5	69.0	70.5	72.0	73.5	75.0	76.5	78.0
19	51.2	54.0	56.8	59.7	61.1	62.5	63.9	65.4	66.8	68.2	69.6	71.1	72.5	73.9
20	48.6	51.3	54.0	56.7	58.1	59.4	60.8	62.1	63.5	64.8	66.2	67.5	68.9	70.2
21	46.3	48.9	51.4	54.0	55.2	56.6	57.8	59.1	60.4	61.7	63.0	64.3	65.5	66.9
22	44.2	46.6	49.1	51.5	52.8	54.0	55.2	56.5	57.7	58.9	60.1	61.4	62.6	63.8
23	42.3	44.6	47.0	49.3	50.5	51.7	52.8	54.0	55.2	56.3	57.5	58.7	59.9	61.0
24	40.5	42.8	45.0	47.3	48.4	49.5	50.6	51.8	52.9	54.0	55.1	56.3	57.4	58.5
25	38.9	41.0	43.2	45.4	46.4	47.5	48.6	49.7	50.8	51.8	52.9	54.0	55.1	56.2
26	37.4	39.5	41.5	43.6	44.6	45.7	46.7	47.8	48.8	49.9	50.9	51.9	53.0	54.0
28	34.7	36.6	38.6	40.5	41.5	42.4	43.4	44.4	45.3	46.3	47.3	48.2	49.2	50.1
30	32.4	34.2	36.0	37.8	38.7	39.6	40.5	41.4	42.3	43.2	44.1	45.0	45.9	46.8
32	30.4	32.1	33.8	35.4	36.3	37.1	38.0	38.8	39.7	40.5	41.3	42.2	43.0	43.9
34	28.6	30.1	31.8	33.4	34.1	34.9	35.7	36.5	37.3	38.1	38.9	39.7	40.5	41.3
36	27.0	28.5	30.0	31.5	32.3	33.0	33.8	34.5	35.3	36.0	36.8	37.5	38.3	39.0

GEARING AND EFFICIENCY

Correct gearing doesn't just improve pedaling; it also improves your efficiency. This is especially noticeable when riding in a group. Those who consistently find the right gears have a definite advantage, because any vehicle with limited power benefits greatly from operating at its optimal rpm. The point is clear from recent automotive engineering changes: the vastly overpowered V-8 automobiles of the pre-emissions-control era needed only three forward gears; today's smaller economy cars use four or five gears, spaced more closely, which allow the engine to turn at its best speed in any situation. The same point is suggested by the fact that since the sixties racing cyclists have moved from ten- to twelve- to fourteen-speed bicycles. Broadly speaking, with underpowered vehicles it's a case of the more gears the better—assuming they are well selected and easily available.

HUB GEARS

The Sturmey-Archer type of enclosed hub gear is amazingly reliable and very convenient for commuting and knocking around, but it does not offer the range and options of the derailleur system. Its range can be raised or lowered by changing the rear cog, but you have to

THREE-SPEED ADJUSTER CHAIN
Gears are adjusted by loosening the knurled locknut, then adjusting cable tension. When you find an adjustment that allows all three gears to work, tighten the lock nut. Neat and simple.

take the thing for the self-contained unit it is. The three-speed offers a high gear 33 percent above the middle gear, and a low gear 25 percent below. On the open road, those big between-gear jumps are a problem, because they totally change pedaling cadence. The rarely seen five-speed is better because it gives more range with narrower jumps between gears, but it is less reliable. There are also hub gears by Bendix, Dana, and Shimano and others, but none are significant improvements over the original.

The hub gear is excellent for short distances, and perfect for people who don't want to be bothered with a dérailleur. It is simple to use and almost indestructible, being well protected from the elements. Few people have the courage to disassemble the intricate mechanism, but it is rarely necessary. Adjustment of the tiny chain mechanism that comes through the hollow axle is simple and positive, and lubrication with the manufacturer's oil keeps these gears rolling almost forever. Shifting is done with a device on the handlebars and is very simple. When the lever is out, you have high gear; the middle position is second; all the way in is low. One advantage is that you stop pedaling during the shift, which means that gears can be changed at a stop light. Most people learn to shift a hub gear in a few minutes. The Sturmey-Archer hub can also be used in conjunction with a derailleur, as described later, an arrangement that yields no end of gears.

THE DERAILLEUR SYSTEM

Derailleurs are a different matter, a tinkerer's paradise with endless possibilities. Early derailleurs were not much fun, and only the best ones worked well. Japanese innovations of the seventies changed that dramatically, and today the problem is more in people's heads than in the hardware.

The derailleur is operated by levers and cables and springs somewhat like those of caliper brakes. It changes gears by lifting the chain from cog to cog (rear) and chainring to chainring (front). It is an ancient system, obscurely conceived in the 19th century, championed by Velocio, endlessly refined, and full of compromises. The chain-line is imperfect, and owing to this, certain gears are best avoided. And components that should apparently work together frequently don't.

The great virtue of the derailleur system is that most riders can come close to a perfect gearing setup with available hardware. The more you ride, the better you understand the advantages of this, and the derailleur is the racing and touring standard all over the world because of it.

DERAILLEUR SHIFTING TECHNIQUE: GENERAL

The first thing to do is to make sure the gears are working. If you've just bought a bike and are unfamiliar with shifting, get the shop mechanic to put the bike in a repair stand and show you the technique; seeing it done helps. Then move the levers yourself while the cranks are turning, and you will get the feel of how to make a shift. Take a few minutes. You can do it yourself on a repair stand or any device that will get the rear wheel off the floor, such as a Turbo-trainer or Racer-mate. Watch the mechanism while you shift; the process is very simple. If no stand is available, have an experienced rider make sure the gears are working.

GETTING IT DOWN

Practice is the key to smooth shifts, but few beginners ever actually practice shifting enough to master it. In the long run, this is time well spent. Do your practicing in an out-of-the-way place, on level ground, and you will learn the feel and sound that indicate a good shift. The easiest way to learn is on a Racer-mate or Turbo-trainer, which hold the bike upright as you pedal. Of course, people were shifting dérailleurs long before these devices were available; they just make the first steps easier.

SHIFT LEVERS

Shift levers may be located on the down tube (the traditional place), bar ends (good for touring, because your hands stay on the bars), on the bars themselves ("thumb-shifters"), or at the stem, as on cheaper bikes. Wherever they are located, the left lever controls the front (chainring) shifter, the right controls the rear. Almost invariably, pulling a lever back (against the spring) lifts the chain to a larger cog or chainring; the reverse drops it onto a smaller one.

Shifting is done by touch and sound, and despite the efforts of inventors, it apparently always will be. The dérailleur responds to a careful touch and will not be bullied; force it, and you get grinding

SHIFT LEVERS

All these different items do the same thing—shift the derailleurs. Clockwise from upper left: Down-tube mounting (1) is the classic; short cables give quick, precise shifts. Bar-end shifters (2) are often used by tourists because you can shift without moving your hands off the bars and reaching down, which changes balance. Thumb-shifters (3) came in with mountain bikes and are the best raised-bar option. Stem-shifters (4) are what you get on lower price bikes. Note handy wingbolt adjustment on down-tube and thumb-shifters. Keep these tight; a loose one will snafu the whole system.

sounds and missed shifts. Take time while learning; you will get a sense of how far the lever must move. Most shifting problems come from overshifting—moving the lever too far.

Remember this too: A derailleur shift cannot be made with full pedal pressure; the pedals must turn, but pressure must be eased. You won't notice this on a test stand, but on the road you will grind gears if you try to pedal hard and shift at the same time.

SHIFTING THE FRONT DERAILLEUR

The front (chainring) shift is simple: to downshift (from big ring to small), ease up on the pedals but keep them turning, and push the left lever forward all the way. To upshift (small to big ring), pull back. (A few derailleurs reverse this process, but not many.) With triple chainrings, the shifts are similar, but the getting to middle ring can require some fishing around.

It's a good idea to keep the chain on a middle cog in the rear and practice the front shift until it is smooth. Don't practice shifting in the road—if you are preoccupied with shifting, you tend to ignore traffic; the empty parking lot is ideal.

SHIFTING THE REAR DERAILLEUR

The rear shift is more subtle, and the motion is shorter. Pulling back the right shift lever puts you onto a larger cog, giving a lower gear. Pushing it forward drops you onto a smaller cog and gives you a higher gear. Since there are anywhere from five to seven cogs, with no "stops" between them, it is not uncommon to overshift past the one you want. The secret is to ease the lever firmly but gently. If you are pedaling too hard as you do this, there will be grinding noises, but unless you really force the situation, there should be no damage. If there is a clicking noise after the shift, this indicates slight misalignment, which means that you may slip out of gear; try moving the lever back and forth very slightly until the sound goes away. With practice this becomes second nature. Competition derailleurs are generally more positive in action and require less of this adjusting than touring derailleurs.

COMMON PROBLEMS

OVERSHIFTING

Overshifting is caused by moving the lever too far, and it can drop you into a very unexpected and awkward gear. It can also leave you in no gear at all, which will let the pedals turn freely in both directions without moving the bike forward. Don't be alarmed; a small correcting movement of the lever in either direction will almost always put you in a gear, though it may not be the one you want. The worst that can happen is that you coast to a stop.

RUSHED SHIFTING

Rushed shifts are another beginner's problem. Good equipment in the hands of an experienced rider allows almost instant shifts, but riders who delay shifting until the last minute often miss the shift, especially on hills. Any shift to a larger cog takes a second or two, during which you lose some speed; an inexperienced rider can roll to a standstill while fishing for gears. Because of this, the rule is to shift before it becomes necessary. When you see a hill coming up, don't wait until you lose momentum; a last-minute shift may end with the bike stopping.

LOOSE SHIFT LEVERS

Slipping out of gear is another common annoyance. This is caused by a loose shift lever, and is fixed by tightening the lever; some require a screwdriver, others can be tightened when riding without tools.

SKIPPING

This problem is as old as the freewheel, but there's no excuse for it with a modern bike. It can be caused by a partial overshift, which keeps the chain trying to hop off the cog, or by the internal workings of the freewheel (rarely), or by chain and/or cog wear, which is to be expected after 1500–2500 miles, depending on conditions. (Often only one cog skips, and can be replaced.)

CHAIN RUB

Despite the best attempts of dedicated engineers, derailleur chains continue to rub against the cage of the front derailleur as rear shifts move the chain from one side to the other. When you notice this, correct the front derailleur slightly; after a while you will do this automatically.

DRIVE TRAIN MAINTENANCE

ADJUSTMENTS

Positioning derailleurs exactly right is a complex procedure that varies somewhat with design, but adjustments are basically similar. These are made by screws that limit how far the cage can travel. On the front derailleur, these screws keep the chain from going off the inner chainring (irritating), or sliding down between crank and outer chainring (bad). On a rear derailleur, they keep it from going off the small cog and against the frame (annoying) or into the spokes (the worst). Since a jumped chain can wedge itself very securely in the wrong place, these adjustments are quite important. Chewed-up spokes are bad news.

Loosening a set screw widens the travel of the cage; tightening one closes it down. Getting oriented is easier when the screws are labeled (usually they aren't), but once you have located them it is easy to figure out which does what by looking closely. Small (¼-turn) adjustments are often enough; proceed cautiously.

DERAILLEUR ADJUSTMENT "SET" SCREWS
These come in pairs, and patience will lead you to whatever location the manufacturer has chosen. One screw stops movement to the inside, one to the outside; establish which is which and adjust cautiously. Careless adjustment can drop the chain into various wrong places; a chain in the spokes can chew them up—not to mention wedging itself in very securely.

CLEANING AND LUBRICATION

Some of the commonest derailleur problems are caused by cable-stretch, dirt, and corrosion. A stretched cable often makes it difficult or impossible to shift to the largest cog or ring. The cable should be tight when the shift lever is in the forward position, and must be firmly anchored. If it's slack, loosen it at the derailleur end, where it will be attached by some kind of anchor bolt, much as brake cables are (Chapter 9). With the lever in the forward position, pull the end of the cable until it is taut, then tighten the bolt securely.

Dirt and corrosion are best handled with blasts of WD-40, using the (easily lost) plastic tube that comes with the can. Cages and jockey wheels must move freely, and a solvent-lubricant is the quick way to achieve this. An old toothbrush is helpful with caked-on gunk.

WEAR

Excessive wear on rings, cogs, or chain will also affect shifting. If you can lift the chain away from the large chainring with your fingers, you know the chain is worn. If the ring teeth are worn to sharp points, the ring is worn. Worn freewheel cogs are harder to spot visually; "skipping" is the usual clue. When freewheels fail internally, they may either fail to freewheel or do so in both directions; sometimes they will grab at the chain when you coast. A flaky one should be replaced or repaired immediately (no easy job); it's likely to fail at just the wrong time and leave you stranded somewhere.

Persistent shifting problems with modern, undamaged equipment are almost always caused by poor technique, incorrect installation, or poor alignment, and the last may not be the fault of the equipment. If a rear derailleur is attached to a bent dropout, it has to be straightened before you'll get smooth shifts.

DESIGN ASPECTS

CHAINRINGS AND FREEWHEELS

Easy shifting depends first of all on having good derailleurs properly mounted on a well-aligned frame, but there are other factors. The wider the difference or "jump" between rings or cogs, the slower the shift, especially the upshift, because the derailleur has to lift the chain further. As a rule of thumb, anything more than a 13-tooth jump between rings (52–39, for example) will upshift a bit slowly. Similarly, a one- or two-tooth jump on the freewheel (16–18, for example) will be quicker and easier to shift than a jump of three or more teeth.

CHAIN-LINE

As mentioned before, chain-line is a factor in any derailleur system. Rarely if ever is the chain perfectly aligned front to rear, and when chain-line is extreme the system usually doesn't work very well. The derailleur resists, the chain may jump out of gear or make aggravated noises, and all parts involved tend to grind a bit and wear faster. In a double-chainring setup this usually eliminates two gears; with a triple, as many as four may not work, depending on alignment and the sizes of rings and cogs.

BAD CHAIN-LINE
This chain is running from the small (inner) chainring to the small (outermost) cog; this puts a severe bend in the chain and causes alignment problems. Everything grinds more, and derailleurs get cranky. Large-ring-to-big-cog is worse yet.

FRAME DESIGN

Chainstay length also affects shifting. The very short stays typical of modern racing bikes are designed for quick response to hard pedaling, and are fine with the narrow-range gearing they're designed for. They are not so fine for wide-range touring setups though, because they shorten the length of the chain and thus increase the chain-line angle.

CHAIN LENGTH

New bikes usually have chains with the correct number of links, but a used bike may have a link too many or too few. Too many links create "chain-slop" and too few links may not allow you to use certain gears without damaging equipment. Follow the derailleur manufacturer's directions and talk to a mechanic if in doubt.

TRIPLE CHAINRINGS

There is a school of thought that favors triple chainrings, which can yield (in theory) as many as 21 gears. Another school feels that with the six- and seven-cog clusters now available, and with gears as low as 30 inches easily obtainable with two rings, there is usually no point to the added hardware.

Triples date back to the days when there was no other way to get a

TRIPLE-RING CRANKSET
Triple cranks are often overkill, and setting them up to work smoothly and simply is not easy. However, for off-road bikes and truly wide-range, load-hauling gears, the triple is the way to go. This Sugino set is solid and reliable.

wide range of gears. Tried and discarded in competition, they are mandatory for off-road bikes and heavy touring, but converting from double to triple rings is usually expensive, and there can be exasperating complications. On the other hand, if you happen to like mechanical challenges and don't mind the expense, you can enjoy bragging rights to the lowest gears in town.

TYPES OF DERAILLEURS

If and when you get around to rearranging your gears, you'll find that derailleurs themselves, while basically similar, differ substantially. They are designed for different applications, and the differences can be significant. Changing them can improve performance, but it's very unwise to switch before understanding some basics.

FRONT DERAILLEURS

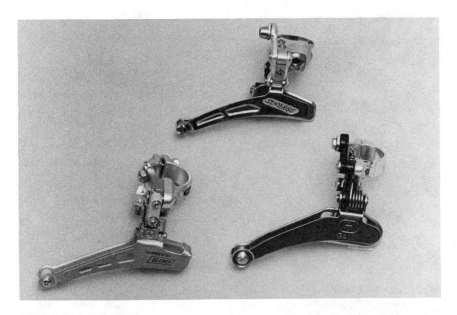

FRONT DERAILLEURS
SunTour Superbe (top) and Shimano 600 (lower left) are good general-purpose derailleurs; the Galli is built for competition. There are differences in strength and lateral movement, but front derailleurs are fairly similar and can usually be interchanged.

The front derailleur is usually attached to the seat tube with a bolt-on, wraparound fitting. The outside plate should be aligned parallel to the big chainring, and positioned 1/16"–3/16" above the big ring. Knowledgeable mechanics will sometimes initiate you into the mysteries of bending the outer plate to improve performance; it often works wonders.

Front derailleurs differ in three ways, of which strength is one. Some are beefy, some not, and of all the places to save weight, this is among the worst; a derailleur that bends isn't shifting correctly. Front derailleurs also vary in how wide a difference in chainring sizes they can handle; some will shift between rings with as much as a 16-tooth difference (50 and 34, for example) without complaint, while others have problems with more than 12. Finally, some have sufficient lateral movement to handle triple chainrings, and some do not.

REAR DERAILLEURS

Rear derailleurs vary even more, and any attempt to deal with them briefly and accurately is doomed to failure. Short-cage derailleurs (in

REAR DERAILLEURS
To handle big cogs, the cage and its jockey wheels must hang low enough to clear them, and the cage must be long enough to take up chain slack created by wide-range system. Long-cage SunTour Superbe and VGT (left) can handle very big cogs easily. Medium-cage Shimano Crane and Campagnolo Record (middle) handle enough for most uses. Early model Campagnolo Super Record and SunTour Cyclone (right) have limited capacity and are for racing.

which the jockey wheels are close together) will handle only the small cogs (up to 24 teeth) used for racing. A long-cage model offers a much wider range by taking up more chain slack and making room for cogs with as many as 34–38 teeth. Between these is the medium-cage type, perfected in competition but adaptable to most situations. Tough and quick-shifting, it is a useful all-around piece of equipment, capable of handling a cog with as many as 26 or 28 teeth—enough for many riders. Recently Mavic has developed a quality racing derailleur with a cage that can also be adjusted to handle large touring cogs.

LONG-CAGE REAR DERAILLEURS

The inexpensive long-cage, wide-range touring derailleur, standard for mass-market bikes, did not become genuinely reliable until the Japanese firms of SunTour (Maeda) and Shimano developed what is sometimes called the "pantograph" system during the early seventies;

CURRENT INNOVATION
Europe strikes back: Japanese inroads have sparked European creativity. Wide-range Huret Duopar (left) has a unique double-parallelogram cage that is very good with extra-big cogs. The Mavic derailleur to the right was used by five teams in the 1984 Tour de France—but unlike other racing derailleurs, it can be adjusted to take big touring cogs. Handy.

the old European style used the parallelogram system, which is more limited in its capacity.

It was the great leap forward in wide-range derailleurs, for which the pantograph system is ideal. For ten dollars you could buy a well-built, alloy, touring derailleur that really worked. For about the same price you could also buy a basic racing dérailleur that wasn't bad at one-third the cost of the better European models. European manufacturers ignored the innovations for a while, then responded by improving their own touring equipment. The Huret Duopar is a good current example of this.

The wide-range derailleur is the province of the heavy tourist, and it brings the off-road mountain bike to life, giving it the low-range power to negotiate situations that would stop another bike. The weakness of the long-cage derailleur is that, being larger, it is more flexible and less precise. It does not shift as quickly, and in some circumstances this can be irritating. Often each shift requires slight follow-up adjustment. Quick, smooth shifts are gratifying; missed shifts are annoying, especially if your friends ride off and leave you behind.

SMALL-CAGE REAR DERAILLEUR

Small, neat, light, and quick-shifting, designed for racing, this is for strong riders only; its limited range provides no "easy" gears by normal standards. Usually these derailleurs are of the parallelogram design, shift quickly but do not handle extra-big cogs. If your equipment can't handle anything bigger than a 24-tooth cog, you had better be strong, or live in a fairly flat part of the country. The limited cog-handling capacity of a short-cage derailleur makes it a specialty item.

MEDIUM-CAGE REAR DERAILLEUR

This derailleur is more lenient; its 28- to 30-tooth capacity comes very near to providing the sainted Velocio's gear recommendations (page 209), as modified for USA roads. A perusal of the gear chart (page 108) shows that a 38-tooth ring to a 28-tooth cog (38 × 28) yields a 36.6-inch gear, which many semifit people find adequate, except with a touring load. Basically race-derived equipment, this type of derailleur also shifts quickly; it may be of pantograph or parallelogram design.

REPLACEMENT

Clearly, different derailleurs are for different kinds of riding. When the time comes to replace yours, consider the way you ride and purchase accordingly. But don't feel you have to replace your derailleur to improve your gears; the typical stock wide-range derailleur in good working order can handle almost anything; it is the cluster and rings where the first and most basic changes are made.

FINDING YOUR GEARS

Gearing possibilities are more or less infinite, which has encouraged some highly suspect conclusions. Proceed with caution. When you read a magazine article that suggests that Dick and Jane Bikerider have real use for gears similar to those used by a Greg Le Mond, don't swallow it whole. Pushing gears is not the same as turning them smoothly; it demands less skill than learning to pedal, but your knees and back bear the brunt of the effort. Very few people need those gears, and most of those people are making a living racing bicycles. A recreational cyclist who spins out a 54 × 12 on a long descent is often going faster than he or she can really manage. It's not very safe, especially if there are panniers or bags on the bike and some gravel on the turns.

ESTABLISHING YOUR BASIC RANGE

After you've been on enough rides that you're beginning to have some feel for the bike, try to locate the gears you favor consistently. If you find yourself spending a lot of time in a 70-inch gear, make sure it's built into your new setup. Your most-used gear is the heart of your range; build around it. Velocio named 72 inches as his favorite, and if you find yourself much higher than that, remember that Velocio was a very fit, experienced rider. (Casual riders who insist that 81 is their natural gear haven't learned how to pedal.)

Build around your most preferred gear; make sure that you have easily reached gears closely adjacent to it. Also establish your top and bottom gears; then spread your gears as evenly as possible in the high and mid ranges. If you're not particularly athletic, spread them wider toward the bottom; these are your gears of last resort, used when cadence is sacrificed to survival.

HIGHS AND LOWS

Establish your bottom gear realistically; if you can really handle the toughest hills on a 44-inch gear, don't bother with anything lower. But don't go with that 44 out of macho, because it can load most legs with lactic acid on a hard climb, making any ensuing climbs progressively harder. Establish the high end with equal humility. When you start thinking about gears over 100 inches, remember that your knees have to live with what your ego decrees. Those ligaments, cartilage, and muscles are the real you.

And, unless the need is real, don't complicate your system with the extra gears available through triple rings and/or split-shifting. The real starting point is your own body; if you don't need those gears or can't get at them conveniently, they're pure clutter.

FREEWHEEL GEAR CLUSTERS
These five- and six-speed clusters by Maillard, SunTour, and Regina show the wide variety available. The tiny 13–18 (upper left) is for racing in flat country; the big 13–32 is for long hills under load. Those in between work out best for most people most of the time.

IMPROVEMENTS IN GEARING

Unless you are technically inclined, some of what follows will seem complicated until you've ridden a derailleur bike. It's not necessary to understand it as a beginner, but as you sense the limitations of stock equipment, the rest of this chapter should be of definite interest. It approaches derailleurs, freewheel, chain and chainrings as a system. To our knowledge, no other book explores the advantages of recent technology in terms of simplifying the use of the derailleur, making it relatively foolproof, and matching gears to individual ability.

THE TWO-TOOTH JUMP

It is an article of faith among café-racers, real racers, mechanics, and *cyclo-sportif* types that anything more than a two-tooth difference (jump) between cogs on the gear cluster is pretty much a bad thing. It's not just that derailleurs prefer smaller jumps; the legs do, too. These smaller jumps make it easier to maintain pedaling cadence without use of the front derailleur.

Like any rule connected with the derailleur system, it needs some bending, but for a majority of riders it's a sound approach. It's not for heavy touring or off-roaders, but under normal conditions it leads to quick, simple shifting for the average rider, as developed below. Bigger jumps are reserved for the low (climbing) range, where cadence tends to break down with most recreational riders.

CASSETTE SYSTEM FREEWHEEL
Good thinking by Zeus: Old style freewheels have each cog screwed onto the body; replacement is tedious and often difficult. This Zeus (and others like it) requires only that the outer cog be unscrewed, after which the rest slip off easily. A number of manufacturers have gone to this system, and it is a real boon to those with limited tools.

ELIMINATING THE SPLIT-SHIFT

When you've lived with your bike for a while and have developed some level of skill and fitness, you'll begin to notice that some gears are always in use, some very rarely. You may also notice that certain useful gears can be reached only through a tedious process involving both shift levers. This is the so-called "split-shift." You have arrived at the point where theory bumps into practice; in theory you "have" the gear you need; in practice you also want it easily available.

A gear that requires the use of both levers is not easily available to most riders. Because there are twice as many chances to blow the shift, these split-shifts can be tricky, and they are slower than those accomplished with one shift lever. This means that the bike may slow down markedly, especially on hills; if the shift is *really* slow, you may roll to a stop while your friends continue on their way. It's been over a decade since split-shifting was used in serious competition; the civilians are just starting to catch up.

As delivered, many stock bicycles require that you split-shift to get to the gears you want. Here is a typical example of gearing, given by the inches system for a 27″ wheel, on a mass-market bike:

	COGS					
	14	17	20	24	28	32
52	100	83	70	59	50	—
CHAINRINGS 40	—	64	54	45	39	34

The 52 × 32 and 40 × 14 gears are not listed because of the chain-line problem discussed previously.

A close look at this arrangement reveals a much-too-big jump down from the 100 gear to the 83, and another huge jump down to the 70. These gears are too spread out for most riders. Also note that if you are cruising in the 70 gear, to get down to the 64 you must use both levers—a split-shift. Getting back and forth from the 54 to the 59 also requires using both levers.

These are gears most riders would use frequently, and all this split-shifting is awkward. It's also confusing to many people, because there's an additional thinking step as you figure out how to get to your next lower or higher gear. Under stress, these unnecessary mental and physical steps can be distracting.

This kind of gear setup is basically a mess, and this is why you see people with their gear ratios written on strips of paper taped to the top tube or stem. They can't keep track of things any other way. Other riders just don't bother trying for the right gear. They simply stay on the small ring for hills and on the large one for descents or with following winds. In other words, they use the rings as a dual-range system, accepting awkward jumps in gear that make it impossible to maintain cadence.

"Most people naturally think in terms of a dual-range system," observes John Allis, "and when I explain gears to people, this is the natural way to explain it. Until you have quite a lot of experience, all that (split) shifting is very confusing, and there's too much chance for error. When I started racing, bikes were set up that way for competition, but not anymore; it's more complicated, and there's no necessity with current equipment."

Allis is correct—and split-shifting is for people who enjoy problems. Limitations of early derailleurs created the need for split-shifting, but the basic problems have long since been solved.

THE DUAL-RANGE SYSTEM

There is a better way. As mentioned earlier, current options include six- and seven-speed freewheels that can make the right gears more easily available. In this (dual-range) approach, the gears are set up so that almost all shifting is done with the rear derailleur. In practice, this simplification is a real boon: Hills and headwinds are handled on the small ring; descents, flat terrain and following winds use the large ring. The ratios produced (i.e., the spacing or jumps between gears) are also advantageous. Here are some examples:

MODEL A:

A simple change of freewheels can do wonders. By switching to a custom freewheel, this easy to use set-up is possible. Compare it to the earlier example:

	COGS					
	14	16	18	20	24	30
52	100	88	78	70	59	—
CHAINRINGS 40	—	68	60	54	45	36

This is not the sort of arrangement theoreticians would like, because the 70/68 and 60/59 are virtual duplicates. It doesn't matter much, though; what really matters is that the high- and mid-range gears are more closely spaced (which makes it easier to hold cadence), and are much more convenient to use. The big leap down to the 30 cog is a well-known expedient—it provides the semifit rider with real relief when he needs it most, on hard climbing. This bottom cog, which gives the lowest gear, is known as a *granny*, as in gears your grandmother would require.

This setup is very simple to operate; in favorable conditions you can stay with the big ring, and the rest of the time you should be on the small one. The ratios can be described as neither fish nor fowl (too wide for racing, not wide enough for heavy touring), but they are very nice indeed in terms of an average person enjoying the bicycle.

Where do you find a 14–16–18–20–24–30 freewheel? You have it made up. Prices will vary a lot; shop around.

MODEL B:

A stronger rider might opt for something like the arrangement below, still without changing chainrings. This setup is not too far from competitive gearing for mountainous terrain. Its ratios are perfect for

GEAR RANGES

Because people vary enormously in strength and fitness, gearing is a very personal thing. Racing gears (about 47–120 inches these days) are used by very strong athletes who do not need to gear down as much for climbing. Their gear clusters are small, chainrings big. Out-of-shape tourists with piles of baggage use wide-range gears down as low as 30 inches, requiring larger cogs and smaller rings. Many stock bikes these days come with wide-range gears, but the answer for most riders is something between these extremes. The gear ranges below reflect conventional thinking as worked out over the better part of a century, and provide useful orientation:

90–plus: *genuinely high gears—gears that take real strength to turn efficiently for periods of time. Except on downgrades, or with a strong wind behind them, most people aren't really up to these gears; they are even prohibited in junior racing.*

75–90: *very important high-range gears for almost any cyclist, competitive or otherwise. Fit athletes can handle many hills in the low end of this range.*

55–75: *an equally important cruising and easy climbing range for most noncompetition riders.*

many athletic men and women who do better by pedaling up the hills than muscling the bike in bigger gears.

| | COGS | | | | | |
	14	16	18	20	23	26
CHAINRINGS 52	100	88	78	70	61	—
40	—	68	60	54	47	41

MODEL C:

If you are really strong and fit, you can go a step further; this is just slightly backed off from a typical racing cluster.

| | COGS | | | | | |
	13	15	17	19	21	24
CHAINRINGS 52	108	94	83	74	67	—
40	—	72	64	57	51	45

40–55: *This is for more serious climbing, and with an unloaded bike this is as low as athletic riders need to go.*
30–40: *Velocio drew the bottom line at 35 inches, and few people actually benefit by going much lower than 30 except under very heavy loads. Direct drive (one pedal revolution = one wheel revolution) comes out to 27 inches, and it can be done; a 36 ring to a 36 cog is no problem with today's equipment. Keeping a loaded bike upright at the walking speeds such gears produce is something else.*

Velocio had his own ideas about appropriate gearing, developed over hundreds of thousands of miles. Riding the heavier bikes of his time on poor surfaces and roads that routinely included steeper grades than those in the modern U.S. road system, he explored gears from below 30 inches to above 120. This early champion of the dérailleur then defined the really useful gearing range as being between 35 and 85 inches, naming 72 as the single most useful gear. These suggestions have an uncanny accuracy about them, indicating a remarkable instinct for the ergonomic realities. Allowing for improved bicycles and the shallower grades typical of the U.S. road system, many sportif *types would raise that to something like 40–100 inches. As the French are fond of pointing out, the more things seem to change, the less they really do.*

ADVANTAGES

These are setups you can live with, simple, reliable, useful gears that enable you to hold pedaling cadence where you want it. If you choose to vary ratios by switching chainrings, the change is quick and easy.

THE "FIND-YOUR-FREEWHEEL" APPROACH

Some people just ride until they learn their basic parameters, embody these in a freewheel, and make all changes at the chainrings. Surprising flexibility is possible. The 14–26 freewheel (Model B) combined with 53–44 rings amounts to a hilly road race setup. With 50–40 rings it is much less demanding, and with 50–34 rings it is, for many, a light touring setup with a low gear of 35 inches. The chainring upshift won't be quick, but because most shifting is done at the rear this doesn't matter much.

Extra chainrings can be expensive, but they are much easier to switch than cogs or freewheels, and no special tools are required. This approach is very convenient for people who ride regularly and adapt gearing to variations in seasonal fitness, as explained below.

The one problem you may encounter is in the crankset itself; this setup depends on equipment that will accept a wide range of chainrings. Many do not, including most high-quality racing equipment. T.A., some Stronglight models and a number of good new Japanese sets will, however. Because a good set of cranks will usually cost somewhere in the vicinity of $100 to replace, this is definitely something to ask about when you buy a bicycle. Fit, athletic people can usually handle the typical 52–42 racing crankset but most riders are better off with something that allows more flexibility.

One good point of this system is that once chain and freewheel have mated, you won't be changing either of them. You might have to add or drop a link or two from the chain, though, when making a major change. Note that the new seven-speed freewheels discussed later make this approach even more attractive to the less athletic rider by providing wider range.

DESIGN FACTORS

Before consulting your gear chart and rushing out to revise everything in the drive train, consider these observations by Sheldon Brown, definitely one of the more experienced gear gurus to be found in the U.S.

"You can't forget the mechanical aspect of the system. It's built on cogs and chains, and they can be misused. You want to make sure the chain is wrapping around the freewheel cogs. People will look at a gear chart and see that they can use very small cogs and rings to get the gears they want; often they like the idea of saving weight here, but this has its disadvantages. With very small cogs, you may get very little chain-wrap, which means that perhaps one or two links are in contact with one or two cogs. That's not as good as having contact at three or four points; it doesn't give you a smooth, long-wearing system. Also, you can feel it when you ride; a small ring driving an 11 or 12 cog does not feel the same as a larger one driving a 14, even though the gear is the same.

"There's also a problem with these very small chainrings in that chain stress is definitely higher; you're putting the chain through a lot at both ends, so it stretches and wears cogs and rings faster. If you do a lot of riding, it's annoying to have to replace a chain after a thousand miles."

NARROW FREEWHEEL CLUSTERS

As mentioned previously, a given frame is built to accept either a "standard five" (120mm) or "standard six" (126mm) rear hub. Most mid-priced bicycles take the five; most expensive bicycles the six. One of the more significant developments of recent years is the "narrow cluster," which fits an extra cog into a standard rear fork-width. Thus, with a SunTour Ultra 6 or equivalent, a "standard five" becomes a six-speed. (This is why all the preceding models are based on six-speeds.) And the "standard six" becomes a seven.

SEVEN-SPEED CLUSTERS

The new seven-speed clusters, designed to fit the 126mm hub found on most quality bikes, open new options. Originally intended for racing, the seven-speed cluster had limited use for most riders because the range was narrow and the small cog had to be a 13, 12, or 11(!). With standard chainrings, such small cogs produce huge gears. The options have expanded, and today's seven-speed freewheel can produce very wide-range, well-distributed gears, suitable to almost any kind of terrain or load. Stick to the 13 cog rather than 12 or 11, and don't forget that any narrow cluster needs a narrow chain like the Sidisport.

MODEL D:

Here is an example of what can be done with a seven-speed setup combining medium-ratio jumps in upper and middle ranges with low gears sufficient for much touring.

	COGS						
	13	15	17	19	22	25	30
CHAINRINGS 48	100	86	76	68	59	52	—
38	—	68	60	54	46	41	34

LIMITATIONS OF HARDWARE

In the search for perfection, you will discover the odd and sometimes frustrating realities of the hardware itself. Alignment varies from frame to frame and you may need to add or remove spacers here and there to make things work. You may "lose" three gears rather than only two if you are using a seven-speed.

Current information comes from consumer magazines, manufacturers, experienced riders, and good mechanics. Don't buy anything before finding out if it can work, or making arrangements to return it for credit if it won't fit.

TOURING

At some point, extra-wide gears will force you to split-shifting, but not necessarily to triple rings, though many prefer them (see current cycling magazines) and they offer a better chain-line. Current long-cage derailleurs will get gears as low as 30 inches using double rings, as below:

MODEL E:

		COGS					
		14	16	19	22	26	32
	50	96	84	71	61	52	
CHAINRINGS	36	—	61	51	44	37	30

A setup along these lines will get most people up most hills even under a fair load, without complex shift patterns.

THE ULTIMATE

For those who want to know just how far gearing can be pushed, the answer is provided by Ivar T. Tonneson, who toured the world with Mai-Britt Johannson in the late seventies, using a single 34-tooth chainring and four cogs combined with a customized Sturmey-Archer five-speed hub. Unlike the usual triple-ring setup, it offered close ratios and simple shifting. Between them Tonneson and Johannson wore out 18 chains in 32,424 kilometers, but had no serious transmission problems.

		COGS			
		14	15	16	34
HUB GEAR	1	98	92	86	41
	2	83	78	73	34
	3	66	61	57	27
	4	52	48	45	21
	5	44	41	38	18

CRANK LENGTH

Crank-arm length is a hot topic of the eighties. The normal road length has long been 170 mm, but cranks can be as short as 160 or as long as 185 mm, usually graduated in 2.5 mm steps. Long cranks do give greater leverage, allowing a slightly larger gear to be turned and giving mechanical advantage on a hill, but this is gained at a price. Long cranks just don't spin as smoothly, and for many, smooth is the name of the game. The normal range for road (as opposed to track, where short cranks are common) is 167.5 to 172.5, with 175 mm as a respected outside limit even for long-legged riders, though 6'5" Czech racer Hynek Dvoraceck used 180 mm cranks on hilly stages of Colorado's 1983 Coors Classic race.

Farrel's Fit Kit comes up with very similar recommendations, based on full (floor to crotch) inseam:

up to 29½"	*170 mm or less*
29½"–33"	*170 mm*
33"–36"	*172.5 mm*
over 36"	*175 mm or more*

Coaches and experienced riders are conservative because they value the knee, and so should you. Used regularly for long, hard rides, extra-long cranks can create hyperstress here. Slow, heavy pedaling also tends to tense the muscles and impede blood flow, thus allowing waste products to build up. Lower-back pain is another symptom of the long-crank/big-gear syndrome. All this notwithstanding, there is an American school that recommends superlong cranks for riders of average leg length. Most riders are better off learning to pedal.

SEASONAL VARIATION

Everyone knows that hilly terrain means lower gears; so does cool weather and lack of basic fitness. Warm weather and conditioning let you roll bigger gears later in the season; it's common knowledge that if you ride regularly, a freewheel that feels good with 50–40 rings in early spring may feel about the same with 53–42 in summer.

Sticking to a freewheel that gives you nice ratios is popular with experienced riders because they can easily vary the gearing to seasonal fitness by switching rings. Others get more or less the same result by switching freewheels in spring and fall. Of course, having a set of winter wheels with appropriate gears is even more convenient; if you have bicycle fever you find a way to justify the cost.

9.
BASIC MAINTENANCE

There are plenty of technical manuals on bicycles, some quite good, but because they are written by people with an affinity for hardware they often don't take the average rider into account. This average rider may be much better at selling houses, teaching school, or designing molecules than bicycle repair. He or she is also more interested in riding than fixing a bicycle. Bearing all this in mind, the priorities for this chapter were set by necessity and simplicity.

It's in the nature of the bicycle that cables will stretch, tires will puncture, spokes will pop, and even sealed lubricants will dry up or be washed away. These and similar matters are dealt with in detail, but bottom bracket and headset are not; these will easily last out a season when properly installed, are difficult to work on, and require expensive and specialized tools. Likewise, there is no instruction on wheel building, one of the high arts of the bicycle. After you've had your bike a month, you'll know if you want to get into more difficult jobs and seasonal maintenance. At the end of the chapter you'll find several good sources of information, along with a list of tools for routine maintenance.

When things go wrong, deal with them; bicycles tend to either improve or slowly go to pieces. Like household pets, some bikes have happy homes, others seem to cringe. This says something about the owner, at least to fellow riders. Experienced riders avoid ramshackle bikes exactly the way drivers shun the rolling wreck. It's an accident waiting to happen.

PERILS OF THE CHEAP BIKE

It sometimes happens that nuts and bolts strip, parts don't fit, and things keep going wrong with a bicycle. Sometimes this is congenital with the bicycle, sometimes the owner. Bargain bikes are not cost effective because they're not designed to be repaired; they are designed to be sold and then to fall apart. The suggestions in Chapter 4 should save you from this misery, but even a good bike does not go on forever. It loosens up. The first rule of maintenance is to check your bike out to make sure nothing is loose. If you've bought a new bike and your dealer has some kind of post-purchase checkout, take advantage of it. In particular, spokes often need tightening after a few hundred miles; this is called trueing, and will make the wheel last much longer. Unless you have mechanical talent, don't try it yourself; it's no job for a beginner. But you can easily learn to handle routine brake adjustments and flat tires.

MECHANICAL APTITUDE VS. PERSPECTIVE

Some people enjoy working on bikes as much as they do riding them. Some years ago the U.S. national team had one member so adept at servicing bottom brackets that he would fix another rider's for free; he went around spinning cranks and pointing out deficiencies in this crucial (to him) area.

In point of fact, his labors were largely wasted; assuming reasonable parameters of adjustment and lubrication, very little energy is lost here. In fact, not much energy is lost through bearings in general; it is a much-overlooked fact that all these moving surfaces are low-speed bearings. They don't really need fussing over except in unusual weather conditions, and most of them can go a full season on one servicing. If they are dry, it's no sin to simply squirt some oil into them from time to time rather than completely disassemble and repack with grease; some of the best hubs have a little hole just for this purpose. But be aware that this is a temporary measure; oil will dissolve what grease remains, so that you must then lubricate on a regular basis— every week or two, depending on mileage, and immediately after the bike has been ridden in the rain.

MINIMAL MAINTENANCE

Calculated neglect requires that you know what you're doing, and when it's time to stop. A bike that's never serviced goes into decline, and this decline follows a certain pattern. Soft tires subject the rim to battering; the rim develops flat spots, and spokes loosen up. If the chain is dry, it squeaks, wears, and develops stiff links that affect shifting; if it's loaded with oil, it collects dirt that turns into black gunk that gets on your pants and clogs dérailleur pulleys. Brake cables loosen and fray; bumped dérailleurs develop problems. When the bike gets to the shop, all this takes time to repair. Minimal maintenance is based on the notion that once a year a qualified mechanic will go over the bike carefully, repacking and adjusting bearings, and so forth. Do this at the end of the riding season, then hang the bike up for the winter in a clean dry place, to avoid rust and save tires.

There are certain basic repairs and adjustments that are essential to master. Flat tires spareth no man, woman, or child; cable-stretch and dry chains are universal, and spoke failure is a guaranteed eventuality. You can make these and other minor repairs with the basic tool kit (see p. 247), which will also handle other light maintenance without butchering your bike. If you use cheap tools, you'll have more problems; this is no place to save money. If you need more complex repairs, good relations with your bike shop will pay off. Constant changes in components make it impossible for any book to explain everything, but mechanics are sometimes willing to tell you what's going on.

WHEELS AND TIRES

Changing a clincher tire is tedious, and patching a tube is more so, but recent technology makes it a lot easier. If you carry a tube, you save about half the time because you don't need to patch then and there; if you carry a fold-up casing, you can replace one that's been blown out. These items can be carried under the seat in a small nylon bag. You should also carry a patch kit, frame pump, and tire levers; if your bike has no quick release, you'll need a wrench to loosen the wheel nuts. Schraeder valves have a removable core, and it's a good idea to carry a spare.

Check the valve first. The time-honored method is to seal it with saliva after pumping some air in the tire; if it bubbles, you have a bad valve. Schraeder cores screw out with a metal valve cap; replace the core, and you are all set. Some Presta valves are removable too, but this

REMOVING A SCHRAEDER VALVE
This automobile-style valve is still common on less expensive bikes. Sometimes the valve core is defective; you can check it for leaks by sealing the valve with saliva. If it bubbles, there's a leak. The core unscrews with the metal cap (rare these days) or a special tool; just screw in a new one.

innovation is far from standard, alas. If the valve is the problem and cannot be replaced, you must remove the wheel.

REMOVING THE FRONT WHEEL

At this point you will come to appreciate the quick-release concept. The brake release opens to widen caliper clearance, which makes it easier to get the wheel past the brake blocks. If the hub has a quick release, simply throw the lever outward, hit the top of the tire with the heel of your hand, and it will pop out. Do not unscrew the quick release, except to adjust it. After you replace the wheel, tighten the quick release by putting the lever back to its original position; then hit the top of the tire again to make sure the wheel is in solidly. There are also several wheel-retaining devices mandated by the Consumer Products Safety Commission; these vary, but are not very complicated. Many riders remove them after learning how to lock a wheel on properly.

QUICK-RELEASES

The brake quick-release (left) spreads the calipers; the hub quick-release (right) loosens the wheel. Pull levers to open, press tight to close. This is a reliable mechanism, found on virtually all quality road bicycles, but it's not idiot-proof: failure to adjust and/or lock the brake quick-release can result in no brakes; failure to lock the front wheel can result in a *very* bad crash when the wheel jumps loose on a bump. A loose one on the rear wheel lets the wheel pull to one side and rub against the frame.

REMOVING THE FRONT WHEEL

Wheels sometimes don't want to come out. Hitting the tire with the heel of your hand after you've loosened the hub quick-release will do the trick.

If the wheel is held by nuts on a solid axle, loosen the nuts with a wrench and follow the same procedure.

REAR WHEEL

Front wheels are easy, rear wheels are messy, because of the chain (and derailleur, if there is one). With a derailleur bike, begin by

REMOVING THE REAR WHEEL
With a derailleur bike, be sure the chain is on the smallest cog before starting. A sharp forward-and-down motion will dislodge the wheel. Getting the hub past the chain can be messy, and the trick is to calmly observe what you're doing. You must work the freewheel side of the hub past the derailleur cage and chain. Reverse the procedure to put the wheel back on. Be careful not to rest the bike on the derailleur when the wheel is off; you can knock it out of line. If you learn to do this at home first, it's much easier on the road.

shifting the chain to the outside (smallest) cog. Then open the brake quick release. After this, loosen the hub quick release or retaining nuts, and hit the wheel sharply from the rear, so that it falls forward and down. When it is clear of the dropouts, lift the chain off the cog and remove the wheel, being careful not to wrench the derailleur (or rest the bike on it). Seeing this done makes it easier. Bad alignment of the dropouts makes it harder, but most shops can align them to let the wheel come out freely. Race mechanics change rear wheels in ten seconds, but the job is tedious first time around.

Nonderailleur bikes follow a basically similar procedure; if the dropout opens to the rear, you may have to slide the wheel forward first, lift the chain clear of chainwheel and cog, and then slide it out.

CHANGING TUBULARS ON THE ROAD

One great virtue of tubular tires is instant replacement. Starting at the far side of the valve, you simply strip the glued-on tire off the rim, being careful not to damage the valve. Then insert the valve of your spare into the valve hole (making sure it is upright), and stretch the tire onto the rim. The remaining glue on the rim will hold the tire in place when it is inflated, if you ride carefully.

Et voilà! as the French say. Very continental until you get home and consider that while the tubular can be replaced in no time, repair is comparable to minor surgery, the vital organ being a diaphanous white latex tube that is reached by unsewing the sewup, which must later be resewed. This is the price you pay for super performance.

GLUING TUBULARS

Gluing on tubulars is no pleasure either; wear your oldest clothes. A new rim should be roughened with a coarse file to give the glue better purchase, and the portion of the tire that meets the rim (the rim-strip) should also get a layer of glue. Join the pair when the glue is tacky, and make sure to have some solvent around to clean up with; it's messy. Clement is a standard European glue, and 3M Fastack is a popular U.S. product, though it sticks so well it tends to pull the rim-strip off the tire.

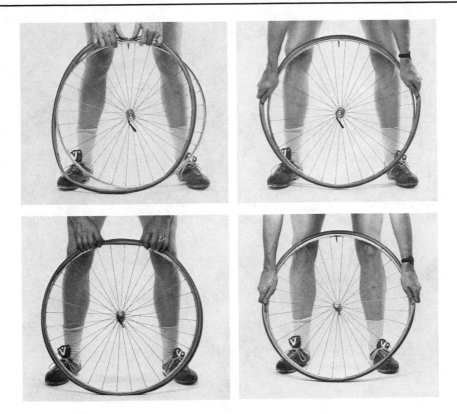

STRETCHING ON A TUBULAR

Tubulars strip off easily; you peel them away starting opposite the valve, being careful not to injure the tire around the valve. Installing tight new tubulars can be more difficult, but they usually loosen up at warm temperature. Make sure there is glue on both tire and tube, and that the tire is centered on the rim all the way around. Clockwise from upper left: (1) insert the valve; (2, 3) work the tire onto the rim, constantly stretching it toward the far side; otherwise the final stretch (4) won't get the tire onto the rim. Full pressure is crucial to keeping the tire on the rim, *especially when glue is questionable.*

CLINCHERS

Clincher tubes can be repaired in the field. Begin by inspecting the exterior of the casing. If you can find what caused the puncture, remove it, and mark the spot; it will help you locate the tube puncture later on. If there is still air in the tire, let it out. Then carefully insert the rounded end of a tire lever (*not* a screwdriver, which will usually damage the tube) between bead and rim, at the opposite side from the

REMOVING A CLINCHER TIRE

Make haste slowly, and work further from the valve than this mechanic. Tire levers can damage the tube. Clockwise from upper left: (1) insert the first lever carefully, with just enough of it under the bead to lift it; pry casing off rim and lock lever on spoke; (2) do likewise with the second lever, about 4″–6″ away; this will loosen many tires enough that you can remove one lever and repeat the prying action further away, but a third lever makes this easier; (3) when tire is loose on rim, slide your fingers under the bead, then (4) remove tube, being careful of the valve. Always check rim for protruding spokes and inside of casing for nails, glass, etc.

valve. You can puncture a tube by pinching it with a lever, so pry the bead off carefully. Then hook the lever on a spoke.

Now insert the second lever about two spokes away and carefully repeat the procedure, again locking the lever on a spoke. At this point the casing may be loose enough to work off by hand; if not, repeat the procedure with a third lever. Now slide your fingers under the bead and run them around the tire, so that the bead is outside the rim all the way around. If you found a nail or some glass in the casing, mark the corresponding spot on the tube. After this, remove the casing completely; this will make it easier to get the valve out.

Before going any further, run your fingers slowly along the inside of the casing to locate anything that might have caused this or some future problem, and remove it. Now inspect the side of the rim that faces the tube. It will be covered with cloth or rubber rim tape, but spokes can force themselves through. If so, the protruding spoke must be filed down, or it will cause another puncture. If you carry a spare tube, skip ahead to *Mounting;* otherwise you patch.

PATCHING

Ideally, you have a tub, basin, or bucket of water. Bubbles from the submerged tube indicate where the leak is. Field expedients are the mark you made on the casing, a faint hissing sound you will soon learn to hear, and intuition. Running your hand carefully over the tube while it is full of air will often reveal the leak. Saliva spread over suspicious areas provides final evidence. Slow "pinhole" leaks are tricky; if one person pumps air into the tube while another inspects it, the leak is easier to find. If the area around the valve is leaking, patching usually does not work.

When the puncture is located, mark it; pens will mark even the

PATCHING
(1) Lightly roughen an area larger than the patch. (2) Cover it smoothly with cement. While the glue sets, peel the backing off the patch, being careful not to touch the sticky part. (3) When the glue sets (appears to dry), press tacky side of patch onto it (right). Cleanliness is second to nothing in getting patches to stick; body oil from the hands can interfere with the bond.

darkest tube. You can also stick a toothpick into the hole to mark the spot. Now clean the tube, roughen the area (larger than the patch) with sandpaper or grater from the patch kit, and keep it clean of everything, including fingerprints. Working on the tube is easier if it is stretched over a solid object; your knee will do.

Finally, spread a thin layer of glue over the roughened area and allow it to set until it appears dry. Strip the backing from the patch carefully, again avoiding finger contact, and press it on the roughened area, making sure it is in contact all around and holding it in place for a minute. Let another minute pass, test at low pressure, and you are ready to remount the tire.

MOUNTING

Begin by working one of the beads over the rim; some casing/rim combinations go on easily by hand, others do not. Now insert the tube, with just enough air in it so that it retains its shape. Put the valve through the hole in the rim, making sure it is upright and stays that way; bent-over valves tend to fail after a while. Take time to adjust tube and casing so that the valve is set correctly. Be sure that the tube is tucked all the way into the casing.

Now work the other bead onto the rim, starting at the valve, and work it on as far as you can. When the going gets tough, you have reached the critical point; some casings don't want to go onto some rims. Finger strength and experience can be important, and the thumb is the strongest finger. Make sure the tube is well tucked in, and try letting out some air. Push hard; everyone agrees that tire levers have no role here. Sometimes they are used, but risk of pinching (and re-puncturing) is high. When the casing is on, put in 20–30 pounds of air, and check that the casing is seated. Some seat automatically, others don't, and full pressure in an unseated casing means blowing out a tube—creating a big hole that can't be patched. Seating is easy to check by eye; if one area is lifted, bulging, or out of line, let out the air, massage that section further into the rim and start again. Don't be in a hurry; if the tire was seated before, it will reseat. If the tire was really difficult to mount and/or seat, talk to your dealer about which tires are most compatible with your rims. Proliferation of tire and rim widths has been very beneficial in terms of performance, but some "semi-mismatches" do exist. (See page 105.)

MOUNTING A CLINCHER TIRE
Clockwise from upper left: (1) Starting with just enough air in the tube to give it some shape, insert the valve through the protective strip and rim, making sure it is upright. (2) Stuff the tube back into the casing. (3) Work one bead onto the rim all the way around, then empty tube completely. (4) Work the other bead onto the rim. The last push may tempt you to use a lever; don't. Chances of pinching (and puncturing) are quite high. Refill in stages, checking to see that casing seats properly.

KEEPING IT SIMPLE

Three things are for sure: A new tube beats field patching; fold-up casings can save the day; and tubulars are marvelous if you can afford to toss them when they puncture.

BRAKES

Brakes are a popular area of neglect, and there are plenty of folks who would just as soon ride with one as two. You can get away with this until you have to stop in a hurry; the rear brake just can't do it, and the front one alone is liable to flip you if the wheel is even slightly turned or your weight is forward. This is known as doing an *end-o* and is quite dangerous.

QUICK ADJUSTMENT

This is simple to do with a few inexpensive tools, and if there are no hidden problems, it can be very quick. Minor adjustments on good brakes require no tools at all, being made with the built-in barrel-adjuster mechanism, which is finger adjustable by a knurled knob. It can be located at either end of the cable, usually at the caliper. Cables stretch though, and when you come to the end of this adjustment you must take up the slack. This requires (1) a small wrench (two for center-pull brakes) to loosen the nut that holds cable to caliper, (2) pliers to pull the cable taut, and (3) some way to hold the calipers against the rim, such as a Third Hand or toe strap.

Start by locating the barrel adjuster and tightening it down; then open the quick release, which will put slack in the cable. Now clamp

BARREL ADJUSTERS
Dia-Compe's side-pull barrel adjuster assembly is just above quick-release. Turning it allows you to fine-adjust brakes by turning; the lock nut sets the adjustment. Older Mafac center pulls (right) have barrel adjuster at brake lever, but it does the same thing.

the brake blocks tight to the rim with Third Hand or toe strap. If you have side-pull brakes, loosen the anchor bolt that holds the cable to the caliper. If you have center-pulls, use one wrench on each side of the yoke, and loosen the anchor nut just enough to let the cable slide. Then grasp the cable with your pliers and gently but firmly pull it taut; the process is easy with side-pulls, much less so with the double-wrench procedure required by the yoke on a center-pull. When the cable is taut, tighten the anchor bolt.

Free the calipers and tighten the quick release. In some cases, the brakes will be too tight, and will not release from the rims. If so, very gently squeeze the lever; if the cable is not locked down at the caliper, it may be induced to release a bit of cable by careful squeezing. If not, clamp the calipers down again, loosen the cable slightly and feed

BRAKE ADJUSTMENT
Toe strap tightens blocks to rim for adjustment. Pliers pull cable taut, wrench tightens anchor-nut holding cable. This is a typical side-pull assembly; others are slightly different, but the process is basically the same.

back about ⅛″ of cable. Ideally, brake blocks are adjusted to just barely clear the rims, which gives maximum braking power, but wobbly out-of-true wheels won't allow this. What it comes down to is getting the blocks as close as possible without having them rub. When you are sure of your adjustment, tighten the cable very securely and squeeze

CANTILEVER CENTER-PULL SYSTEM
Cantilever fittings are brazed to the frame, making them extra-solid; they are found on off-road, tandem, cyclo-cross and better touring bikes. These Mafacs work like any center-pulls: cable feeds through hanger (above), and anchors on a yoke cable that pulls up on both calipers. You need two wrenches to work on any center-pull anchor bolt; It's trickier than a side-pull. But cantilevers are the ultimate anchors, short of discs or drums.

the brake lever *very hard,* as in a panic stop. Inexperienced mechanics often do everything right, but they hesitate on torquing down this crucial bolt. Afterward, tin the cable end with a soldering iron, or screw a spoke nipple onto it to prevent fraying. A drop or two of epoxy is the space-tech approach. Frayed cables are a mess.

RELATED PROBLEMS

Brakes often drift off center, causing them to rub on one side, and making adjustment more or less impossible. Some brakes are centered

CENTERING CALIPERS
Often one caliper drags while the other is free. Tapping the spring behind the calipers will center them unless there is a serious problem; tap lightly at first.

TOEING IN BRAKE BLOCKS
Brake squeal can usually be cured by bending calipers very slightly so that the front end of the block touches the rim just before the rear. Take your time, bending calipers very slightly, or you can weaken them. Taking out the wheel lets you work lower down on the caliper, which distributes stress better.

with a cone wrench, but all respond to a sharp downward tap on the spring that is pulling the block too far from the rim. If this doesn't work, the spring (or caliper assembly) may have worked loose; tighten whatever is loose.

Brake squeak is another common ailment; it usually responds to slight "toe-in," which is created by holding the caliper with a wrench and bending the forward part inward. Obviously, you don't want to overdo this because it can weaken the calipers. If the squeak persists, it is usually caused by the composition of brake blocks as they interface with the material your rim is made of; try different blocks. "Sticky" brakes can be caused by weak springs, but a smooth cable line is essential. Cables do not like to go around sharp corners, so adjust housings to allow free movement.

BRAKE BLOCKS

Whenever working on the brakes, check the blocks, also called pads. These usually slide into metal shoes, which are bolted to the calipers. The blocks should line up parallel with the rims; the nuts holding them should be secure and the blocks should be seated securely in the shoe, *with the closed end of the shoe forward.* They must not overlap the tire, or they can wear through. When blocks show obvious wear, they should be replaced. For wet weather and/or the heavy loads of touring, with alloy rims try composition blocks like those made by Mathauser. If you have steel rims, chrome-leather blocks are your best bet in the rain, according to Whitt and Wilson's authoritative text, *Bicycling Science* (MIT Press: Cambridge, MA, 1982).

BRAKE LEVER POSITION

As pointed out in Chapter 7, lever position is very important because the hands rest on the brake hoods much of the time; how the lever assembly is positioned has a lot to do with comfort. If you decide to reposition levers, start by peeling away enough bar tape to give you room to slide the assembly up or down on the bars. Loosen cables as explained before; with the cables slack you will find there is just enough room to access the bolt under the lever. Loosen it just enough to allow movement, slide the lever to where you want it, and tighten the bolt firmly. After rewrapping the bars, bring calipers together with Third Hand or toe strap and proceed as in the adjustment described earlier.

MOVING BRAKE-LEVER ASSEMBLY
Left, an empty film cartridge makes a handy tape holder; center the adjusting bolt (sometimes a screw) is reachable after loosening the brake cable; right, be sure to tighten the bolt very firmly. Re-wrap bars and reset brake cable.

OVERHAUL

Replacing cables and housings is a more complicated task, less frequently required. Battered housings and corrosion brought on by exposure are more often the culprits than wear. Frayed cables and sticky brakes are indications that it's time for replacement. Cables and housings are not costly, but the job is labor intensive, particularly the first time, and the little ferrules that hold the cable at each end resemble ball bearings in their tendency to disappear. Be sure to remove and grease cables thoroughly if you decide to do this job; it retards corrosion. Teflon-lined housing is even better, greatly reducing the corrosion effect. It can also make up for less-than-perfect cable-line and weak caliper springs.

HUBS

As suggested earlier, there are two approaches to hubs—benign semi-neglect or loving care. Likewise there are two kinds of hubs—those with open and sealed bearings. Fisher's best MountainBikes come with rugged Phil Wood or Cook Brothers sealed hubs, which are better able to deal with the dust, mud, and hyperstress of off-roading,

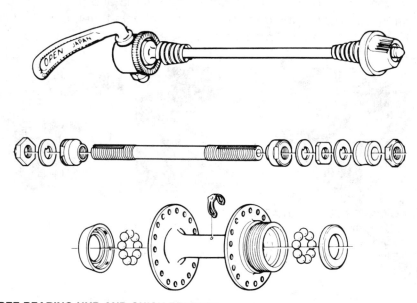

FREE-BEARING HUB AND QUICK RELEASE
Properly adjusted free-bearing hubs can last a very long time, but they are vulnerable to rain and grit. The ball bearings and adjustable cones with locknuts are common to headset, bottom bracket and pedals. With a pair of cone wrenches you can get at all the hub parts for maintenance: you can pack them with grease and adjust them for pennies, though it takes some time. Note handy oil hole in exploded view. Above is quick-release, which removes from hub during overhaul.

and Mavic's sealed bearings were used by five teams in the 1984 Tour de France. When a sealed hub fails, though, you must be able to remove the bearings, usually with a special tool, and find a replacement. Each brand is different.

The classic free-bearing hub is easier to service, and of course you can oil it at any time. This tried and true component uses ball bearings riding on races and cones, packed in somewhat waterproof (usually lithium) grease. The grease eventually gets dirty or washes away, but this is not critical, nor is the type of grease, though some people would have you think so. Ideally, the dry hub is immediately repacked with grease, but these being low-speed bearings, it is no sin to deal with a dry hub "externally" by squirting in medium to heavy machine oil. As mentioned earlier though, you must do so regularly until the wheels are repacked. If the hub does not have an oil hole, tilt the wheel, squirt in a small amount of oil, spin the wheel, and carefully wipe away the excess. Then repeat on the other side. When newborn experts criticize, point out that track racers have been running on oil for generations, and that you bought the thing to ride.

GROT

Grot is whatever causes unsmoothness in mechanical things. Oil will hold dryness at bay, but a grotty sound indicates debris grinding away. You can take the hub apart, clean and repack, but you will need a pair of specialized and rather expensive cone wrenches plus some patience to do this. The alternative is to simply tilt the wheel to a horizontal position and carefully squirt kerosene or solvent or WD-40 through until the hub runs clean. Then clean up the excess, let the hub dry out for several hours, and oil it with ordinary medium-weight machine oil.

ADJUSTMENT

Bad adjustment is serious, but occurs mostly in new or newly-packed hubs that have not been correctly assembled; a correct adjustment here should last indefinitely. A tight hub or one that wobbles is grinding away at its races and cones, and sometimes crunching the bearings. To fix this you need cone wrenches (though sizes vary with hub manufacturers), and a repack is usually in order while you are at it. The manuals at the end of the chapter tell you how to do this; a shop will usually charge around $6–$8 for the job.

SPOKE FAILURE

This is an emergency situation and has to be dealt with on the spot because a popped spoke often throws the wheel out of line enough to make the bike unridable. An enterprising loose spoke can even get into the derailleur. The first thing to do is to work the spoke out of the hub if possible; otherwise, wrap it around another spoke to get it out of the way. Now open the quick-release on the brake, which spreads the calipers; if you then tighten down slightly on the adjuster barrel you may also retain some braking as you limp home. (Good racing side-pulls have quick releases that hold in any position, for just this situation.) Though ridable the wheel will be damaged if you continue riding it this way, and it will become very difficult to true.

If the wheel is so far out of true that you can't ride the bike, a spoke wrench can save the day. Limit yourself to first aid, and don't decide to true the wheel. Simply *loosen* the two spokes adjacent to the broken one (which are pulling the wheel out of line) by turning the spoke nipple counterclockwise half a turn each; then *tighten* the next two (clockwise) slightly, which will pull the wheel back to the side of the broken spoke. Don't be a perfectionist; the idea is to adjust stress, make the wheel ridable, and save the rim. Then get to a good shop A.S.A.P., because even with this treatment, the rim is suffering.

THE CHAIN

No one, including mechanics, really wants to have much to do with chains. The chain is the dirtiest part of the bike, an engineering marvel with all the appeal of a waste disposal plant. But the neglected chain either collects gunk (and grit) or dries out, and in either case it wears, stretches, loosens up, and stops cooperating, especially with derailleur bikes.

Chain lore is amazing. There are about fourteen kinds of lubes and twenty methods of applying them. The only thing anyone agrees on is that the chain should be as clean as possible, and there is great emphasis among machine-oil advocates on wiping away excess completely. This is because only the lubricant *inside* the chain prevents wear; the stuff on the outside just collects dirt. Because removing a derailleur chain requires a special tool and a somewhat tricky procedure, light, spray-on lubricants are more and more popular. WD-40 does not give the ultimate protection, but if you use it every few days it does the job. Tri-Flo is similar, but lasts longer. The main advantage of these and similar lubricants is that they are clean and quick, and don't collect grit.

Traditionalists dote on their chains, applying a single tiny drop of oil to each of the 120-odd links (and wiping away excess, of course). They also remove the chain from time to time, rinse it thoroughly in kerosene or solvent, then cook it at very low heat in heavy oil or light grease for an hour or so. Then they hang it in the sun to drip and clean it meticulously. Sounds ridiculous, but no more eccentric than Ferrari's practice (finally discontinued in the mid-fifties) of using animal fat for certain aspects of lubrication. Actually, there is no better (or more waterproof) chain treatment than cooking, because the heat gets heavy lube into the bearings where it belongs.

CHAIN PROBLEMS

Even the best-cared-for chain eventually stretches, and this causes "skipping" on derailleur bikes, along with increased wear on cogs and chainrings. If you pull your chain away from the forward part of the big ring and it lifts more than 3/16″, it should be replaced. You can also measure the chain; the rivet heads are 1/2″ apart. If a foot of chain has stretched more than 1/32″, it's worn. When you replace it, you will find that some chains and freewheels mate monogamously. If the new chain does not break in to your old freewheel within twenty miles, you may have to buy a new freewheel, or replace the worn cogs. It may be time to figure out a new cluster anyway; chains usually last 1,500–2,500 miles, and by then, you'll have ridden enough to know which cluster will yield the gears you need.

Another problem is the stiff or frozen link, usually caused by neglect (i.e., corrosion) or incorrect installation (a chain tool in the wrong hands often tightens a link). Both will affect derailleur shifting and cause skipping. You can spot the frozen link by running the chain around the smallest cog, and it can usually be loosened by dousing in WD-40 or solvent and flexing the chain laterally (opposite the normal operating motion).

CHAIN REMOVAL

Derailleur chainlinks are ½″ × ³⁄₃₂″—narrower than three-speed links, and not interchangeable with them. The chain is removed by driving a rivet part way through a link using a special tool. It requires skill that can only be obtained by practice. The technique is clearly described in most manuals; the problem for novice chain-tool users is that rivets are easily driven too far, creating a whole new problem—getting the rivet back into the chain. A botched job can create the stiff link mentioned above or weaken the chain. You may not want to get down with your chain to the extent of mastering this skill, in which case installing a master link (RLL Super Link, available through Ten Speed Drive, Tallahassee, FL) provides an easier way to remove the chain. (Make sure you get the one that fits your chain.) If you're going on tour, though, learn to use the chain tool; if your chain fails in the middle of nowhere, you need a way to get rid of the bad link.

Generally speaking, Regina chains work well with standard European freewheels; Sedisport chains seem to work smoothly on any kind. Japanese chains don't measure up to their other components.

Three-speed chain is ½″ × ⅛″, and uses a master link, usually held by a spring clip, which is removed with needle-nose pliers or pried off with screwdriver or knife. (There are several types.) This is a convenient system except that the clip occasionally fails, which can leave you stranded unless you happen to have another one in your wallet, as many commuters do. Install it with the closed section facing forward into the normal motion of the chain. These clips have a way of flying loose when pried off, so beware.

FREEWHEEL

This cluster of cogs gets as dirty as the chain and is harder to deal with. It is removed with a special tool, which varies with the manufacturer, and just getting it off can be a challenge, owing to the fact that threaded surfaces under stress tend to bind together or "freeze." Except with newer "cassette-type" freewheels (see page 205) like that of the Shimano Freehub, changing cogs is another knucklebuster, and going inside the freewheel itself to deal with pawls and hairsprings is on the order of Sturmey-Archer dissection. Nor are all freewheels made

SPLINED FREEWHEEL WITH GROT
This is the preferred system for conventional freewheels; splines (center) make
removal easier and much less prone to damage a stuck freewheel. Things like this
become important when you're on tour.

the same way. But one thing is certain—to replace or repair it you have
to get the thing off, and the spline system makes this easier.

Among conventional freewheels, the SunTour New Winner has a
system approach that is hard to argue with: Using one body, you can
build a standard five or narrow six (120 mm rear fork), and a standard
six or narrow seven (126 mm rear fork). Sprockets from 13 to 32 fit the
five and six speeds; the seven speed will take a 12.

If a freewheel starts to "catch" (fail to spin freely), or begins freewheeling both ways, and you lack tools or expertise, the innards can
sometimes be cleared of debris by simultaneously flushing with kerosene or WD-40 (directed with the plastic tube), and spinning the freewheel. (If it's broken, you're out of luck.) If you used kerosene, follow
with light oil or WD-40, but do not take continued success for
granted—get a new one. Repair is not cost effective unless you're
gifted with talent and tools.

Actually, freewheels are generally reliable, and a bad one tends to
show up quickly. Cogs, though, wear gradually; after some thousands
of miles, the most frequently used ones will sometimes start skipping.
In this case, replacement of individual cogs usually solves the problem,
but this is a job for a well-equipped mechanic, except with the cassette-type freewheel.

CRANKS

New cotterless cranks need to be checked frequently while seating on (forming to) the axle, or they can be ruined. Tighten them when

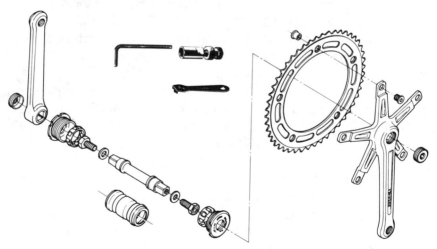

COTTERLESS CRANKS
Cotterless cranks being tightened here (top) usually set onto an axle permanently after a few hundred miles, but should be checked frequently when new. Caps over bolts remove with screwdriver or Allen wrench, and should be kept in place to protect threads. Exploded view (bottom) shows bottom-bracket parts.

necessary, but not super hard; 30 foot-pounds is enough. Tools to do this vary and are usually supplied with the crankset.

While cotterless cranks tend to seat permanently, old-style cottered cranks (rare except on three-speeds) give more trouble with age. Because cotters come in a great variety of lengths, diameters, and bevels, and are difficult to remove and install, most riders leave this to a shop. Loose cranks of either variety are easy to identify; there is play, and it can be felt if you hold one crank and move the other; it can also be felt in pedaling, as a jerking forward during the stroke. Whatever kind of cranks you have, all bolts and cotters should be checked periodically.

Cotterless crank removal, like freewheel removal, is done with a special tool, and while it is somewhat easier, it is only necessary for access to the bottom bracket bearings, which are normally serviced seasonally. Be sure to remount them in their original position.

CHAINRINGS

Even on new bicycles chainrings may be slightly bent. This can be almost invisible to a casual eye, but it affects shifting, and, with an inexperienced rider, it can throw the chain. There is a tool made which slips over the chainring allowing you to bend it. The tool is basically a long slot which grasps the chainwheel deeply when straightening it. Chainrings also wear at very different rates, depending on alloy quality (Campagnolo is still the best) and other factors like torque levels, chain condition, and the presence of abrasive grit.

BOTTOM BRACKET

This is not exactly no-man's-land, but servicing usually requires specialized and expensive tools you may not want to buy. What can happen on the road, though, is loosening of the adjustable (left) cup; rarely the fixed (right) one. In the absence of a proper tool, a big screwdriver can be used to tighten the cup, by placing it into a notch and tapping carefully in a clockwise direction. This does some slight damage, but if you distribute it between two or more notches, it is minimized. Don't count on this field repair to hold, and if this happens to a new bike it can be very bad news, suggesting flawed threading of the bracket. If it happens again after tightening with proper tools, negotiate

TIGHTENING CUP WITH PUNCH OR SCREWDRIVER
This is a field expedient. Tap clockwise, fairly hard, but avoid violence, which can deform the cup. Then get to a shop and have it done right.

for a new bicycle; the bracket is probably defective, and repair is very expensive.

HEADSET

Headset repairs are not entered into lightly or with ordinary tools. Like the bottom bracket, it can generally go for a season without attention once correctly and securely adjusted. The usual sign of trouble is a looseness at the front end, and clunking sounds when you pick up the front end of the bike and drop it back to the road. New ones sometimes come loose, but there is no real harm done unless you ignore the problem. Simply tightening the top nut doesn't work because this is locked against a lower one, like the cone and locknut on a hub. Designs vary, but getting the right adjustment usually requires two very large wrenches; you work with them until the bars turns freely with no play in the bearings. Don't get experimental away from home; if you loosen everything too much, bearings may fall out. Even if a field adjustment seems all right, have a mechanic check it out; it may loosen up.

HEADSET

Design varies widely. The inside (lower) of the two nuts on top sets the adjustment, the outside (upper) one locks it. Big wrenches are required; vise-grips and giant pliers will usually work but leave scars. Exploded view is of traditional ball-bearing type; roller and sealed-bearing units are also available.

PEDALS

Pedal problems are not uncommon, especially if you ride hard and long. Sometimes this is due to poor assembly, more often to basic

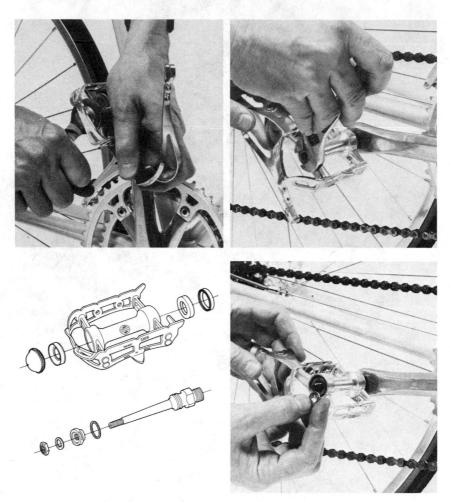

ADJUSTING PEDAL CONES
Pedals can be difficult to remove, and doing so requires a long, tight-fitting wrench. A field adjustment can be done, though. Clockwise from upper left: (1) Start by removing the cap; under it are a cone and lock nut similar to that of a hub. (2) After separating cone (inside) and lock nut (outside), adjust cone for free movement with just a hair of play. Hold cone in place while tightening lock nut; this MKS has a slotted axle and fitted washer between lock nut and cone, which makes adjustment easier. When lock nut is tight, adjustment will be closer than before. (4) Design of many makes is basically similar; this one is by Zeus.

quality. Pedals take high, complex, and uneven stresses, especially with big people who pedal badly; all but the best seem to come apart or wear fairly fast. Very cheap pedals are disposable in that they have no provision for adjustment. Their axles often bend, after which they wobble, and there is no cure for this; the pedal must be replaced. The replacement must match in thread size and direction. Also, right and left pedals are not interchangeable. Japanese and English pedals are marked L and R; French pedals are marked D (right) and G (left); Italian pedals are marked D (right) and S (left). Most bikes these days have English-Italian $\frac{9}{16}''$ × 20 tpi, but the French persist with 14 mm × 1.25. You can have cranks retapped for English-Italian threading, which will give you easier access to replacements, but it's no job for an amateur.

Removing pedals requires a beefy wrench of exactly the right size, because the pedals seem to bond with cranks. The direction you turn to loosen them can be confusing; the trick is to always turn the wrench over the top and to the rear of the bicycle. Adjustment can often be done without removal, though. Quite often, pedals simply start to come apart because the lock nut is not secure; this leads first to loosening, then to accelerated wear, then to broken bearings. If you catch this in time and tighten the lock nut you can often save the pedal.

What you are dealing with is a miniature version of a hub, usually covered by a cap on the outboard side of the pedal. This can be removed with your adjustable wrench, or a special wrench made by the manufacturer. Once inside, your key item is some tool that will turn and hold the cone; an adjustable wrench will work on the locknut. As with hubs, you want a free but not loose, adjustment. Also as with hubs, most pedals have free bearings that are grease packed; oil will do if they go dry, but then they must be oiled every week or two until the pedal is repacked. Don't be surprised if inexpensive pedals continue to give problems, or if the axle bends (which you will feel when pedaling). Quality is a good investment here if you use your bike a lot.

GENERAL MAINTENANCE

One reason for owning a basic set of tools is that you can tighten the miscellaneous nuts and bolts that inevitably work loose over the months. With a new bike especially, it's a good idea to check everything carefully. Bikes assembled in the heat of the selling season tend to have something loose. There are an amazing number of nuts and bolts, and if you find the loose ones early, you prevent damage. A derailleur that floats up into the rear wheel can destroy itself, and the wheel, and even damage the dropout if you're unlucky. Brake cables that seem fine can slip in a panic stop; seats can come loose, and pedals can disintegrate. With good tools that don't damage the parts, you can make a good bike go on forever.

IMMERSION THERAPY

What you do with your bike after it's been ridden in the rain is at least equal in importance to seasonal maintenance. Your best move is to start by washing it clean of the inevitable mud; a little mild detergent in warm water does it quickly, but *don't* hose it down afterward; the blast of a hose can blow out more lubrication than hours in the rain. A gentle spray from above like that from a watering can is safe. Race mechanics do hose down bikes, but those bikes are also serviced on a very regular basis, and are reckoned to have a somewhat limited life span. You can get rid of the grit with a light spray, an old towel, and some elbow grease. When you've got the bike clean and as dry as possible, spray it down thoroughly with WD-40, which gets under the remaining water and leaves a thin, protective, antirust film that is also a light lubricant; it should go everywhere the rain went, especially the chain and cable housings. Removing the wheels to keep WD-40 off the rims (i.e., braking surfaces) is a good idea.

If the grease has been washed away you should get a little oil into the hubs and pedals and hit brakes and derailleurs with WD-40. If the freewheel sounds grotty, clean it as described earlier and lube with WD-40 or light oil. If you had an unprotected leather saddle on a bike without fenders, the best thing you can do is rub the underside with Brooks Proofide and hope for the best.

THE THOROUGH APPROACH

The next step up from this basic treatment is the equivalent of yearly maintenance: Repack hubs, pedals, bottom bracket, headset, and brake cables with waterproof grease; oil small moving parts; and cook chain in oil or grease if you're a purist. (Replace it if you have any doubts.) Spraying WD-40 into all the inside frame tubes that can be reached is also a good idea. Add wheel-trueing to this list and you have the typical yearly maintenance.

GETTING SERIOUS

If you are serious about mastering bicycle mechanics, the corner-stone of reliable information is *Sutherland's Handbook* (Chapter 4), which is densely packed with information about components, threads, gauges, compatibility, etc. Along with this you need a step-by-step, "how-to" book geared specifically to maintenance. *Anybody's Bike Book* (Ten Speed Press: Berkeley, CA, 1979) is an inexpensive low-key classic of the seventies' bike boom which covers the basics in a down-home way. *The Ten-Speed Bicycle* (Rodale Press: Emmaus, PA, 1979) is a gentrified, more elaborate, sometimes more complete approach with good illustrations but less good opinions. (It assumes the five-speed freewheel standard when sixes and sevens are the new facts of life and by implication recommends the four-cross wheel, etc.) Eugene A. Sloan's revised *All New Complete Book of Cycling* (about $12.50) is good too.

TOOLS

Raleigh and others make a special all-around bicycle wrench that fits almost everything on a bike, and can be very useful. Certain com-ponents require special tools; discuss this with your dealer, but buy only what you really need at first. Also note that additional tools are needed for touring, as discussed in Chapter 11. Cone wrenches, free-wheel removers, and chain tools are inexpensive and useful additions. If you do all your own repairs, an inexpensive stand like the Minoura is almost necessary; a Turbo-trainer or similar device doubles as an exercise and repair stand. Beyond this lie handsome sets of box/open-end wrenches, large adjustable ones, and an expensive array of sub-stantial items for dealing with headset and bottom bracket. Campag-nolo makes an excellent tool kit that will solve any and all problems of their components while providing a modest tax shelter.

THE BASIC TOOL KIT

Quality is extremely important in tools; poor ones destroy nuts and bolts, leading to added repair costs when a shop mechanic extracts and replaces the ruined parts. This minimum kit is predicated on the idea that all the tools are of good quality. If they're not, you'll have problems.

Needle-nose pliers: To be applied only as needed, when no wrench will do the job.

Screwdrivers: One medium standard type (actually, one large and one small is preferable) and one Phillips type. Check them against the bolts on your bike to make sure they fit.

Six-inch crescent (adjustable) wrench: Even a good one with hardened jaws and precise adjustment will tend to slip; tighten it on carefully.

Cable clipper: The notched type is best, the kind built into a pair of pliers the worst. Use carefully; sloppy cable-clipping leads to loose strands and related complications.

Small and large "Y" wrenches: These inexpensive tools give you six socket wrenches that will fit any nut on the bike.

Lubricants: (1) WD-40 or equivalent. This light spray-lubricant penetrates, prevents rust, and will do temporarily for heavier jobs when nothing else is available; (2) Light machine oil or equivalent for bearings and chain, preferably in the kind of container that can (a) be sealed and (b) deliver very small amounts; (3) Sturmey-Archer oil (if you own a three-speed); (4) waterproof grease (if you pack your own hubs, etc.).

Patch kit: Thin patches with beveled edges like those for tubulars are best; light clinchers repaired with fat patches will thump. If you ride tubulars, get the special kit with needle and thread. And make sure the glue hasn't dried in the tube.

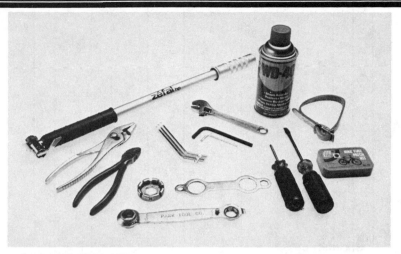

BASIC TOOL KIT
This is a start. Clippers shown are not the best; the kind that places the cable in a small notch usually cuts cleaner. Needlenose pliers "would do less damage" according to bike builder Peter Mooney, but there's no substitute for the right wrench. New plastic tire-removal tools are said to be better; to each his own. The main thing is to have the right tools for your particular bike.

Spoke wrench: *This must fit your spoke nipples precisely; there are several sizes. It takes an expert to true a wheel, but you can make your bike ridable after popping a spoke easily enough with this tool.*

Third Hand or toe strap: *One-use items that make brake adjustment much easier by holding calipers together while both hands are occupied.*

Hex (Allen) wrenches: *Examine your bike and make sure you have one of these to fit anything secured by this increasingly popular method, such as chainrings, dérailleurs, stem, seatpost, brakes, etc.*

Frame pump: *This is discussed as an accessory in Chapter 10, but a pump is a tool in the sense that without one you can't get rolling after a flat.*

MAINTENANCE AND REPAIR PRIORITY CHART

There will never be complete agreement on how much an owner really needs to know about fixing a bike. Our priorities are based on the likelihood of having the problem, the difficulty of repair, and the tools and time involved. Priority ratings: 1 = Necessary skill, 5 = Average rider doesn't need to learn; Difficulty ratings: A = easy; E = a job that requires special tools or trained skills.

COMPONENT	ADJUST OR REPAIR	TOOLS NEEDED	PRIORITY	DIFFICULTY
Brakes	Barrel adjustment	None	1	A
	Adjustment via cable-reset at caliper	Toe strap and small wrench or screwdriver, pliers	1	B
	Toe-in	Crescent wrench	2	B
	Move levers	Toe strap, wrench, screwdriver, pliers	2	C
	Overhaul, replace cable	Toe strap, wrench, screwdriver, pliers	3	D
	Replace blocks	Wrench	2	B
Wheel	Change	None with quick-release; wrench otherwise	1	front: A rear: B
Tires Clincher	Remove and remount	Tire levers	1	C
	Patch	Patch kit	2	C
Tubular	Remove and remount	None in field; glue for permanent mount	1	A
			1	C
	Repair puncture	Patch kit, small knife	3	E
Cranks Cotterless	Tighten	Manufacturers tool or socket wrench	1	A
	Remove	As above, plus crank removal tool	4	D

Component	Task	Special tool (or improvise)		
Pedal	Replace cotter		4	E
	Adjust cone (in field)	Manufacturer's dust-cap tool, small wrench, small screwdriver	2	C
	Remove/replace	Long, high quality wrench	3	C
Freewheel (conventional)	Remove/replace	Manufacturers tool	4	D-E
	Change cogs	Special tool	2	5E
Hub Conventional	Pack and adjust	Cone wrenches, grease, new bearings	4	D
	oil	None	1	A
Sealed	Change bearings	Much variety	2	C-E
Headset	Field adjust	Big wrenches	3	2B
	Pack and adjust	Big wrenches & parts	5	E
Bottom bracket axle assembly	Tighten (emergency)	Big screwdriver or punch, hammer	1	B
	Pack and adjust	Socket wrench, crank-remover, special tool	5	E
Chain	Light lube	Aerosol lube	1	A
derailleur	Remove	Chain tool	3	D
3-speed	Remove	Screwdriver	3	B
Derailleur	Adjust and lube	Screwdriver, WD-40	1	A
	Install/repair	Chain tool, wrenches	4	D

10.
CLOTHING AND
ACCESSORIES

As architect Mies van der Rohe observed, *Less Is More,* and this definitely holds true for the bicycle. There is an awesome variety of bicycle accessories on the market, some invaluable, some useless junk. You can usually tell the junk because it looks wrong; it looks wrong because it's unnecessary, and necessity is the first rule about add-ons. The second rule is that accessories, like components, should be strong, light, and well designed.

Safety is an obvious priority, as with any vehicle. Helmets, lights, reflectors, etc., are important; gadgets are not. Shop owners sometimes hesitate to suggest these items because there is a truism that safety talk does not sell bikes. On the other hand, there is the personal experience of editor Ed Pavelka, of *Velo-news,* a cycling journal. After a helmet saved him a trip to the hospital, he wrote in favor of them. The hard core wrote back that he was a traitor; some digressed to offer tips on guerrilla-style methods of getting around the law.

SAFETY-RELATED ACCESSORIES

HELMETS

Pavelka was right, and the statistics are unequivocal. Next to handling skill and a roadworthy bike, a good helmet is your best protection against serious injury. It's the cycling equivalent to the automobile seat-belt. Doctors support the protective hard helmet overwhelmingly, but many traditionalist (and all guerrilla-style) riders reject the hard helmet. Their forebears also rejected the dérailleur and the freewheel, not to mention the Safety bicycle itself, which was regarded with suspicion for years.

Bikies clearly don't know everything; unless you are very well-coordinated, daring, and fatalistic, don't let your sense of style make the helmet decision for you. The guy without a helmet who goes by you slipping through traffic like an eel may have thousands of racing miles behind him, plus the fine-honed peripheral vision and reflexes racing develops. He might be a bike-messenger, who does this all day, every day. He might also be somebody due for a skull fracture sooner or later; anybody can make a mistake.

WHAT TO LOOK FOR

With the growth of recreational cycling, helmet manufacturers have become very serious about researching and improving their products,

HELMETS
Clockwise from upper left: Skid Lid, Bell, Pro-tec and Bailen helmets. This is a representative collection; all run in the $40–$50 range. There is also a new Bell racing type with open ventilation like the Skidlid, but with a rigid design.

and the results are apparent: lighter weight, better ventilation, and more comfortable design. All helmets are not the same, though; check for fit, thickness and density of padding, effective cooling, and any interference with vision and hearing. (Also check to be sure that the strap will hold it on.)

You will find that there is a trade-off between total physical protection and other considerations. At one end of the spectrum are the sturdy Bells, and Bailens—solid, reliable equipment that performs exceptionally well in laboratory testing. At the other end is what racers call the "leather hairnet," mandated by the U.S. Cycling Federation, but no help at all except with abrasions. In between are the light, well-ventilated SkidLid and Bell V-1 which hardly feel like hard helmets at all, but which are better protection than many cheap ones, some of which have no effective padding at all and flex freely in all directions. Bell also makes a good child's helmet.

RELATED ITEMS

Shatterproof sunglasses are an inexpensive and useful item. They keep dust and bugs out of your eyes and reduce glare (a factor in mental fatigue). There's a valid tradition: Pictures of Fausto Coppi and Louison Bobet leading the Tour de France show them with dark glasses. Colorado's Olympic gold medalist Alexi Grewal often wears them, too. There are also small rearview mirrors that mount on glasses or helmet; Mirrycle makes a good one that mounts at the brake lever assembly. You may feel that your ears tell you what you need to know, but a mirror can be helpful in traffic.

VISIBILITY

REFLECTORS

Bikes sold in the U.S. arrive festooned with reflectors, which are mandated by law and look it. So do the cheap and ugly brackets, and this tempts riders to strip their bikes. If you can't abide the el cheapos provided by most manufacturers, find one you can live with.

Reflectors are better than nothing, but they are a stopgap approach to night safety, and very misleading. They work only when struck by headlights, which they won't be at dusk. They fail to command attention in all but near-total darkness when drivers are un-distracted by other traffic and ambient light. In many countries it is illegal to operate at night without lights. Pedal reflectors are more effective than stationary ones because their movement catches light from different angles—and only a fool would ride without a rear reflector.

LIGHTING

The real solution, ignored by the Consumer Product Safety Commission, is effective lighting. It is a plain and obvious fact that motorists expect vehicles and objects in the road to be lit up at night. Lighting is the only way for a bicycle to be visible at dusk and after dark, and it is the great leap forward from reflectors to real safety.

LIGHTING
Clockwise from upper left: (1) Per-lux system (around $125 complete with charge unit and dual taillights) is impressive; you can actually see the road, potholes and glass quite clearly. (2) Kearney strobe flash taillight (about $35) is the best and brightest of its kind; his headlights are also formidable. (3) Bottom-bracket-mounted Sanyo generator (about $20–25) combined with (4) Union halogen bulb (another $20–25) don't match Per-lux or Kearney systems but are much brighter than most bike lights and don't weigh much.

TAILLIGHTS

Never mind that the law does not require taillights; with cars moving at about 80 feet per second at the legal limit, you definitely want to let them know where you are. The best protection comes from the type of system described below, but even if you don't plan night riding you need at least some protection. The absolute minimum requirement is an armlight or a strobe-flasher. The armlight works best strapped below the left knee, where its movement draws the eye; the flasher can be fastened to clothes or bike, but frame-shock can affect it, so it's best attached to the body.

The best of the strobe units may be that from ZTS Photonetics, P.O. Box 262, Loveland, OH 45140. At $35 it is about two to three times as expensive as cheaper units, but is brighter, and you can get nickel-cadmium batteries and a charger for it. Schwinn makes a highly rated strobe unit that is bright, easy on batteries and can flash 96 times per minute. (A high flash rate equals greater visibility.)

HEADLIGHTS

The next step is a headlight that will really let you see the road ahead. The typical bike light, working off a pair of D cells, doesn't come close. Until recently, the best thing was a three- or four-cell waterproof flashlight of the kind favored by the French for their midnight rallies. Now halogen bulbs combined with big, long-lasting batteries put the bicycle at about the same level as a moped. This is possible largely because a halogen bulb yields about half again as much light as conventional sealed beam units with the same power. (These in turn are many times superior to typical make-do cycling equipment.)

At time of writing, halogen bulbs are available for both generators and high-quality battery lighting systems of the type offered by Ed Kearney's Bicycle Lighting Systems (718 North Vermont Street, Arlington, VA 22203; 703–527–4164) and Perlux (c/o Master-Line, P.O. Box 90529 Palms, CA 92277; 714–362–4261). Expensive and somewhat weighty, powered by rechargeable nickel-cadmium or conventional batteries, they let you see where you are going, and are perfect for dawn and dusk commuting. Lights of this type start around $40, but the best bet is a rechargeable front/rear system, which will run two or three times that. The new Velo-lux system uses a lighter rechargeable battery (built into the halogen-type headlight) in conjunction with an under-bracket generator; $100 for battery, head-, and taillights. (Velo-lux Corp., 1412 Alice Street, Davis, CA 95616.)

GENERATORS

If Kearney or Perlux is not your cup of tea, your alternative is a generator. Generators run on friction drive off a tire and are not nearly as effective as the better battery systems, but they are an occasional-use option. They vary considerably both in brightness and in how much drag they apply to the wheel. Those which drive off the sidewall are definitely *not* for use with light skinwall tires or tubulars. Whatever kind you use, you will feel the drag of the drive wheel, so generators are no great fun for long periods. They have their uses though, especially since the halogen bulb has been adapted to bicycle use. Halogen takes the generator from very marginal to acceptable, within limitations.

The "block" generator that mounts to the fork and drives off the front wheel is the simplest, but it has two vices: It drives off the side of the tire (less efficient and rough on the tire), and unless mounted onto its own brazed-on fitting it tends to slide down the fork (and sometimes into the spokes). This is extremely dangerous. The next step is side-wall drive, rear-wheel mounting. Schwinn and Mitsuba make good, more or less identical conventional systems.

State of the art in generators is rear-wheel drive combined with bottom-bracket mounting, as with the Sanyo Dynapower; this allows the drive wheel to face the tread directly rather than at an angle. This safer and more convenient design reduces bearing wear and friction, and allows the use of light tires. Soubitez makes reliable under-bracket and conventional systems.

Unfortunately, these and all generators depend on wheel speed, and the light fades at slower speeds. Despite improved leveling of output at varied speeds in recent models, the problem still exists, and when you stop there's no light at all. This dependence on speed is the generator's Achilles heel, and it is a serious one: A taillight that goes dim at low speeds (exactly when you need it most) is *very* bad news. If you rely on any kind of generator, be absolutely sure to have additional, battery-powered lighting to the rear—the best you can find. And remember that even with halogen bulbs, generators don't equal the big, battery-powered halogen systems.

APPAREL

Bike riders are second only to people in show business when it comes to talking about clothing, but for very different reasons. For the cyclist, clothing is equipment first, personal statement second. When it's wrong you notice it: the light-colored slacks with the chain-grease stain, the groin-strangling designer jeans, the too-short jersey that lets a chill into your lower back, the hood on a flapping parka-like contrivance that drives you crazy because it blocks your view to the rear.

Likewise, you may not feel like clacking your cleats into a restaurant and having people stare at your skin-tight lycra shorts and pink Giro d'Italia Leader's Jersey. Most people wish they'd worn something like an old Lacoste shirt and some kind of shoes you can walk in without looking like a duck. The right clothes let you feel less conspicuous, more in control, more able to relax and enjoy yourself off the bike. This is getting easier to do. Sports clothing manufacturers are turning out all kinds of new casual bike clothing for the noncompetitor, some of it very well designed.

APPROACHES

There are as many approaches to clothing as there are to the bicycle, and they make sense in their own terms. At one end you find the hard-line dropped-bar derailleur operators—café racers in cleated shoes, white socks, black shorts, and team jerseys. They are into riding hard, and this is the way you dress for it. Far removed from this is the three-speed commuter who manages to get from home to office in a blue three-piece suit complete with tie, never quite raising a sweat. (Dark suits are favored; they don't show the inevitable chain spot.) Somewhere between is where most people want to be, wearing clothes that feel right both on and off the bike.

THE CLASSIC APPROACH

Race-type clothing may be of more interest to you than you'd think; it represents the purely functional realities, having evolved as a response to specific needs. If you plan to be on the bike for long periods, it all makes sense: chamois-padded shorts, racing shoes, and wool or polypropyline jersey wicks away sweat while allowing the body to work freely with no binding or chafing. Body temperature holds quite level under most conditions, and with the addition of leg-warmers, arm-warmers or long-sleeved jersey, hat, and a "breathable" waterproof jacket (*impermeabile* in Italy) you are fairly well protected from the elements, though not for a whole day's ride in heavy rain. As with equipment for any sport, it is simple ergonomics; clothing is constantly being reevaluated in terms of function, comfort, and durability. For long-term consistency of quality and fit, Italy's (wool) Sergal clothing is an industry standard. Assos is another good European name. This kind of gear is not cheap, but it is a good investment. It also feels very, very good, which you learn to appreciate on long rides. Recent (and accepted) innovations include nylon-soled shoes, lycra stretch-shorts (not good in cool weather), fast-drying "synthetic chamois," and synthetic-blend jersey fabrics.

ERGONOMICS OF THE BICYCLE SHOE

Cyclists don't have the problems runners do with their feet, but shoes are equally important to performance because the foot is the interface point for energy and machine. The fit is crucial for those who ride long distances. Many European racing cyclists have shoes custom-made.

THE BASIC SHOE

The classic cycling shoe is designed for comfort and efficiency when used with toe clips and quill pedals. It is built on a thick, almost rigid sole, with a light, glovelike upper that conforms closely to the foot and fits tightly. The sole may be reinforced leather, wood, or plastic; all have their advocates. The upper is usually leather, sometimes nylon. Expensive shoes do tend to be superior, but you can often find a good pair in the $50 range. What you are looking for is a snug fit (tighter than that of a walking shoe) both length- and width-wise; and you want this for both feet—almost invariably one is slightly larger. Try on both shoes.

Leather tends to conform to the foot with time, and this is an advantage when feet vary in size. Nylon shoes are getting very good, with mesh uppers that form and breathe quite well. If a pair of nylon shoes fits really well, buy them; they will last. If they don't fit from the start though, they won't change shape the way leather does. This is the great virtue of leather, and if you want to speed it up, wet the shoes and go for a ride. If they're good shoes, they won't fall apart; they're de-

THE CLASSIC BICYCLE SHOE
Once you get into the bike for longer rides, there's nothing quite like a good European shoe (no matter whose name is on it). Clockwise from upper left: Maresi, Vittoria, Vittoria, Coq Sportif. Other excellent shoes come from Duegi, Detto Pietro, Sidi, et al. The range for good ones is usually $60 (if you're lucky) and up. Each company has its own ideas about how feet are shaped; look for a snug fit.

signed for European conditions, where rain is the usual thing. Nor will they start to bend, because a supportive shank between the layers of leather distributes the stress to the entire front sole.

This type of shoe is designed to work with cleats (Chapter 7) which greatly improve on-bike performance but prevent much walking. Even without cleats, you should avoid walking in this kind of shoe; it weakens that firm sole. Rigid, heelless, and tight, a bike shoe is the world's worst walking shoe, anyway, and this has resulted in a new kind of combination walk/ride shoe, discussed below.

WALK/RIDE SHOES

Shoes intended for both riding and walking are a more recent development, and many riders are very happy about it. While these shoes represent a compromise, they also fill a real need. This kind of shoe usually has a slightly raised heel, which allows normal walking, and it is also more flexible than a true cycling shoe. This is all horrifying to the purist because it lets the foot slop around somewhat while pedaling, but the crux of the matter is at the ball of the foot. If the shoe is firm enough that you don't feel the pedal coming through the sole when you bear down, it is at least on the way to being acceptable. From there your decision rests on other factors.

First of all, you have to decide whether the shoe is primarily for walking or riding, because the compromise will lean one way or the other. Think in terms of 20-, 40-, or 60-mile shoes and make your choice on that basis; shoes adequate for an hour on the bike often reveal weakness and poor fit on a long ride. When you are sure the fit is right (i.e., snug), go to what may have been your first priority—whether you can stand to look at them. These walk/ride shoes come in a wild variety

WALK/RIDE SHOES
Unlike classic cycling shoes, these differ radically. Clockwise from the top: Coq Sportif, Bata, Rivat and Vittoria. Batas run as low as $20 and are a good buy; others are more stylish but average about twice that. Finding a compromise between the tight, rigid, pure bike shoe and the looser, more flexible sneaker-type depends on how hard you pedal and how far you ride. Vittoria and Avocet tend toward the traditional; Cannondale and Duegi less so.This market is changing rapidly.

of colors and styles from utility black to red, white and blue. They are made from cloth, rubber, plastic, suede, and leather. Don't rush to make a choice, because many dealers just can't keep up with the new (and often experimental) products.

SOCKS

Socks are also important. Traditionally, wool, silk, and cotton were the favorites because they don't irritate the skin. White is the favored color, because the absence of dye tends to prevent infection, and if you're caught out at night they are more visible. Colored socks may bother your café-racer friends, but if they are the right kind of socks, they'll feel fine. What you want to avoid is hot, irritating, artificial fibers, especially on long rides in warm weather.

SHORTS

The more you ride, the more you appreciate how much well-made shorts have to do with basic comfort. A good pair of shorts should fit like a second skin, coming well down the thigh and well up the back, allowing free movement and breathing. Stitched into the seat is a large, smooth chamois (sometimes synthetic) pad, on which rides the perineum, which is subject to abrasion. The single pocket is exactly where it belongs, on the upper hip, out of the way. Suspenders are popular with shorts because they allow freer breathing.

Wool has been the favored material for shorts more or less forever because it wicks away sweat, forms to the body, and tends to balance body temperature. Around 1980, lycra shorts appeared, and soon the top professionals were wearing them, often in the form of "bib" shorts, which have built-in suspenders. Now there are breathable polypropylene-lycra blends that outwick wool, and the choice is largely a matter of taste. There are also colors too, finally. Ultima makes a comfortable chamois-lined pair, with red or blue side panels, that comes in a wide range of sizes; the medium-tone panels work out better than full-colored (or light-colored) shorts because they aren't soiled as soon as you put them on.

CHAMOIS

The perineum is a sensitive place, and you pay for what feels good. Chamois is expensive, dries slowly after washing, and requires special preparation, though some ignore this successfully. Chamois pads have been with us since the early days of the sport, but the new synthetics are turning out to be acceptable to most riders, and they're showing up in racing too. They machine-wash (cold) and air-dry quickly.

Not so chamois-lined shorts, which should be hand-washed in warm water with a mild soap like Woolite. Experienced riders usually lubricate the natural chamois to avoid irritation. Jecovital, a European preparation, has been the standard for many riders; A and D Ointment is used by many; Greg Le Mond uses Noxema, which gradually forms a fine, dry powder.

CARE

It's important to wash shorts frequently to discourage bacteria. Keeping them out of the dryer is equally important. If you are riding frequently, you'll find you need two pair. Lower cost and quick drying time favor the new synthetic chamois pad; what matters is how your skin reacts.

TOURING OR SPORT SHORTS

For decades you could get riding shorts in any color you wanted, as long as it was black. The classic snug fit was all you could buy, and your snug black shorts had one pocket. All this is breaking down, and in the last few years, touring shorts in different colors and cuts by Coq Sportif, Descente, Cannondale, and others have been appearing on the market, some good, some not very good. As with walk/ride shoes, some are more suited to the bike, others to walking. After you've settled on a pair that you like, check them out by the same standards as traditional riding shorts: Begin with the chamois or pad and compare it with that in a pair of racing shorts. Try them on and test them for freedom of movement; stretch fabrics are very desirable. The shorts will be snugger than you might want, to keep fabric from bunching up at the seat. Don't try to duplicate the look of Bermuda or hiking shorts, because the fit will be wrong. Also avoid white, which will never again be white. Hard-finish fabrics that resist stains are good.

PANTS

Shorts, of course, are not the whole story, and long pants suitable for cycling are not easy to find. Dark colors are common; the problem is more in the cut. Models ride bicycles in tight jeans for TV commercials,

SPORT GEAR
(1) Cotton shirt by Cannondale (about $25), shorts by Coq Sportif (under $40). (2) Rugby shirt and shorts by Cannondale (about $25 each), shoes by Vittoria (about $30). (3) Shorts by Descente (about $40), wind jacket by Cannondale ($32). (4) Foul weather gear: Ascente's bright yellow vented Gore-tex Cascade suit (about $140) goes over almost anything; it's really waterproof and visible.

but not when they're actually out for a ride, because anything that binds feels all wrong. What you want is something fairly loose down to the knee, but definitely not bell-bottoms. Something more like moderate zoot-suit pants from the forties. Light, inexpensive cotton painter pants allow very free movement and are good all round. They also come in many colors. What you don't want is belled, low-rider jeans. And don't forget some kind of pants clip; the reflective cloth type with velcro are comfortable on your leg and in your pocket. Tiffany's offers a silver one you can put your name on.

THE SKINSUIT
This one-piece design began as a track racing outfit, moved into road racing, and is now modified for triathlon use. Descente's sells for about $150.

JERSEYS

The traditional cycling jersey is a well-thought-out piece of clothing. The three pockets in back will hold a map, a few tools, and enough food for a day's ride. Like good shorts, good jerseys look tight, but are cut to allow the rider to lean forward onto dropped bars. The back is cut long, to keep wind off the lower spine. As with shorts, the traditional material is wool, which breathes and wicks away moisture. This is important, because in hilly country the chill of long descents is made worse by little pools of sweat that would have been soaked up and dissipated by a good jersey.

OTHER FIBERS

Early cotton and artificial-fiber jerseys were not very popular because they did not wick, but recently synthetic jerseys have begun to appear in competition—a sure sign that the problem is being overcome at least partly. Avocet offers polypropylene (which is even more absorbent than wool), and Coq Sportif uses "Climalite," a two-layer fabric. European racing cyclists usually wear a thin wool undervest beneath the jersey, which is really good in cool weather. (Professional racer David Mayer-Oakes says that the hotter U.S. weather makes them— and wool jerseys—unnecessary.) Wool undervests are almost a thing of the past, but polypropylene is available and does the same thing.

The best thing about a good jersey is that it feels just right on the bike. The worst thing is that it is exactly what it is, and proclaims itself as such even at times when you might not feel like making the big *sportif* impression. Less gaudy, jerseylike garments are coming out now, cut for comfort and more conservatively styled.

THE JERSEY/SHIRT

The closest thing to a real jersey, oddly enough, is the Lacoste-type tennis shirt; the next closest thing is a well-fitted natural-fiber rugby shirt. Variations on these and other styles are available through cycle-clothing manufacturers, some of them wool and polypropylene blends with good wicking capacity. *Sans* pockets, lurid color combinations, and team advertising, these garments are versatile enough that you might end up wearing them on days you don't ride.

In functional terms, judge these garments as you would a jersey, in terms of length, fit, and fabric. Some of these jersey/shirts can be hot washed, but few survive the dryer without some shrinkage; check the label. Whatever you choose, it should be on the long side, to cover the base of the spine, as a jersey does.

ADD-ONS AND ALTERNATIVES: BEATING THE CHILL

Cool weather used to mean a long-sleeved jersey over the short-sleeved one, and a layer of newspaper between the two. To protect the

TRADITIONAL WEAR AND ADD-ONS

Dressing in layers is basic. Clockwise from upper left: (1) Shoes by Maresi (about $65), poly-cotton jersey and lycra shorts (both Descente, about $35 and $25). Underneath, a light wool or polypropylene undershirt stops sweat from pooling and chilling. (2) For cooler weather add cap, second jersey (Coq Sportif, about $40) and/ or dickey, plus legwarmers (Protogs, about $12) and a layer of newspaper between jerseys (no charge). Shoes by Vittoria this time. (3) Next comes some kind of wind jacket, preferably waterproof. This is Descente's version of the *impermeabile* (about $55) with breathable stretch-fabric panels. You'll need warm gloves with fingers too, and shoe-covers help. (4) Bottom half of Descente's suit (about $45) on the legs plus wool cap get you warmer yet. It's also quite light and waterproof, with nothing to flap around.

legs you wore tight, chamois-lined pants that fit like the shorts they replaced. It still works, but there are other ways. Many prefer arm- and leg-warmers, which can be removed and stuffed into pockets if the temperature rises. The European-style waterproof or *impermeabile* is another useful item, a featherweight windbreaker that folds down to pocket size. Less eccentric looking are "windjackets" made by Cannondale and others; Ultima makes one that is warm, waterproof, and breathable, with pockets in back. Like the *impermeabile,* these jackets are cut long enough to fit the dropped-bar position.

DICKEYS AND SWEATERS

The dickey is great; it weighs almost nothing, folds small enough to fit anywhere, and keeps you warm where you need protection, at the throat and chest. It combines with a wool shirt in spring and fall to keep you warm without a lot of bulk. Sweaters are good too, especially in wool, and a turtleneck protects the throat.

HATS

Another useful item is something to cover your head, often overlooked. Not only are some people very sensitive to the midday sun, but in winter a great deal of body heat is lost via the head. If you can't live with a helmet, the cotton cap is a very good idea; the bill will keep sun out of your eyes. Some prefer headbands, which keep sweat out of the eyes. There are also wool winter cycling caps (a watch cap does the job too), waterproof caps, and for the hardiest souls, balaclava helmets.

GLOVES

Fingerless summer riding gloves prevent irritation, and if they are well padded, absorb some road shock. If you happen to spill, they also prevent abrasions to the palms, otherwise hard to avoid. Most experienced riders use these; after a day's ride without them, you'll know why.

Winter gloves are different, having both fingers and insulation. Without them, cold-weather riding is painful, and even dangerous, because circulation to the fingers is limited. Unlike summer gloves, they are not standardized. Look for an in-between fit, neither sloppy-loose or very tight, with leather at least on the palms and the kind of insulation

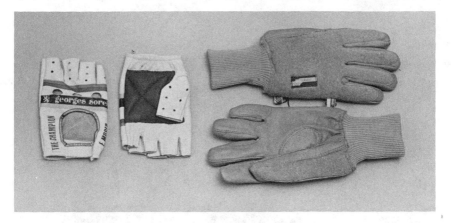

CYCLING GLOVES
People who ride more than an hour at a time usually end up wearing some version of the fingerless, padded glove in summer; price is usually in the $10–$12 range. You'll need full gloves in cold weather, though.

that has little bulk; you need freedom to work the brake and shift levers. If it's very cold, thin wool or silk liners make them more effective.

KEEPING THE LEGS WARM

Knickers and long wool socks were not a bad solution for keeping the legs warm, but these haven't been in vogue since the thirties. The leg-warmers mentioned earlier are inexpensive and can be covered by a pair of painter pants for added warmth. There are also form-fit cycling "longs" with a windbreaker front and breathable back. For those who want to show up at the office more low-key, dark, wool pants clipped at the bottom are good.

FOR REALLY COLD WEATHER

There are brave people who ride in all kinds of weather, and there are those who draw the line at some point. Above 40°F, the above measures are effective; below that temperature, each couple of degrees seems to make things markedly worse, and you can't safely ignore the problem; hypothermia is no joke. The problem is wind-chill, created by the movement of the bike, combined with limited bodily movement. Runners move much more slowly, and their feet get a flexing workout that keeps them warm. On the bike the point of diminishing returns comes faster, and you can't just keep adding layers. Not only will you

ULTIMA WINTER GEAR
Warmer yet. Top to bottom: Waterproof nylon-covered cap ($10), windproof nylon-face knit jacket ($55), chamois-lined knit tights ($40), Brancale wind-and-waterproof gloves and shoe-covers (about $20 each).

feel too clumsy to ride well, you'll get into a sweat/chill cycle that is both uncomfortable and draining.

Really good insulated gloves, with liners, are essential, and feet need extra protection too; lack of movement slows circulation, as do tight cycling shoes, and much heat can be lost at the ankle. The traditional solution is an old pair of heavy wool socks over the shoes, but this may not be enough. Lined winter shoes are available (buy large enough to accommodate heavier socks) along with several kinds of spats-like, waterproof shoe covers. Talk to your dealer about which are best.

LONG JOHNS, ETC.

Underwear is much discussed by people who ride through the winter. For decades there was fine, light wool underwear available in Europe at reasonable cost. Then it was mixed with plastics, which made it less fine. Just as it was disappearing, polypropylene began to be available, developed largely at the behest of skiers. It is very good in most applications, especially the light, long-sleeved tops like the Lifa Super, but quality and fit vary. The best is formfitting but nonconstricting. But because it tends to irritate the perineum, it's best to wear a pair of lined shorts under polypropylene long johns; good wool is less abrasive.

One word of caution about really cold weather: If you happen to have sensitive lungs, you may have to figure out a way of warming the air you breathe to avoid exercise-induced asthma. Spray-paint masks help somewhat, and so does a cautious approach. If your lungs are good for an easy hour, don't push long and hard; they'll have to deal with much more cold air.

RAIN GEAR

As with clothing in general, there are two schools of thought about rain gear. There are the minimalists (or fatalists), and there is the traveling-tent school. The minimalists will tell you there is just no staying dry on a bike in a serious rain, but those favoring heavy-weather gear are more determined. Either way, it's just a matter of temperament and style, and in any case it's hard to choose between the calculated wetness of the minimalists and the dank humidity that can build up under rubberized ponchos and similar garments. If you're the determined type, you will want more elaborate gear; if an hour or two is your max for rainy riding, you can get by with much less. Help is on the way, in the form of Gore-tex, and the new lightweight Gore-tex is even better. It is pricey but long lasting and light, and provides a presentable jacket that has uses off the bicycle.

Whatever your choice, remember this: In cold wet weather, maintaining the right body temperature may be much more important than actually staying dry. You don't want to seal yourself in; the clothing must "breathe," or at least be ventilated. Wool clothing keeps you warm even when wet, and when the rain lets up it will dry as you ride. Finally, avoid

LIGHTWEIGHT GORE-TEX
This light and well-cut waterproof suit by Ascente stuffs very small. Well made but pricey, it is hard to beat; jacket is fine off the bike as well.

anything that hampers pedaling or flaps around. Loose fabric often gets caught in the wind and sometimes in the wheels. Quite dangerous either way.

THE *IMPERMEABILE*

The waterproof or *impermeabile* mentioned earlier is the minimalist favorite, waterproof where the rain hits, but vented at the sides, so you don't overheat. It is a low-drag, race-derived piece of clothing that stuffs into a pocket, and the good ones are very well designed. Add a waterproof hat and wool leg warmers, and while you won't be dry, the combination makes rain tolerable at moderate temperatures. It also keeps body temperature in a good range. As a combination rain and wind jacket the *impermeabile* is very convenient. State of the art seems to be Descente's stretch-fit model, which has matching pants and comes in a highly visible yellow; the pair cost about $100. (See page 267.)

HEAVIER GEAR

Ponchos and similar items are favored by slower riders and tourists. They have the advantage of keeping you drier, but have greater bulk, weight, and wind resistance. In gusty sidewinds the poncho can add a whole new element of adventure that you will not enjoy. Many have hoods, which don't work very well, because they obscure vision when you turn your head. But if there is no dry room and shower waiting for you at the end of your ride, something like Ascente's Gore-tex suits can be very appealing.

FENDERS

Fenders or mudguards are not clothing, but they are essential rain gear; there's nothing else that will keep the rear wheel from throwing a muddy stripe up your back. They also keep mud out of your brakes, etc. Back in the early seventies fenders clashed with the New Image of the Bicycle created by the bike boom, but they are understood and accepted in Europe, where wet-weather cycling is routine. Even racing cyclists use them in Europe for wet, early-season training rides, partly because it is extremely unpleasant to ride behind a wheel that is throwing mud in your face. If all this sounds convincing, make sure the bike you buy has brazed-on eyelets front and rear; without these, fitting fenders is much more difficult.

Fenders make showers tolerable and are absolutely essential in heavy rain. Touring without them is madness, unless you like the mudman look. Like much else, fenders have improved a lot recently. Today most are flexible plastic, and some are quickly detachable. The best ones are also reflective, and nearly indestructible. Avoid the tiny plastic or alloy pseudo-fender; it keeps your brakes clear of mud, but that's about all.

One final note: some close-tolerance racing frames just don't have room for any kind of fenders; they don't have mounting eyelets either.

BAR BAGS AND SEATPACKS

There's just so much you can stuff into your jersey pockets, and most cyclists find themselves looking for some way to add to this

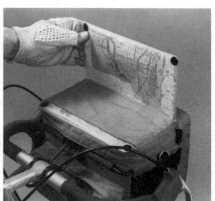

BAR BAGS AND SEAT PACKS
Of dozens available, these are among the best. Clockwise from upper left: (1) Kirtland and (2) Eclipse mid-size bar bags in $50 range. Solid mounting and construction, map cases and separate compartments make them useful and reliable. (3) Eclipse makes their bar bag into a seat pack with a clamp called The Thing ($14); Kirtland makes three of these Faspack underseat bags (4) with excellent three-point velcro mounting; this is the ($30) middle size.

sooner or later. These days, the bar bag is very popular. It has improved enormously since the entry of research-minded U.S. manufacturers who have applied backpack technology and common sense. A good bar bag should be stable, nearly waterproof, and easily detachable. It should also have some kind of internal structure to keep it from sagging, a transparent map case on top, and a small independent compartment for sunscreen and other small items. Big bar bags are tempting, but not a wise decision; all that weight way up in the air can make the bike top-heavy and headstrong, especially if it has a short wheelbase and steep angles.

Seatpacks are another option, and much the same rules apply. They range from very small ones for odds and ends to humungous things that can destabilize the bike. Kirtland has taken a completely new tack on this with their neatly designed Faspak, which comes in three sizes and tucks neatly out of the way. Another option is the Eclipse "Thing," which converts a bar bag into a seatpack. Chapter 11 covers racks and panniers for touring.

CAR CARRIERS

At some point you may want to pack the bike itself and escape to some sunnier place. You can get a bike into most cars by taking off the

ALLEN RACK
This economical (about $30) and reliable rack adapts to most vehicles. Getting two bikes arranged so they don't chew each other up isn't easy though, and the bike is vulnerable to a rear-end collision.

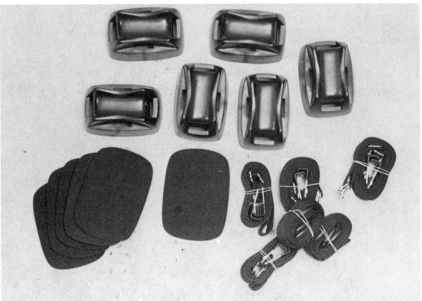

CAR-TOP RACKS

More expensive racks like these take bikes up and out of the way; most can handle three or four. Clockwise from upper left: (1) Steel Prealpina (about $100 with mounting for two bikes) is a classic seen around the world; it's solid and durable, but it takes a while to get all those parts together. (2) The Stratos (about $120 with two-bike mounting) is a lighter, simplified aluminum version of this approach. (3) The rugged

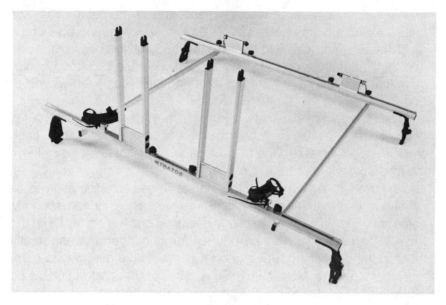

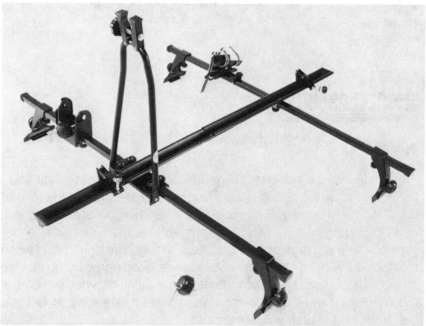

Thule (about $100 for two bikes) is designed to handle canoes and boats as well as bikes, which it carries upside down or right side up. It also has a clever system of locking both rack and bikes ($25). (4) The Zulu is an inexpensive ($25) and compact design using straps, blocks, and pads.

front wheel, but it takes up a lot of space, and it's a bit of a mess. Two bikes take up a great deal of space, and most people end up using a rack. These are divided into the kind that hang off the back of the car, and the kind that go on top. They are also divisible into good equipment that's easy to work with and annoying junk you'll wish you never bought.

Rear-mount racks are not elegant, but they will carry a pair of bikes on most cars if you don't mind some dings where they rest against each other. They do not protect the bikes in case of a minor rear-end collision though. Cost is about $25. A car-top rack will carry up to four bikes, and there are many brands on the market. These are several times as expensive as the rear-mount type. Some are easy to attach securely, some not. From time to time a poorly designed one will simply fly off the top of a car, an unnerving experience for all concerned, especially those in the car behind. But a good roof rack is the best way to carry more than one bike. Make sure it will fit; cars vary in construction, as do racks. It's reasonable to ask the shop owner to check your installation, and, to allow you a trade-in if the thing doesn't happen to fit your particular car.

MISCELLANEOUS:

PUMPS

Outside these general categories are several accessories you'll find it hard to do without. A reliable pump is definitely one of these, and the choice is wide. If you ride tubulars (often built on latex tubes that need to be pumped up daily), you probably want a floor pump. A decent one with a gauge costs about $20, though you can spend twice that for a really good one. More essential is a good frame pump that fits on the bike; you can't fix a flat without one. In an emergency you can fill tubulars from a gas station pump if you have a Presta adaptor, but you can blow the tire up if you're not careful.

The low end on frame pumps is the cheap alloy item often found as standard equipment on mid-price European ten-speeds. This pump is identified by a flexible rubber connecter of great unreliability. On average, these pumps work about 49 percent of the time, and when they

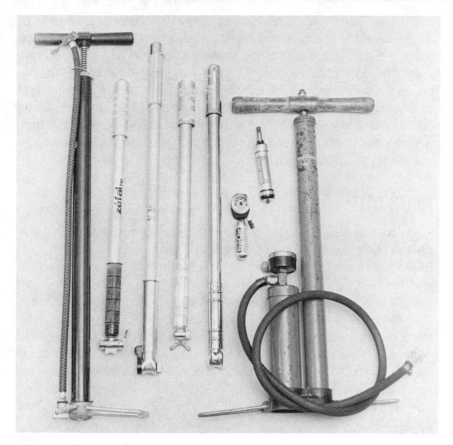

PUMPS

Unless you ride tubulars (which often have natural rubber tubes that lose air overnight) you may not need a floor pump (right and left); these run from under $20 to near $40. Anyone out on the road needs a frame pump though. The plastic Silcas (4th and 5th from right) are the racer's standard, usually about $25 with preferred Campagnolo head. Zefal (2nd from left) is rugged, all metal, less expensive (about $12) and comes with fittings for both Presta and Schraeder valves. Plastic Zefal to its right also adapts to both kinds of valves, and sets tire pressure automatically. The two small units by Schwinn and Spair work from CO_2 cartridges; these units run about $25–$30, cartridges about $1.75.

do, they rarely deliver full pressure. Avoid this product of outmoded technology.

The most popular racer's pump is the frame-fit plastic Silca, preferably with the Campagnolo metal head, pricey though it is (about $25 for the combination). The similar Nagusi is less elegant, less expensive, and more efficient, but for most riders, the slightly heavier all-alloy Zefal

H.P. is the best deal. This comes with a clip-on head (Presta or Schraeder) and is a sturdier piece of equipment. Its heft and balance make it a decent antidog piece as well. At around $12 it's a real bargain. The final portable option (favored by triathlon competitors because it is superquick) is the CO_2 powered inflator; it's handy, light, and compact enough to carry in a pocket. Spair makes a popular one that comes with either Presta or Schraeder fitting. At $30 it costs more than a frame pump, and if your tires need to be pumped up frequently, it's not cheap.

WATER BOTTLE

Water bottle and cage are two more standard accessories if you plan to ride more than five or ten miles at a time. Aside from saving you the money spent on soda, or other beverages, it lets you choose what you want to drink. Buy a standard bottle that fits a standard cage and clean it frequently. Replacing an odd-shaped bottle can be a problem.

The usual place for mounting a bottle is on the down tube, where there is room for two if you are into really long trips. You can also mount them on the seat tube if you don't have a frame pump there, and some touring bikes mount a second cage under the down tube, but this is a last alternative; it's a messy place.

LOCKS

Last but not least, some kind of lock is a virtual necessity for most riders. This can be a light, collapsible "deterrent," consisting of a small lock and cable, a hardened chain with heavy padlock, or the U-bar type that fits on the frame. The latter two provide much more security.

A lot depends on where you live and what the bike is worth. The inexpensive lock-and-cable will thwart a tempted twelve-year-old, but a bike thief will clip it in seconds. The hardened chain in combination with a big, expensive lock is formidable but heavy; so are the popular U-bar locks made by Kryptonite, Citadel, etc. Nevertheless, a good bike in a bad neighborhood needs serious protection. Bear in mind also that you need to protect the wheels; many an inner-city resident has failed to remove the front wheel and lost it. The bar or chain must pass through *both wheels and frame* to be effective. While any lock can be picked or broken, recent models of the U-bar are pretty effective, given that the thief must work in full view of passersby.

RIGHT AND WRONG USE OF U-BAR LOCK
Kryptonite was first on the scene with this heavy-duty approach to protecting your bike. U-bar locks weigh about two pounds and cost about $30, whether by Kryptonite, Citadel, or other maker, and you need one in most cities. Kryptonite's is as strong as any, and recent models have been redesigned for convenience. Correct use (1) of this or any lock involves securing both wheels and frame; otherwise (2) you can lose most of your bike.

THINGS YOU CAN LIVE WITHOUT

Beyond these basics is a sea of options, some curious, some silly. They arrive on the market at the whim of some inventor or market researcher, often to disappear. Most of these accessories are harmless, some useless, others potentially dangerous—like the kiddie-seat. This places as much as thirty pounds of unpredictable weight quite high, and far enough back to further destabilize the bike—which is often ridden by someone without the strength and skill to cope with the problem. Make sure you have full control before going on the road with one of these, and be absolutely sure the child has a really good helmet, correctly attached.

THE ZZIPPER FAIRING

For some sixty years man has been proving and reproving that fairings (streamlining devices) make a bike faster, but rarely do you see an enclosed bicycle on the road, because of weight, stability, and heat problems.

The Zzipper has pretty much avoided these problems and manages to streamline a bike substantially while violating no basic rule. The 22 percent drag reduction is described by most riders as making a bike ridable "one gear higher" under most conditions—by which they mean a one-tooth difference on the cog. It's enough advantage that the Zzipper is illegal in normal competition. At 10–12 mph it makes a difference; at 15–20 mph it makes a big difference.

ZZIPPER FAIRING AND PANNIERS

Equally important, it keeps both hands and torso much warmer in cold weather, and it definitely makes the bike more visible. (A wider, reflective edging would be better yet.) Because it can be removed from the bike in about 50 seconds, it is usable by commuters. To this end, Zzipper also puts out the streamlined panniers seen with it. These, too, reduce drag. For tourists who like to move right along they create interesting possibilities.

The Zzipper is made of very flexible Lexan, weighs 14 ounces, and attaches easily without tools, using velcro. And it doesn't restrict hand positions. In other words, inventor Glenn Brown knows about bikes. The Zzipper won't get you up a hill, and you may not want it on the bike in superhot weather, but it definitely has its uses.

11.
TRAVELING BY BIKE

The most important thing to bear in mind is that travel of any kind is an individual art. Fifty years ago travel writer Peter Fleming penetrated far into the jungles of Brazil and crossed Tibet traveling his own way, improvising skillfully: "Our supplies and equipment, though they would have made any modern expedition sick with laughter, proved completely adequate to our needs and to conditions on the road. . . . we had with us no single thing which proved itself superfluous." Fleming rode camels, ponies, and canoes, but these criteria are valid for anyone traveling by bicycle.

There are so many approaches to "bicycle touring" that the term is almost meaningless. A middle-aged doctor decides to cross the U.S. and averages 85 miles a day, traveling light, eating mostly at restaurants, and sleeping with a roof over his head; Bikecentennial's June and Greg Siple rode the Americas from Alaska to Patagonia, largely on impossible roads in primitive areas—a very different experience. A New York couple spends a week in New England on bikes furnished by Vermont Bicycle Touring (see page 311), and another couple in California escapes the automobile every weekend on mountain bikes. A group of students piles on tent, stove, sleeping bags and pads, and grinds over the continental divide.

This last style is the best known in the U.S.; it's something like bicycle-backpacking along side roads, but it does present its own difficulties. Grinding away in low gears from dawn to dusk on a heavily loaded bike can take it out of you. Americans have accepted the idea that hauling 40-odd pounds 60 or 70 miles, followed by a cookout and a night in a tent is the way to go, no matter how bone weary or nearly

TOURING
These people are definitely away from their usual world; their baggage is in a sag wagon that follows the tour. Very nice idea, especially for beginners in the New England hills.

sick you feel. This is dangerous nonsense; a sedentary over-thirty body may need all the rest it can get after a day on a bike, especially when chilled, wet, or both. That heavily loaded fifteen-speed, popping spokes as it struggles through the Rockies and across parched plains, is not the only way to go; it just happens to be the best advertised.

AVOIDING DISASTER

Actually, the first requirement of enjoying bike travel is to think about it until you have a definite and concrete idea of what you want to experience, and then subordinate everything to that. If you want to be provided with a bike, guide, sag wagon (following vehicle with baggage), and pleasant watering holes, why not? It's more expensive, but it's not a bad way to start. Having things take care of themselves is just great at the end of a long ride when your legs are full of lactic acid and your blood sugar level is sloping off uncertainly. Ask any racer.

INFORMATION

Consumer books and magazines still tend to deal largely with the conventional approach. Check them out, but then let your imagination run loose a bit, think about places to go. Then contact one or more of the organizations listed at the end of this chapter for information. You want to know the best time of year to go, and what the terrain and weather will be like. You need appropriate maps, described below. With luck, you will hear of someone who has ridden the area. Listen to what they say; good advice, good maps, and reliable equipment matter more than anything else.

LIMITS

The other essential is knowing yourself in a very basic way—knowing what you can actually do, physically, and what you really want to do. If you have a firm grasp on that, you can avoid the madness that overcomes inexperienced tourists as they hammer away, deplete their stamina, and try to enjoy something they just aren't ready for.

They finish the day in bonked-out desperation as dusk falls, and they are still fifteen miles from a place to camp. At this point, it is time to stop at a motel, farmhouse, or whatever will put a roof over their heads. Even Velocio came to rest comfortably after his epic overnight sagas. Like any continental, he knew the value of relaxing over a good meal and a night's sleep under a roof—especially after the kind of really hard riding he favored.

ATTITUDE

Velocio's seventh commandment, herein freely translated as "don't show off," has also been taken to mean "don't pedal out of vanity" (or vainglory, or ego). It has to do with staying within your ability, and how you pay for pushing yourself beyond it. Craig Hoyt, M.D., medical editor of the old *Bike World* magazine, describes the results perfectly: "I often cycle from dawn to dusk. Unless you are out to break some record, this is not recommended. . . . on one tour I rode so hard that I developed cold sores, lost my appetite, and finally collapsed in a French inn for a 20-hour sleep."

The rider who pushes himself through a hundred-miler on Saturday can recoup on Sunday, but the semifit rider who insists on trying to do it day after day often rides him or herself into the twilight zone so well described by Dr. Hoyt. This rider is no fun to travel with unless you are very fit. The riding becomes too competitive. Of course, it's hard to believe that even Velocio was completely without vanity, but it was apparently under good control. He was fun to ride with.

APPROACHES

LLOYD SUMNER

Lloyd Sumner demonstrates the individualism of bike travel as well as anyone, and his round-the-world expedition in the early seventies had a style all its own: strange foods, stranger languages, sinister bandidos, dervishes, hookahs, close shaves, and cash-flow problems. Sumner took off for his 4-year, 28,000-mile world tour without ever really checking himself out on a bicycle or making any serious preparation. He did it, he said, after a study of endangered species had led him to the conclusion all wild animals ought to be free, adding that he "could find no reason why (he) should be an exception." His other principle was not to bother other people or be dependent on them.

Unlike most unprepared attempts, Sumner's trip was a success, largely because, like writer Fleming, he was flexible. His philosophy of the bicycle is interesting: he observes that cars, buses, motorcycles, etc. provide "an abstraction of movement, removing you from lands and people," and that "letting things come to you, each in its individual way" was the way to appreciate your trip. Thinking along these lines, Sumner was never bored, adapted fast, survived classic gastrointestinal problems, and never got off the road "for anybody." He ate local food including whole pig brain on rice and sheep testicles, and learned to touch no food in Asia with the left hand.

OFF-ROAD

Lloyd Sumner rode the ten-speed of his time, but in spirit he was an off-road man, ready to go anywhere. Today's off-road bike allows this, and with solid racks and panniers, you can really get to that world beyond the highways. After six or eight months of indoor activity this may be the one thing you really want to do. Traveling the modern U.S. road system, it is hard to hold civilization at a distance, but a fat-tire bike frees you. The still-evolving rules of this game require survival skills adequate to your distance from civilization, and uniformly rugged equipment. Off-road, you do your own repairs.

ALL-TERRAIN TOURER
This MountainBike rig will get you far enough from civilization that you should put some extra thought into medical and tool kits. Off-road touring is "different and terrific" with "much more freedom" in the words of one convert. Katherine Dienes and Réanne Douglas used bikes like these on a recent Latin American tour to Tierra del Fuego.

CYCLO-SPORTIF

The hard-riding *cyclo-sportif* is into the bicycle itself and fights complications. Such people feel that time spent puttering around campsites is very different from time on the bike or in a bistro. They know just how much weight they can carry before the bicycle stops feeling good, and they also know exactly where that weight belongs.

These are the riders that break your heart by making you realize you really don't know how to ride very well. They roll the gears, get up hills without coming unstuck, sometimes do outrageously long rides at surprising speeds. As a group, they are more wine than wheat germ people, and, until recently, more likely to be found in France than the U.S. Their bicycles are race-bred but adapted for extended travel.

TRADITIONAL

Essentially this is backpacking on wheels, on paved roads but off major arteries. The dropped-bar derailleur is the favorite because it is at its best at long distances. Techniques and equipment have changed considerably in the last few years in response to a solid market. Racks, panniers, tents, and stoves have improved vastly. Weight distribution and its effect on safety and stability have been thoroughly explored. (See BLACKBURN SIDEBAR.)

TYPES OF TOURING BIKES

Different kinds of touring have developed different kinds of bicycles, and they fall on a continuum. Long distances on poor roads and in foreign countries work out best with either a super-rugged conventional derailleur bike or an off-road bike, because attrition and parts availability make maintenance a top priority. It's been suggested that no human being has the energy to both ride and repair a bicycle, and this really applies for third-world-type touring. Do not be misled by those who genuinely enjoy removing and rebuilding freewheels, etc. under field conditions.

Heavy-gauge tubing, laid-back angles, rugged, wide-range derailleurs, heavy tires, spokes, rims, etc. are what you want for tough conditions. The typical derailleur bike is light because it is designed for paved roads; heavy loads and poor roads can triple stress—and change your riding style to the point where dropped bars are really advantageous only into the wind. For this kind of travel, the ultrawide-range gears offered by triple cranksets are necessary.

A good example of this kind of bike is the pair used by Ivar Tonneson and Mai-Britt Johannson for their 1977 trip, which circled the globe and covered 32,424 km. On Grebart Cykler custom frames constructed on 72 degree parallel angles of sturdy Durifort tubing and Reynolds 531 forks, they hauled over 70 pounds of equipment. Gearing was European style, used a five-speed Sturmey-Archer hub in combination with derailleur as described in Chapter 8. Bars were the inverted "flat" type; saddles were Ideale leather. Titanium bottle holders were the only inconsistency.

The new thing in this field is obviously the off-road mountain bike, because it has been designed from the ground up to take punishment. You can pretty much go where you please on one. The beauty of these bikes is the utter reliability (of the good ones) and the comfort of the ride over the hours. Upright bars put the off-road bike at a disadvantage on paved roads, but not as much as it might appear, and its adaptability makes cross-country and dirt-road excursions a pleasure.

FAST AND LIGHT

The *cyclo-sportif* is the other end of the spectrum, usually riding a bicycle with fairly tight frame geometry; a responsive bicycle, in other

TOURER SPORTIF
Bicycle by Rene Herse, restoration by Peter Mooney. Herse was a top builder who put nothing extra on a bicycle, and knew exactly how to set up a stable, responsive geometry. This bike has no rear rack or provision for one; it's intended for front panniers only. Long-legged owner apparently doesn't mind high-seat, low-bars position.

words, but a stable one. This kind of rider is invariably in love with his bicycle, sometimes to the extent of riding tubulars in the 275–300 gram range, or light, narrow, high-pressure clinchers, both of which feel very good but are somewhat fragile under load. The bike will usually have provision for front panniers and fenders, and it won't be too far from a professional road-racing bike of the late fifties or sixties, before angles went bolt upright.

The Rene Herse pictured is a good example of the type. Equipped with generator, front rack, and fenders, it is still no ordinary "touring bike" by U.S. definition. With its 72.5 parallel geometry, mild fork rake, shortish top tube, 41″ wheelbase, and 22-pound stripped weight it is very close to what Jacques Anquetil might have ridden on a long stage of the Tour de France, but it is not tricky to handle. It is a kind of Porsche or BMW of bicycles, quick and practical; definitely *not* the kind of bike you stick 180 mm cranks on because some exercise physiologist thinks it a good idea.

ROAD TOURER

This is the basic touring bike, and falls somewhere between the Tonneson and Herse described above. If you plan to tour on a stock

AMERICAN STYLE
Bicycle by Mooney, racks by Blackburn, panniers by Cannondale. This is a typical heavy-touring setup, but better balanced than most, though bar bag is pretty hefty. Sleeping bag and tent would go on rear carrier.

bike, you'll find good ones in the $400 range, with frame angles typically in the 71–72 degree range, and a wheelbase of around 42" or more. Weight is not a primary consideration; another pound or two of static weight is hard to feel on the loaded bike, and stability is more important as the load increases. Many upper-mid-price bicycles are well adapted to touring, if they have provisions for adding racks and fenders. Check for necessary braze-ons, described below, and avoid odd-looking bikes with unusual angles; they may act dangerously strange on a fast, long, heavily loaded descent. Brakes are critical.

CUSTOM TOURERS

Ideally, you have a bike built to fit, designed for comfort and reliability. Custom frames are expensive, though, and you won't know what you really need until you've actually been on tour at least once. There are so many new builders in what is now called the high-tech market that you'll have a problem just making up your mind. With some you'll also have a problem in that they have strong views about what they want to build. Reputation passed by word of mouth is a better guide here than fancy ads or breathless reviews by journalists who may not know much more than you. Herse and Singer are still top names, but U.S. builders are getting very good. Either side of the Atlantic, prices may blow you away.

BRAZED-ON FITTINGS

Whatever kind of touring you do, certain brazed-on fittings are virtually essential because they allow you to attach additional equipment securely. Racks are best attached this way with brazed-on eyelets, although Blackburn makes a device that fits in the rear dropout of a racing bike, allowing you to attach a rear pannier rack. Double braze-ons here are much better, because they make it easy to add fenders as well. Fenders are looked down upon by many beginners, but only before being rained on for an hour or two: mud thrown up by the wheels is a real scourge for clothing and equipment. Double water-bottle fittings are another good idea. The body loses much more water than you realize on hot days, and you can carry different liquids in the two bottles— one with water, one with something containing sugar and caffeine, for when you find yourself bonking out in the middle of nowhere.

Some people like a fitting that allows them to bolt a battery or generator light onto the fork. Other options are shift-lever bosses, cable holders, and cantilever brake mountings, all of which improve the bike substantially. These brazed-on fittings add to the price of a bike, but they keep things simple and tight. This is no abstract point; you can get in real trouble if something slips into the wheel at the wrong time, and anything that keeps coming loose or breaking down is a bummer.

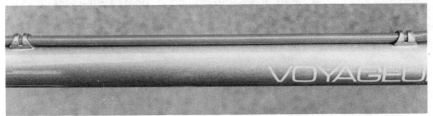
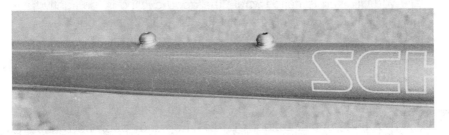

BASIC BRAZE-ONS
Without these fittings it's pretty hard to get things securely attached. These are on the Schwinn Voyageur; Upper left: (1) Shift lever boss (under lever) eliminates need for strap-type mounting. Upper right: (2) Eyelets for rack (in use) and fenders. Middle: (3) Brake cable guides. Bottom: (4) Water-bottle mounts. (Not pictured are useful seat stay fittings for rear rack.) Custom builders will work out just about anything you want, but it can get expensive. These are basic.

WHAT TO BRING

Practically every cyclist and writer on the subject has very definite ideas about what to bring, and the variation is amazing. A few things do crop up as almost absolute essentials, though, even among the lightest travelers: good maps, toilet kit, first-aid items, sunglasses, riding and walking clothes, two pair of shorts minimum, rain gear, cap or hat, shoes you can walk in comfortably, extra jersey or sweater, flashlight, long pants or leg-warmers, at least several pair of proven-comfortable socks, sunscreen, ChapStick (with PABA), and a tool kit, plus some spare parts listed further on.

MAPS

From the beginning of time travelers have lived and died (or experienced serious discomfort) by their maps. It's the same for cyclists. Poor maps send you on poor (for your purposes) roads; good ones make it clear where you really want to ride. Something around a one-inch to five-miles scale is ideal, because all roads can be included. Add topographical information, and you have most of what you need to know, except probable wind direction and strength. Maps made by cyclists themselves, like those from Bikecentennial, are usually best of all.

It's not enough to have good maps though; you need time to look them over and think about where you're going and why. Places that sound great in travel supplements may be all wrong on a bike. After a while you will start to notice where the good cycling is, on lightly traveled roads that wind through small towns. Many maps don't even include them.

Sources of good U.S. maps include the states themselves, Bikecentennial, and the League of American Wheelmen, which publishes an extremely useful list of 220 maps, available for $1.50. For Europe, *The International Cycling Guide* (% Tantivy Press: Magdalan House, 136–148 Tooley Street, London SE1 2TT, England), published annually, has a good list of international organizations. One standard map is the Hallwag auto atlas, purchasable at bookstores and auto clubs, which covers all except Eastern Europe in 90 well-detailed, 6" × 9" maps. Michelin maps can be useful, but generally, don't rely on automobile road maps, which lack the kind of detail you need. Carry one as a supplement to those of higher scale; it will provide perspective.

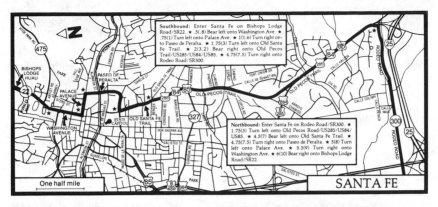

Southbound: Enter Santa Fe on Bishops Lodge Road/SR22. ★ .5(.8) Bear left onto Washington Ave. ★ .75(1) Turn left onto Palace Ave. ★ 1(1.6) Turn right onto Paseo de Peralta. ★ 1.75(3) Turn left onto Old Santa Fe Trail. ★ 2(3.2). Bear right onto Old Pecos Trail/US285/US84/US85. ★ 4.75(7.5) Turn right onto Rodeo Road/SR300.

Northbound: Enter Santa Fe on Rodeo Road/SR300. ★ 1.75(3) Turn left onto Old Pecos Road/US285/US84/US85. ★ 4.5(7) Bear left onto Old Santa Fe Trail. ★ 4.75(7.5) Turn right onto Paseo de Peralta. ★ 5(8) Turn left onto Palace Ave. ★ 5.5(9) Turn right onto Washington Ave. ★ 6(10) Bear right onto Bishops Lodge Road/SR22.

One half mile   SANTA FE

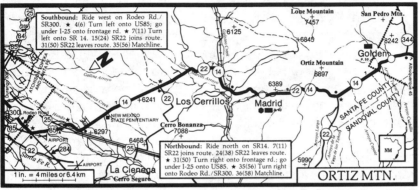

Southbound: Ride west on Rodeo Rd./SR300. ★ 4(6) Turn left onto US85; go under I-25 onto frontage rd. ★ 7(11) Turn left onto SR 14. 15(24) SR22 joins route. 31(50) SR22 leaves route. 35(56) Matchline.

Northbound: Ride north on SR14. 7(11) SR22 joins route. 24(38) SR22 leaves route. ★ 31(50) Turn right onto frontage rd.; go under I-25 onto US85. ★ 35(56) Turn right onto Rodeo Rd./SR300. 36(58) Matchline.

1 in. = 4 miles or 6.4 km   ORTIZ MTN.

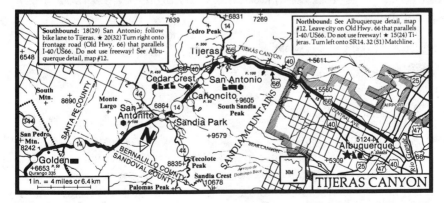

Southbound: 18(29) San Antonio; follow bike lane to Tijeras. ★ 20(32) Turn right onto frontage road (Old Hwy. 66) that parallels I-40/US66. Do not use freeway! See Albuquerque detail, map #12.

Northbound: See Albuquerque detail, map #12. Leave city on Old Hwy. 66 that parallels I-40/US66. Do not use freeway! ★ 15(24) Tijeras. Turn left onto SR14. 32 (51) Matchline.

1 in. = 4 miles or 6.4 km   TIJERAS CANYON

BIKECENTENNIAL MAP

Detail is everything, and Bikecentennial maps are among the very best. The very detailed information is gathered by cyclists—hence, useful to cyclists.

CUTHBERTSON WIND MAPS

Because winds follow patterns, Tom Cuthbertson's pioneer wind maps of the U.S. can be very useful, indicating general patterns and seasonal variations. On long rides, consistent negative wind can raise the level of effort as much as prolonged climbing, and most people find it more unpleasant. Cuthbertson includes 57 cities and towns, and by comparing a road map and a Cuthbertson map for the correct season, you can figure conditions for almost any area. The maps, derived from U.S. Government originals, appear in Cuthbertson's *Bike Tripping* (Ten Speed Press: Berkeley, CA). They require some thought, but it's definitely worth your time.

MEDICAL

Obviously it is a good idea to start with a recent tetanus shot, and you should not travel without Lomotil or something else that will stop diarrhea. Sunscreen for skin and lips is essential, even if you don't usually burn. You should also carry some large adhesive bandages, some cortisone cream, a wide-band antibiotic, a roll of adhesive tape, and a roll of 1½-inch wide bandage. If you fall and scrape yourself, soap and water will get it as clean as anything, but you may need a brush to get out all the grit. If possible, leave road rash open to the air; if not, cover it with the gauze bandage, and soak this off after about two days. What you bring beyond these items should be defined by how far you are from civilization, and where. Campers may want a snake-bite kit in some areas, and mosquito repellent is extremely desirable if you sleep out.

Bailen's $6 medical kit is another good idea; it is well equipped for road rash, including antibiotic ointment and alcohol for cleaning the scraped area.

TOOLS AND SPARE PARTS

At least one member of any group traveling by bike should be a decent mechanic, able to replace a spoke, rough-true a wheel, patch a tire, and replace a cable or freewheel. Skill is not enough though; you need certain spare parts and tools. There is no definitive tourist's tool kit; the stronger the bike and the nearer you are to civilization, the less you need to bring. The tool kit in Chapter 9 is basic, and to this should be added at least these basics:

Freewheel remover and Cyclesport Pocket Vise: The latter will usually get a freewheel off without the aid of a five-pound wrench.

Inner tube and patch kit.

THE POCKET VISE
This odd-shaped aluminum tool between rod and freewheel cluster is handy on tour;
in combination with a freewheel remover it will let you get a defective freewheel off.
($6–8, from Cyclesports Inc., 20102 Cedar Valley Road, Lynnwood, WA 98036.)

Foldable clincher casing: Definitely known to fit your rims (or several spare tubulars if you use these).

Rear brake and derailleur cables: These can be shortened for use on the front.

Half-a-dozen extra spokes of the right sizes.

Chain tool and some spare links.

Cone and pedal wrenches.

WD-40.

Pair of brake blocks.

CAMPING GEAR

The popularity of backpacking has had an important spin-off for touring cyclists in that sleeping bags, pads, air mattresses, tents and cooking gear have all improved amazingly (if expensively) in the last few years. This is still an evolving field in which valid innovations continue. Magazines like *Outside* are a good source of information, as are the bicycle journals. You'll pay for lightness and quality, but it's generally worth it.

STOVES AND STAPLES

Butane and liquid fuel (not white gas) stoves are the basic options, and each has its advantages. Liquid fuel is a bit more efficient and easier to obtain; Coleman is an old favorite, but the lighter Svea stove is popular with cyclists, though it's a little trickier. MSR makes an all-fuel stove that will burn anything including jet fuel, which would be very handy on a long tour through unfamiliar territory.

Butane comes in metal cylinders which make it a little heavier than liquid fuel, but it's easier to use. The Bluett S-200 is a good bike-touring model, as is the Gaz Globe Trotter which packs compactly with its little set of pots. With backpack equipment still changing rapidly, it's worth looking around. Talk to someone with experience if you can.

The usual cooking gear minimally includes a metal or plastic cup, spoon, knife, bowl (a flattish one that doubles as a plate is best) and two saucepans—one for food, one for drink. (Hot tea will put you back

THE BIG BREAKFAST
When you travel in a group, cooking out is more fun, and the weight of stove, pots, etc. can be spread around. It definitely saves money.

together and stave off hypothermia as well as anything, which is why Himalayan expeditions seem to revolve around it.) Cooking oil, sugar (you burn it off before it does much harm), salt, matches and scouring pads are other basics, and anything added to these should be closely considered. Dried foods are light, and often pricey, canned foods amazingly heavy.

TENTS

A good tent has zippered, insect-proof door flaps, with outer flaps for rainy weather. It should also have two screened openings for cross

TENTS
Today's tents can be surprisingly light, compact, and dry. Eureka Wisp 1 (top, $141) weighs 3 pounds, 4 ounces; the two-person version ($175) weighs 4 pounds, 5 ounces. Moss's 3-pound, 10-ounce Solus (bottom, $170) sleeps one; their 4-pound, 12 ounce Starlet ($220) sleeps two. These are well-made, waterproof, ventilated tents.

ventilation, and an integral waterproof floor. Double-wall construction (an inner, breathable layer and an outer, waterproof "fly") is basic to comfort; totally waterproof tents collect moisture inside. One-layer tube-tents seem like a good idea, but most tend to sweat and aren't much better than a tarp or bivy bag. As with rain clothes, Gore-tex may ultimately be the solution, being waterproof (when seams are sealed) but breathable.

A tent for two people should weigh no more than five pounds, and a single should weigh about three. Don't get a superlight tent no one has ever heard of; it may be no bargain. Ease of assembly is very important, as is basic quality of workmanship and materials. Tents that don't work are very annoying; hassles at the end of a day's ride are exactly what you don't need. It's difficult to find good, light tents under $150, but the Sierra Starflight, Eureka Wisp, Moss Solus and others are available in this range. If you're going to spend every night in your tent, get a good one.

SLEEPING BAGS

Down and Hollofil are both used in good-quality sleeping bags, and they are significantly different from each other. Hollofil will keep you warm when wet and let you get some sleep; it's also less expensive, but it's heavier and bulkier. Down weighs much less and stuffs smaller, but it washes out totally when wet. Most cyclists use it anyway, and trust to a good tent to keep them dry.

The price range for light down bags that stuff to very small size runs from $135 to $250, and they are worth it; these bags weigh only two to three pounds and are plenty for any summer trip; usually they are

SLEEPING BAGS
Light, warm, compact, down bags: Camp 7's Meadow ($134) weighs less than two pounds, and is rated down to 40°F. Ascente's Bivy ($154) weighs two pounds five ounces, but is good down to 35°F. If you need extra warmth, think about a Gore-tex shell.

rated to about 40°F. Some are coming out in Gore-tex and similar fabrics, which might actually result in a reasonably waterproof down bag. Camp 7 has an interesting liner/bag/cover system that uses a variety of sophisticated materials (including Gore-tex) to adapt a light bag for a variety of conditions and temperatures. Down Works, Eastern Mountain Sports, Sierra West, North Face, and others all offer good, light, down bags.

Under the bag must go something, and most people find closed-cell Ensolite pads the most comfortable; they're bulky though, and they're not light. The Kelty air mattress is lighter and smaller, and worth thinking about.

TO CAMP OR NOT TO CAMP

Stove, pots, utensils, sleeping bag, pad, and tent add up to considerable weight and bulk. Clearly the commitment to camping and cooking has everything to do with your trip, but it's not an either/or choice. At one end of the spectrum are those who will travel (they hope) in warm dry summer weather, carrying only a light sleeping bag, and using a tiny stove mainly to make tea. They camp when it makes sense and find accommodations when it rains. Others bring a heavier bag, and a small tent. Some groups carry quite big tents and multi-burner stoves. But if you've never done much camping, talk to someone who has (or try it for a few days) before going all the way.

ACCOMMODATIONS

There is a loose network of hostels through both Europe and the U.S. which will put a roof over your head for a very reasonable price. Some people take to them, some don't; it's a matter of temperament, but there's no beating the rates. American Youth Hostels (see page 312) covers the U.S., and has information about Europe. Motels, guesthouses, inns (and in Europe, hotels and pensions) vary wildly in rates and quality. Some cater to cyclists, which means your problems will be understood and no one will show consternation at your appetite.

As always, the best information is from people and organizations with practical experience. Those traveling in the continental U.S. will find the *Cyclists Guide to Overnight Stops* (Ballantine: New York, 1982) invaluable. Information is up-to-date and detailed. Even if you're camping out you may want this book; it offers economical stopovers but it's not just a list of cheap motels—hostels, hotels, and campgrounds are also included, along with cost-effective eateries.

PACKING A BICYCLE

Pack as if for a Himalayan expedition, weighing everything. Experienced riders often decide what panniers and/or packs will be carried, and how much the total should weigh, then draw a hard line. Up to 15 pounds correctly mounted affect the bike little, except on long climbs; 20–25 pounds create a very different experience; 35–40 pounds put you in a whole different category. Unless you are fit and genuinely strong, a really heavy load can force you into very low gears, change the way you ride, and wear you down. Figure a certain amount off your day's mileage for each pound added; if you've been able to handle 75 miles on a stripped bike, 50–60 is a reasonable goal with 20–25 pounds added. If you just aren't a strong rider, pack accordingly; unnecessary weight will deplete you.

WEIGHT

Don't try to save weight with an extra-light bike and components; equipment failure on the road can ruin your trip. And while there's only a few pounds' difference between the average tourer and an off-road bike, the tourist's load can range from under 20 to over 40 pounds. These pounds are attached to the bike rather than being an integral part, and even the tightest pannier setup sways a bit; more weight means less stability.

How weight is attached to the frame has a real impact on stability and handling. Weight that is not tightly mounted shifts and sways, making out-of-saddle climbing awkward; winding descents can become dangerous. Brakes are truly tested. The traditional continental approach—the most experienced, in other words—is based on three general rules: *Light, Low,* and *Forward.* It is a good approach, and front panniers with a small bar bag are the solution. This is fine up to a point, but it doesn't help campers, who are a very large group. Jim Blackburn's recommendations (see p. 339) are indispensable for those who want to go beyond minimum loading.

PANNIERS

Modern equipment is infinitely improved, and U.S. gear is the best available. Panniers are available in small, medium, and large sizes

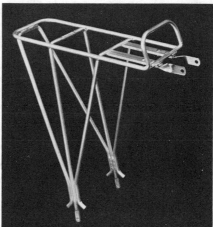

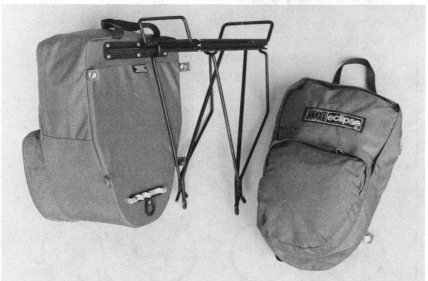

RACKS AND PANNIERS
Bottom: Eclipse rack ($32) and mid-size panniers (about $80) are well thought out and constructed; panniers come in several sizes. The unique slide-on attachment system can be adapted to other racks. Blackburn rack (top right) sells in the $25-$30 range. Good looks and sound design have made it very widely imitated; variants include more complicated low-rider and models that attach to brake bolt. Kirtland mid-size panniers (upper left, about $80) are well-known for quality and convenience; they come in several sizes.

based on capacity (roughly, from 1,000 to 2,500 cubic inches). Small- and medium-size bags are much better in terms of balance. All sizes can be used on the rear, but medium is the limit in front. The usual American-style combination of large rear panniers and large bar bag is cumbersome and can sometimes destabilize a bike dangerously.

Heavy, waterproof nylon is the best pannier material, double-stitched at seams; high quality plastic zippers are standard, and should be covered for better water protection. Alloy or plastic stiffeners and superior mounting systems keep good bags in shape and in place; and they should allow ample heel-clearance when used on the rear. Easy access is a plus. A compact, well-placed load is very advantageous, and there's evidence that well-designed front panniers can actually lower aerodynamic drag, as with the Zzipper model pictured in the last chapter, so that drag of the loaded bike is less than it was before installing the panniers. In addition to the Eclipse and Kirtland

THE WEIGHT ACCORDING TO BLACKBURN

It's safe to say that designer-manufacturer Jim Blackburn knows as much as any American about loading a bicycle. His series of field experiments with experienced cyclists confirms some practices, explodes a few myths, and provides what amount to formulas for weight placement. Blackburn finds the low-and-forward *theory to be not without merit (he now sells a special low-rider front rack), but he goes beyond this. He tells where to place additional weight. Because his very thorough research is a basic*

ACCEPTABLE

IDEAL

source of information that checks out with personal experience, we include illustrations of what Blackburn considers the two best ways to carry substantial weight.

bags pictured, good panniers are made by Cannondale, Kangaroo Baggs, The Touring Cyclist, Velocipac and others.

Despite excellent construction, even the best panniers aren't totally waterproof. If it's raining, line the compartments with heavy plastic bags, and seal them.

BAR AND SEAT PACKS

You're better off with a small bar or seat pack; a heavy backpack above the center of gravity changes handling sharply for the worse. On a sensitive bike, even more so. Most of the load should be at hip level or below, but a small bar pack with a transparent plastic map holder and shoulder strap is handy. It's a place to stow frequently used items— sunscreen, a piece of fruit, camera, glasses case, toilet kit, hat, and sweater. This same weight in a seat pack provides slightly better balance, but the map and contents are a lot harder to get at.

RACKS

It's now possible to buy really good front and rear racks from several manufacturers. The most popular are welded aluminum, like the Blackburn and Eclipse. Make sure that what you buy fits your bike; variations in frame geometry and design can make it difficult or impossible to mount a given rack securely. Simple, positive mounting is very desirable, ideally to eyelets and a brazed-on seat stay fitting; the rear brake mount is another fairly secure upper mount. Avoid cheap, collapsible racks. Loaded panniers sway dangerously no matter how they are mounted because the design is inherently flexible. If you are going off-road, you need heavier racks; Blackburn and others make special heavy-duty models.

If you don't care to pay for state-of-the-art metallurgy, plated steel is fine; some would say it is even better, though the additional strength is rarely needed, and there is a fair weight difference. Make sure it matches up with the pannier mounts. Eclipse has gone the furthest in terms of mounting systems with their very stable slide-in arrangement, but you'll need adapters to fit their panniers to racks made by other manufacturers. On tour you will find that even with lock washers and/or Lock-tite, movement will eventually loosen almost any rack. Check this (along with other things that tend to come loose) and don't let yourself get complacent.

SOLID RACK MOUNT
Attachment to brake bolt is usually adequate, but bolting to the frame fitting as on the
Schwinn Voyageur is better, because it gives four-point suspension—good for heavy
loads and off-roading.

CLOTHING

The recommendations of Chapter 10 still hold, but it can be a
problem keeping warm and reasonably dry under widely varying conditions. Even in summer, mornings and evenings can be cold, especially when it's windy. Rain makes it colder yet. Be sure your clothes
fit the season and weather. Layers of clothing are the answer, because

they are low in bulk, high in adaptability. Beyond this, there's no real consensus on specifics. Partly this is because the available gear is improving so fast, partly because people differ wildly in their ideas about what to wear on a bike tour. It comes down to what you can live with—specific personal knowledge based on your style of touring. Despite this, most experienced riders would agree that:

1) Classic racing-style shorts bind and chafe less than anything else, but have limited utility away from the bike. Lycra washes quickly, but it's terrible in cool weather; wool handles a much wider temperature range. If you're comfortable with synthetic chamois, it will save you drying time. The new touring shorts are good for knocking around, but some wrinkle under the seat and have inferior chamois.

2) Long pants that double comfortably on and off the bike are best; painter pants are comfortable, cheap, and loose enough to fit over shorts and leg-warmers in a cold snap.

3) While colored socks are never found in the Tour de France, they look better with most clothes than white ones.

4) If you're doing big miles, true cycling shoes are best, but you just can't walk in them; Guidebenes and similar driving shoes cost like hell but take almost no space, weigh nothing, and add some panache. Running shoes are much lighter and less bulky than training shoes or sneakers.

5) Some clothes wash and dry like magic, some don't.

6) A dickey makes an open-necked wool shirt or sweater into a much warmer item.

7) Wool and polypropylene sound too warm, but they tend to stabilize body temperature by keeping you dry of sweat. Try cross-country ski shops for this kind of underwear.

8) After a day on the road you finally understand why cycling gloves are made exactly the way they are.

9) While it's virtually impossible to stay dry in a long hard rain, it is essential to stay warm. A waterproof hat or cap makes a big difference. And if you're cold at the end of the day, it's no sin to buy a hot meal and get a roof over your head while you and your gear dry out.

SAFETY

The first thing is not to deceive yourself about your capacities, and not to push yourself into a bonked-out state. If you have, force yourself to drink, eat, and rest even if it means a schedule change. A tired rider becomes a dangerous rider, especially to himself. He gets slow and erratic, and inexperience makes this worse yet. Good drivers don't ignore fatigue, and neither do experienced cyclists

Going on tour without good front *and* rear lights is plain stupid. All it takes is a flat tire to keep you out until dusk, besides which you want to be free to ride when you feel like it. If you don't do much night flying, a halogen-bulb generator combined with a battery-powered flashing taillight is a fair solution. You also need spare bulbs and an extra battery. Pedal and rear reflectors are essential.

MECHANICAL

The bike should be perfect; you don't want to be bothered with flaky equipment. Pack all bearings and give the bike a couple of long shakedown rides. With extra weight on the bike, competition-quality brakes are nice; the cost-efficient move is new, well-greased, heavy-duty cables and the Mathauser composition brake blocks discussed earlier are better, especially in the rain.

If you've been fighting the hard-helmet idea, this is a good time to rethink the subject. You will be riding long distances in unfamiliar conditions.

GEARING

In the days before derailleurs were accepted for competition use, there was a saying: the longer the ride, the lower the gear. As with much antique lore, there is truth in it, and it is reflected in Velocio's recommended gear range of 35–85, which is uncanny in its assessment of long-distance requirements under light loads. But wide variations in physical strength and loads carried make it impossible to generalize. Essentially, you have to find your own way.

For touring under heavy loads, you need smaller chainrings. A typical stock set of rings is 52–40, but something like 50–36 works better on tour. Beyond this, you are into triple rings and split-shifting. One thing you can be sure of is that giving up your high gears is no real loss; few tourists have real use for anything over 90–95 inches. You can really boom down the hills on 52 × 12, but it's really not such a great idea with a loaded bike that's hard to stop.

Strong, fit riders traveling light have a whole different set of rules. If your gears are just right for all but freak situations, it may not be necessary to revamp them completely unless the climbing is really tough. With only 12–15 pounds on the bike, a moderate drop in your regular gearing will often be enough. If your lowest gear for similar terrain is 40 × 24, dropping to a 26 or 28 cog on the rear may be enough; if you're used to a 40 × 26, a 28 or 30 may do it. Anything over twenty pounds on the bike means a wide-range setup for most riders, though.

RIDING IN GROUPS

It may seem obvious, but the first priority is not to knock each other down. Allow a little more room between bikes than seems necessary, especially on descents. Alertness and common sense are important too; don't get in the habit of riding two-up (side by side) when it's not safe. And cultivate your better self. Touring is not racing, and it involves adjusting to the group in large and small ways, even at difficult times. The situation tempts strong riders to rub in their superiority, but bike travel goes better when strength defers to experience. The obvious thing to do when some riders are stronger than others is to shift the load accordingly. It's best to tour with people of fairly equal ability, but this is never quite the case, and athletic ego can rub people the wrong way. Over a period of time it can backfire or quietly erode friendship.

EUROPEAN TRAVEL

Like all foreign travelers, people on bicycles must contend with the language barrier and an unfamiliar environment. Combined, these make for culture shock, which is heightened by fatigue. If you are touring outside the U.S. for the first time, get in touch with people and organizations listed at the end of this chapter. They understand the problems and have useful information.

It's also a good idea to learn at least the basic phrases in whatever language you will need. This gives you a sense of orientation, and it helps you deal with stores and restaurants. Even a very limited vocabulary will get you through most situations.

Likewise it helps greatly to learn all you can about riding conditions in the countries you visit. Americans understand that most of California is reasonably warm most of the year and that New England is hilly but beautiful, but we don't often have this kind of information about foreign countries. Holland, Belgium, and much of France are cold and wet during our spring, for example, as many Americans have found to their dismay. Read about the places you want to go, and try to talk with people who have been there. This will give you some idea when and where the good riding is found, which is the key to enjoying yourself.

Start out with your bike in the best possible condition and carry key spare parts. Foreign bike shops may not have exactly what you need. Currency and passports or visas can be problems, but not if you prepare yourself. Finally, bring a little extra money . . .

MIND AND BODY

Even if you're doing twenty or thirty mile rides on a fairly regular basis, you don't really know what it's like to double or triple that in a strange environment and do it every day with added weight on the bike. It's different. It can become either controlled self-discovery or something less pleasant, the slightly dazed sensation of ongoing hyperstress.

For most beginners, the fourth or fifth day of a two-week trip is crucial. This is the time to think about whether your plans and goals (i.e., mileage) are realistic, and allow some time to check out how you are reacting physically. If there is any doubt in your mind, take a day off and let your system catch up. Rest and relaxation give perspective, and you have a chance to think over changes in plans. Some people need to stop after three days, some after five or six, but most inexperienced and/or semifit tourists are refreshed and cooled out after a day off. If you're bursting with energy you can rent a canoe or go for a hike. Some prefer the happy hour, followed by a movie and a night at a good motel.

SOURCES OF INFORMATION

L.A.W.

The League of American Wheelmen has long been an excellent source of information as well as the oldest and most consistently productive and respected of American cycling organizations. Membership is 20,000 and comprises a wide age and social range. The L.A.W. is a sophisticated organization that publishes a good magazine and has long been the backbone of what could be called the Cyclist's Rights movement, and they are also very helpful about providing information. Current executive director is Don Trantow; Jim Fremont covers information services. Mail address is P.O. Box 988, Baltimore, MD 21203; phone 301-727-2022.

BIKECENTENNIAL

Since 1976, this new group has grown to a membership rivaling that of the L.A.W. They have been gradually developing a kind of cyclist's view of the U.S. by sending experienced riders through various parts of the U.S. to map them. This has resulted in excellent maps of attractive routes; these maps include really useful, current, detailed information on roads, traffic, facilities, stores, etc., en route. Bikecentennial also operates tours ranging from as short as one week to as long as three months, with the stress on camping and cooking out; the day rate averages around $20 per day. There are also an insurance plan and several publications. Write attn. Mac McCoy, P.O. Box 8308, Missoula, MT 59807; phone 406-721-1776.

V.B.T.

Vermont Bicycle Touring was among the first groups to bring bike travel to the U.S. in a way that inexperienced cyclists could enjoy; its approach has been widely copied. For a reasonable fee, John Friedin and company guide you

(continued)

from inn to inn on carefully selected routes; it costs, but it's very well done. Friedin's book 20 Bicycle Tours in Vermont *(New Hampshire Publishing Company, Somersworth, NH, 1979) is accurate and useful. Baggage follows in a VBT sag wagon; short and long tours, graded from very easy to pretty sportif. R.D. 2B, Bristol, VT 05443.*

M.B.T.

Michigan Bicycle Touring organizes short tours for adults and families; beginners are a specialty. Meals and lodging provided. 738 Griswold, Dept. E, Jackson, MI 49203.

THE BICYCLE TOURING GROUP

This is a branch of the bicycle industry. It publishes Bicycle Touring U.S.A. *and distributes touring information. 3509 Grove Avenue, Suite 3-E, Richmond, VA 23221.*

A.Y.H.

The American Youth Hostels are, as their name suggests, an organization of hostels catering to adaptable riders. They can get a roof over your head at a low price, but hostels vary in services provided, and some people don't feel at home with housemothers. A.Y.H. publishes useful guides and a newsletter, and they can put you in touch with European hostels. To take advantage of this network, you must join. Mail goes to American Youth Hostels, National Campus, Delaplane, VA 22025.

INTERNATIONAL:

I.B.T.S.

The International Bicycle Touring Society is a club of 1,000 that runs about a dozen yearly tours in Europe and the U.S., complete with guides, overnight accommodations,

(continued)

and sag wagon. Not cheap, but well worth it if you don't feel like roughing it. A European tour of 2½ weeks costs about $65 a day for food, lodging in very passable hotels, and the handy sag wagon to carry most baggage. Information is available through Dr. Clifford Graves, I.B.T.S., 2115 Paseo Dorado, La Jolla, CA 92037.

C.T.C.

The Cyclists' Touring Club is a British organization, but it is a good source of information on European touring as well. Accommodations from hostels to hotels, bike shop locations, train and ferry schedules, and a bimonthly magazine are available. C.T.C., 69 Meadrow, Godalming, Surrey, England, G07 3HS.

DUTCH TOURIST CLUB (ANWB)

General information and cycling routes in particular are available from this organization, at Wassenaarseweg 220, den Haag, Netherlands. Also try the Dutch Cycle Touring Club (NRTU), which conducts tours: Nederlandse Rejwiel Toer Unie, Postbus 76, Zoetermeer, Netherlands.

FEDERATION FRANCAISE DE CYCLOTOURISME

You can get information on rallies and tours through some of the most beautiful countryside in the world from these people, along with a very useful lodging directory. Write them at 8 Rue de Marie Tago, 75013 Paris, France.

CANADIAN CYCLING ASSOCIATION, ALLIANCE SPRTIVE DU QUEBEC

Between these two you can get basic information on Canadian touring. Write the C.T.A. at 333 River Road, Vanier, Ontario, Canada; the Alliance is at 11652 Alfred Laliberte, Montreal, Canada.

12.
COMPETITION

Bicycle racing is one of the great world sports, with a tradition going back to the 1880s. Americans were among the best at the turn of the century, but the sport here went into a decline that hit bottom after WWII. Not until the mid-seventies did competitive cycling in this country come back to life. Today, bike racing is a sport in rebirth, especially in the U.S. From professional road racing and triathlons to local BMX competition, such barometers as rider registrations, prize lists, and sponsorships have all risen sharply—which is much of the reason for recent American success in the Tour de France and Olympics.

Long a European stronghold, the sport has changed radically in the eighties at both amateur and professional levels, with American, Australian, Irish, Japanese, and Scottish riders appearing prominently in recent years. Until this time, Western Europeans routinely dominated professional cycling, with eastern bloc nations largely in control of Olympic and other amateur cycling. This situation changed considerably in 1982, when Nevada's Greg Le Mond (see p. 319) and Ireland's Sean Kelly took silver and bronze medals at the professional World Championships, and exploded completely when Le Mond won the gold in 1983. Then, in 1984, came a sensational U.S. Olympic effort in which Americans won four out of eight events—the first medals since 1912.

Organized competitive cycling goes back approximately one century, and its longstanding prestige is suggested by the inclusion of seven events at the 1896 Games. There were eight at the 1984 Olympics in Los Angeles, including the first women's event, a road race (won by Colorado's Connie Carpenter). Professional racing is even more prominent as a sport; the three-week Tour de France has long been the largest single spectator event in the world, drawing 15 million live spectators yearly, and easily exceeding soccer's World Cup, the Super Bowl, the World Series, Wimbledon, and the Indianapolis 500. Startling as it is to many Americans, the legendary cyclist Eddy Merckx achieved greater worldwide recognition than even boxer Muhammad Ali, whose career was roughly concurrent.

THE OLD DAYS
A typical turn-of-the-century mass-start track event. Things got wild and physical in such racing, as documented by Major Taylor in his autobiography.

CURRENT DEVELOPMENTS

Performance in the Tour de France is highly indicative of the state of the sport, and in 1984, three of the top five finishers were English-speaking: fifth place Sean Kelly, fourth place Robert Millar, and third place American Greg Le Mond. Australians like Phil Anderson and Danny Clark have also been prominent in current racing, and the Japanese have taken several recent World Championships in track racing, as well as creating their own Keirin event. The net effect has been truly international racing, with the French, Italian, Belgian, and Dutch being challenged seriously on all fronts.

Amateur competition in recent decades has generally been dominated by the Russians, East Germans, Poles, and Czechs. Methodical team selection, training, and support are part of the phenomenon. The other factor is physical maturity; the best Western amateurs turn professional around ages 19 to 21; the Eastern European amateurs are usually older, tougher, and more experienced. This trend toward Eastern amateur dominance culminated in 1980. Until the 1984 Olympics, only East Germany had equaled or surpassed the Russian consistency.

On this side of the Atlantic, Colombia, Canada and the U.S. are the major powers, and in women's racing U.S. riders were acknowledged as dominant before their 1984 Olympic triumph. Mary Anne Martin's victory in the first-ever Women's Tour de France in the same year underscored this American strength. U.S. amateur cycling is governed by the U.S. Cycling Federation, 1750 East Boulder, Colorado Springs, CO, 80909.

TYPES OF RACING

ROAD AND TRACK

Accounts of early racing are always interesting, and occasionally bizarre. Early races were held on the dirt roads of the middle 1800s on high-wheeled Ordinaries and featured frequent mechanical repairs, combined with remarkable distances. With the safety, they increased. Despite the heavy, one-speed bikes, the 1903 Tour de France featured stages in the 400-kilometer range, which meant rising before dawn and riding into the night. As in running, there were also short races, and within very few years the sport was seen as two distinct items: long overland tests and shorter, faster events, held on banked tracks or velodromes. Many riders double on road and track, but track racing demands more speed, and consummate control of the bicycle. Road racing, by contrast, is an endurance sport whose competitors are always at the top in aerobic capacity tests.

ROAD RACING

Unlike the marathon and other endurance sports, road racing has evolved into a genuine team sport. Major professional events pit teams of as many as twelve riders against each other in fields sometimes running over 200, with each team trying to put one of its own across the finish first. Amateur teams are smaller, but the game is the same. Serious races are typically run from six to ten hours for professionals, three to five for amateurs, and can be highly tactical.

Professional emphasis on mass-start road racing has developed a special breed of athlete, usually 130–160 pounds in weight, with great cardiovascular capacity and virtually no body fat. These are true endurance athletes, typically competing between 75 and 100 times per season, sometimes more. The demands are enormous; it is an all-weather sport with a season that begins in late February and does not end until November. Between training and racing, a serious amateur covers 15,000–25,000 kilometers during the year, and pros do far more.

Amateur race distances are usually around 140–180 kilometers for one-day events; pros often double that and race more often. Events are categorized as *time-trials* (raced against the clock), *criteriums* (short, flat races, usually on city streets), long, one-day *Classics*, and multi-day *stage races* which are the ultimate all-around test, and where the biggest reputations are made.

STAGE RACING

Few if any athletic events are as physically and mentally demanding as stage racing. These big professional confrontations roll on as long as three weeks, with daily races (known as stages) averaging around 200–250 kilometers a day—with only one day's rest during the entire ordeal. Even amateur events can last up to twelve days. Within a few days of the beginning of a race, the entire entourage of managers, masseurs, mechanics, press, announcers, TV and film crews, medics, officials, marshalls, support personnel, fans, and groupies moves into a somewhat hysterical zone of its own. Riders collapse at the end of the day's stage, have mini nervous breakdowns, are massaged back to life, and return the next day, again and again.

The stage race is generally accepted as a "climber's game," because the mountain stages are often decisive in determining the overall winner, but there are a lot of ways to score. There are stage victories, team victory, a King of the Mountains, and a "points" winner (deter-

mined basically by consistent sprint performance). The overall individual winner prevails on the basis of total elapsed time, slightly affected
by stage-win time bonuses and an occasional penalty. Except for the
Russians, who are very concerned with collective team performance
for reasons of their own, individual victory is considered the ultimate
goal. For professionals, the Tour de France and Giro d'Italia are the
ultimate tests; for amateurs, there are the eastern European Peace
Race, France's Tour de l'Avenir, Britain's Milk Race and Colorado's
Coors Classic, which has become the unquestioned major event of
U.S. cycling.

THE TOUR DE FRANCE

There is nothing quite like the Tour de France in cycling, or any
other sport, for that matter; it is the largest single spectator event in the
world, and, at about 4,000 kilometers the longest major cycling event. It
goes back to 1903, when it was created by Henri Desgranges as a
promotional device to sell newspapers, and today it is still owned by
l'Equipe, a sports paper. But over the years the Tour has become a
tradition—a French institution that circles the country and creates an

THE TOUR DE FRANCE
This shot from the 1984 Tour shows the world's finest going head-to-head on the
decisive La Plagne stage, which featured three "haute" (top) category climbs, one
after another. Left, Laurent Fignon; center, Greg Le Mond.

endless picnic wherever it goes. And somehow—perhaps out of its media origins—those who run this multi-million-dollar enterprise manage to balance business, sport, and cultural elements to produce an uncompromised event that has become a national institution.

The logistics are amazing. Over a thousand people come and go with each stage, moving on to the next town each day along with about 500 race-connected vehicles—plus a completely separate commercial caravan of one hundred vehicles that precedes it with souvenirs for the crowds that line its roads. Each day over 400 journalists are provided with a huge press room, a computer bank, telexes, and field-installed telephones. Somehow it all works.

The Tour is the ultimate goal of road racers, and it was here that the legends of Coppi, Anquetil, Hinault, and Merckx were forged. Lasting 23 days, passing through Alps and Pyrenees, contested by the finest racing cyclists each year, the Tour is a convincing celebration of the century-old French love affair with the bicycle. Equally important to cycling, it has maintained an invaluable credibility that continues to be a great factor in the sport's international rebirth. If cycling has a home, a place where it draws its life, and which is a haven in hard times, it is the Tour de France. The entry of American Jock Boyer in 1981 was a landmark, and Greg Le Mond's third-place finish in 1984 a solid sign that Americans could truly compete with the very best in this most difficult of events. And for those who disliked the chauvinism of previous editions, which excluded even women reporters, directors Felix Levitan and Jacques Goddet sprang the ultimate surprise in 1984: a women's Tour, won by American Mary Anne Martin.

GREG LE MOND

If there is a single figure that truly represents the resurgence of U.S. cycling it is Nevada's Greg Le Mond, twice a world champion (1979 junior amateur, 1983, professional) and six times a Worlds medalist in various events. When his 1983 championship was followed by a Pernod Prestige trophy he entered the Valhalla that includes such great American champions as Major Taylor and Frank Kramer. When his Dauphine Libéré and Tour de l'Avenir stage race wins (the latter by the biggest margin in the history of the event) are figured in, the still-young (23 at time of writing) Le Mond must be considered the greatest American cyclist since the

(continued)

legendary Albert Augustus "Zimmy" Zimmerman. Only recently, though, through CBS coverage of the Tour de France and Paris-Roubaix, have Americans had a look at Le Mond.

The nature of his 1983 championship prompted Eddy Merckx to remark that never in his life had he been able to win a championship like that. Le Mond's savage attack and long solo breakaway simply crushed all the best cyclists in the world, and it shocked the cycling community on both sides of the Atlantic.

Ironically, teammate Laurent Fignon had won the Tour

1983 WORLD PROFESSIONAL CHAMPION GREG LE MOND WITH DUSTIN HOFFMAN DURING THE 1984 TOUR DE FRANCE.

de France that year, and Le Mond now found himself riding alongside a Frenchman on what was being called "the French national team" by the press. This tricky situation resolved itself when Le Mond came down with bronchitis after running neck-and-neck with Fignon for half a dozen stages. He plunged in the standings, falling out of the top 10. Then he fought his way back up, step by step, and on the final, awesome, La Plagne stage he climbed to third place, which he held to the end, along with the white "best neophyte" jersey. Only two-time winner Fignon and four-time winner Bernard Hinault finished ahead of him.

Le Mond's arrival on the U.S. national scene was equally convincing. In 1977, in Princeton, New Jersey, fellow rider Mark Brandt suggested this writer "talk to Le Mond, the guy who's winning this thing." "This Thing" was the see Junior Worlds trials, in Princeton, New Jersey, where Le Mond (still too young for international competition at fifteen) won easily against a field of much older and more experienced riders. A year later he led the juniors to a first-ever U.S. bronze in the team time trial. Two years later, still a junior, he took gold (road race), silver (pursuit), and bronze (team time trial) medals at the Buenos Aires Junior Worlds.

(continued)

This hat-trick had never been accomplished in the history of the sport, and the assembled Europeans were most respectful.

U.S. withdrawal from the 1980 Olympics removed his final amateur goal, and at eighteen he was negotiating with professional teams. When he joined Californian Jock Boyer on the powerful Renault-Gitane squad led by World professional Champion and Tour de France winner Bernard Hinault in 1981, few observers thought he was ready. But Le Mond won his first pro race at nineteen (a rarity for rookie cyclists) and then went on to a series of consistently high finishes topped by a surprising fourth in the mountainous Dauphine Libéré. In mid-season he came back to the U.S. for the Pro-Am Coors International to meet the all-conquering Soviet Olympic squad. Still tired from the grueling Dauphine, Le Mond slipped as low as sixth, then exploded in the mountain stages to crush the Russians and everyone else. The following year, despite an early-season broken collarbone, he salvaged his season with a silver medal in the World Championships and the Tour de l'Avenir win.

Le Mond is a study in contrasts. A smart, smooth rider who makes very few mistakes, he also rides a fiery, dominating style. Good-natured to a fault, he is "another person on the bike," in the words of father Bob Le Mond, himself an excellent rider. Blocked once too often by U.S. amateur Dale Stetina during the 1981 Coors, he warned him off with a hard punch, after which even the burly Russians pretty much let him alone. Despite success that puts him with the very best of the young professionals, he is still an open, easygoing down-home Sunbelter with a reputation as an unselfish and effective team rider. Off the bike with wife Kathy and son Gregory, he is direct, unaffected, and to the point. Even during the worst days of his difficult 1984 Tour he remained accessible to the media and made no excuses.

Less well known is the fact that Le Mond has had to deal with serious physical disabilities: one of his kidneys is almost dysfunctional, his feet have painful bone spurs that require him to carve out the soles of his shoes, and, most surprisingly, he has a long history of allergies, which are treated by his father-in-law, Dr. David Morris. These disabilities have at times been real handicaps. But along with

(continued)

them is the startling endurance and determination that let him come on strong despite illness in the last week of the Tour. Teammate Hinault and former director Guimard both expect him to win it; so does Tour director Felix Levitan.

THE CLASSICS

The term Classic normally signifies a one-day race, often in flat to rolling terrain where climbs are not necessarily decisive. Some of these races date back to the turn of the century, and winning any one of them sets a rider up for the following season with an improved contract with his sponsor, plus the chance to endorse products and negotiate for "appearance" (start) money at ensuing events.

The Classics require a true road rider, one who thrives on speed and distance (as much as 300 kilometers and more for some professional events), and who can put absolutely everything into a single performance. Because many of these races come early in the season weather can be truly brutal; steady rain in near-freezing temperatures is common, with snow and sleet definite possibilities. This aspect of cycling is represented by such respected events as Paris-Roubaix (France), Milan-San Remo (Italy), Liege-Bastogne-Liege (Belgium), the Amstel Gold (Holland) and the World Road Championships, which move to a different location each year.

PARIS-ROUBAIX

Paris-Roubaix is the most coveted of all the Classics, and more than one great rider has said that winning it outweighs a World Road Championship in ultimate prestige. The race is 260 rain-or-shine kilometers, a gradually accelerating madness, in which the crunch comes when riders move off decently paved roads to medieval cobbles specially preserved in bad condition for the event.

This shift is preceded by a crescendo of attacks as groups of riders attempt to break away from the bunch, because to enter the cobbles behind the top 20 riders usually means one is out of the race. With a huge starting field of as many as 300, escaping the pack is not easy. Once the cobbles are reached, the best path is at the edge, on a strip of packed earth, and the narrowness of this path tends to force the pack into a single line rather than the normal road-filling swarm. Wheels, tires, and even frames simply disintegrate. By the halfway point everyone's face is an agonized mask of dust (or mud, if it's raining).

Rarely do less than great riders win this race, or even show up in the leader's breakaway group, which is why it has become a hallowed tradition. A Worlds course can be anything from nearly flat to a ferocious series of climbs, but Paris-Roubaix is a known thing that varies little, a true test.

THE TIME TRIAL

A time trial is any event, road or track, which is contested against the clock ("contre la montre"). Time trials are regarded as particularly grueling "pain events" because a rider cannot use the slipstream or

TIME TRIALS
Riding against the clock can really take it out of you. This is Kent Bostic after a Coors Stage.

draft effect of his competitors, and because tactics are secondary to pure concentration and physical effort. There are both individual and team time trials; the Kilometer, the Pursuit, the Team Pursuit and the 100 Kilometer team time trials events are examples.

There are also time trials in almost all stage races, crucial to the outcome. Anquetil was famous for squeaking out Tour de France victories through his strength against the clock. The Grand Prix des Nations, a 90-kilometer individual event, and the Barrachi Trophy (raced by teams of two) are both important yearly elements of the professional calendar. The Hour Record, attempted on the track, usually by road specialists, is the ultimate prestige event of this type, and Eddy Merckx said that his record-setting effort in Mexico City was the most demanding of his career. Italy's Francesco Moser shattered Merckx's record in 1983 using a special bicycle with spokeless carbon-fiber wheels which reduced wind resistance dramatically, and were used by the winning Italian Olympic time-trialers in 1984.

THE PERNOD PRESTIGE TROPHY

Although the World Championship road race can fairly be described as something of a crap shoot, the Pernod Prestige Trophy is awarded on a sophisticated system based on points earned in major competition over a season. The Pernod Prestige ratings center on the major Classics and stage races, ignoring short-distance criteriums, which are regarded as incidental. Consistency as well as great single efforts are important, and the Pernod Prestige Trophy is the unofficial World Championship, understood by riders, managers and knowledgeable fans to indicate the best single measure of all-around performance. When Greg Le Mond won this in conjunction with his 1983 World Championship, he was only the fourth rider in the history of the sport to win this "double championship" in a single season.

THE GREATS

COPPI

Italy's Fausto Coppi, France's Jacques Anquetil, and Belgian Eddy Merckx have been described as the holy trinity of modern racing, and among them they exemplify three vastly different approaches that re-

This 1978 U.S. National road team, photographed at the Campagnolo plant in Milan, was the first ever sent by the USCF to campaign in Europe. Managed by Mike Neal, it was very successful. Standing from left: Mark Pringle, Tom Prehn, Tullio Campagnolo, Paul Deem, George Mount. Seated, David Ware, author Rostaing (right).

flect a significant evolution in tactics and techniques. Of the three, Coppi is the most magnetic figure, and a genuinely tragic one. He arrived as a star with the pre-World War II Bianchi team led by Gino Bartali, a unique figure known as the Pious because he stood aloof from the scene, never swore, and went about destroying opponents with sober dedication. It was said that peasants rushed into the road when he passed to kiss his tire tracks. When Bartali missed the crucial breakaway in one race, Coppi went on to win it—a shattering breach in protocol. Coppi remarked that the manager's final instructions to the team were to get the Bianchi green across the finish first, and that he had. From then on it was war between the two.

Coppi's professional career had just begun to take off when it was stopped by World War II; he set the World Hour Record (the ultimate time trial) and went into the army—then spent most of the war in a P.O.W. camp. Like many fine athletes, he lost several of his prime years, but his comeback after the war was spectacular. Beyond his success was an appeal that was genuinely charismatic. Quiet and thoughtful, Coppi was a specialist in the solo breakaway, preferably in the mountains. A poor sprinter, he preferred to finish alone, and often did, even against the very best competition. His resurgence coincided with Italy's long, difficult climb out of the devastation of World War II, and for many he symbolized his country's rebirth.

Coppi's reputation was ruined by his affair with The Lady in White, a married woman, wife of a well-to-do physician, who fell in love with him. The episode continued; the Lady became part of Coppi's life, and many of his followers were outraged. The affair shocked Italy, and the media made the most of it. When Coppi built her a villa just down the road from his family's, his fate was sealed. It all hastened the end of his career, which ended in tragedy: Coppi's last event, really an appearance rather than serious competition, was in North Africa, where he contracted a fever that shortly killed him—after which he was eulogized by the fickle press.

ANQUETIL

With Coppi in North Africa was a young Breton Frenchman named Jacques Anquetil, a completely different kind of person, destined to break a number of Coppi's records. Anquetil had great natural ability, but more important, he was unquestionably the greatest tactician the sport had ever seen. Shrewd and cool, a man who loved a party, Anquetil analyzed road racing to its essentials, and changed it forever. Despite a weakness in the mountains that could be exploited by more talented climbers, Anquetil won a staggering five Tours de France, largely on the basis of his ability against the clock, and his record nine victories in the Grand Prix des Nations (an individual time trial against the clock) may stand forever.

Anquetil, like Coppi, had no real sprint, but timed his moves with utter precision, and while he was not a particularly big man, his silky power in flat and rolling terrain was awesome. He pedaled as well as any man who ever lived. Equally important, his powerful teams were carefully selected, and they controlled the pattern of the race until such time as Anquetil deemed it appropriate to make his move. Somehow the great climbers (often lesser thinkers) could not exploit their talents against him with any consistency. Their stage-race leads would evaporate as he ripped through the time trials taking great chunks of time out of his competition. Once he won a Tour de France by a single second.

In spite of it all, he was not well liked by the press. Cool and ur-

JACQUES ANQUETIL
The French found Anquetil irritating in somewhat the same way American baseball fans were bothered by Ted Williams. He was just too good, and he knew it. But the man loved a party, and his tactical insight changed road racing forever.

bane, he was smarter than most of the writers, and laughed off their overtures. (Today he is a sports journalist himself.) The press of his day preferred the good-natured Raymond Poulidor, an excellent mountainman, who always seemed to finish just behind Anquetil. But it was Anquetil's sophisticated deployment of his team and physical resources that became the pattern for the sport. After him the bravado of ill-advised solo breakaways was much subdued, and using your wits became part of the game.

MERCKX

After Anquetil the Italian *tifosi* (fans) felt confident that the brilliant sprint and strong climbing abilities of Felice Gimondi marked him as

EDDY MERCKX
No one has ever come anywhere near Merckx's record, which included five Tour de
France wins and many six-day wins.

the next Coppi, but he had no sooner taken a Tour and several Classics
than Eddy Merckx arrived from Belgium. A prodigiously physical rider,
Merckx was soon known as the Cannibal for his greed to win. He was
an ergometer-buster who could also win in the maniacal pack sprints
that sometimes end a road race. And he could climb. Tactically he was
workmanlike and effective. Cool and superior, Merckx was not a much
loved figure among fellow riders, partly because of his Olympian manner, partly because on most days during the prime of his career he
could crush any rider in any terrain.

Handsome but cautious of speech, Merckx's style on the bike was
pure power; photos and films show him as a real bike-bender, and tactical analysis of his races shows just how physically superior he was.
Methodical and almost too willing to expend his powers, Merckx sur-
rounded himself with the strongest available team; several of them
could have led teams of their own. But no one ever accused Merckx of
letting other riders take the race to him; longtime British pro Barry
Hoban remarked that if there was a dog up the road, Merckx would
chase it down. His sportsmanship was unquestioned though; when he
crashed badly in the '74 Tour, taking a bad concussion and breaking
his jaw, he drank liquids, stayed in the race, and nearly won the sixth
Tour that would have put him ahead of Anquetil.

THE TRACK

There is no real success on the track without a gift for pure speed, and the short events can be violently anaerobic. Some events are run against the clock, others on a mass-start, first-across-the-line basis. Contact is frequent in mass-start racing, and quick reflexes are a must. The track rider is a physically different type, usually a little bigger and more overtly aggressive than a road rider, but with less talent for hills and distance.

THE BOARDS
Bob George's superb Six-day shot at Montreal's old Paul Sauve Arena shows the non-Olympic side of the track. This is classic board-track racing, and nothing could be further from soloing against the clock than this highly tactical, skill-dependent game of high-speed hand-slings and steep, crowded banking. Pros love the boards because knowledge pays off here.

VELODROMES

Tracks (or velodromes) vary enormously. A wooden indoor board track may be as short as 125 meters, banked very steeply, and its demands create an intensity all its own. There are also huge outdoor tracks of 400 meters with minimal banking which are so totally different that the sport itself is changed substantially. The Olympic 333⅓-meters design allows fast times against the clock and can handle a large crowd, but sacrifices a certain excitement and is not well suited to mass-start racing. The Madison event (below) comes to life better on a short track, where gaining a lap on the field isn't as hard. A good wooden track ("The Boards") is what every track rider loves, but "composition" (concrete) tracks like that of Pennsylvania's Lehigh County (Trexlertown) Velodrome, and that built by 7-11 for the Los Angeles Olympics, can be smooth and fast.

MASS START EVENTS

THE MADISON

Oddly, this is not an Olympic event, though it is the basic event of track cycling, and has been for many years. Hardly any track rider who cannot handle the Madison is ever offered a serious contract by a major pro sponsor. Named after Madison Square Garden, top six-day venue of the twenties and thirties, it is unlike any other event, being contested by two-man teams, of whom only one is in the race at any time, while the other riders circle the track slowly, above or below the action. The "exchanges," by which the fresh rider enters the race, are frequent, tricky, and sometimes unnerving—teammates literally sling each other into the race, in heavy traffic, at top speed. If there is high art in cycling, mastery of the Madison is it. It is a fair race that allows for a wide variety of talents.

THE SIX-DAY

This is the heart of professional track racing, and has an ambience all its own. Usually raced on the classic indoor board track at a smoky European velodrome, it has the intimacy of a sport where you are very close to what is happening.

In essence, the six-day is a series of Madisons, with a running tally kept as to who has lapped whom. But there are also points sprints, so that a pair of teams that are tied in laps gained are still separated by points. European beer, sausage, cigar smoke, and the strange nest of "cabins" around the track where riders rest all create an atmosphere much like that of professional boxing. Down below the velodrome is a world of its own, a warren of tiny rooms where the riders live for a very wild six days. Great roadmen like Merckx have been dominant six-day (i.e., Madison) riders, and six-day King Patrick Sercu (who won more of these events than anyone else in the history of the sport) also won many stages of the Tour de France.

THE SIX-DAY
Along with the match sprint, the Six-day is an ultimate test of track cycling. Americans haven't done badly over the years. Here Jack Simes, now president of PRO, launches partner John Vandevelde into the action.

POINTS RACE

Recently added to Olympic and Worlds competition, this two-man team race has the basic appeal of any mass-start event, but is very different from the Madison. In a points race, both riders are in the competition at all times, and at given intervals during the race they sprint for points; the accumulation of points decides the race, and the final sprint is for double points. Breakaways can and do form, and often they lap the field. It is a wild and hairy kind of racing, with plenty of bumping and crowding, and it takes brains; riders have to keep track of where they stand and figure tactics on that basis.

INDIVIDUAL EVENTS

MATCH SPRINT

The match sprint is a totally different kind of competition, pitting rider against rider in a tactical duel lasting one kilometer, and culminating in a final two hundred meters which can get very down and dirty. It is an event that goes back to the sport's antiquity, and it has endured because of its unique nature. Skill, timing, nerve, intimidation, and ac-

ELLEGARD AND KRAMER
Two tough dudes. Denmark's Ellegard was beating everyone in Europe at the turn of
the century, and had some famous matches with Major Taylor (p. 39). Here he's
pictured with several-time World Champion Frank Kramer. This shot says a lot about
what you needed then for match sprinting. It hasn't changed all that much.

celeration are of the essence. Early heats usually involve several riders,
but the final confrontations are one-on-one matches.

Competition begins with a long series of eliminations, but losers
may re-enter competition for a second chance via a *repechage* system, and the final heats are a lesson in shrewd aggression. Riders stalk
each other carefully, and the early meters are often very slow because
many riders prefer the rear position. Sometimes the result is a *sur-
place,* or standstill, as the front rider tries to force the man in back to
pass. The classic early move is a sudden dive down the banking that
surprises the opponent. The idea is to open a gap, thus breaking the
crucial slipstream or draft effect, which enables a following rider to
expend about 12–15 percent less energy than the leader. But most
often a match sprint is settled in the final 200 meters, in a side-by-side
battle that can feature crowding, elbowing, and *the hook*—a flick of the
leader's rear wheel intended to spill or intimidate the following rider.
Photo finishes are routine.

How rough does it get? American TV viewers saw Canadian Gordon Singleton knocked down several times in the finals at the 1982 Worlds, finally breaking a collarbone, and Sheila Young knocked down fellow American Connie Pareskevin a couple of times before Pareskevin won the duel for the women's gold the same year.

THE KILOMETER

A solo time trial from a standing start, the kilometer is very simple: go flat out for just over a minute. It is famous for leaving riders completely blown out, because the anaerobic capability lasts only 30–40 seconds, after which the rider is hip-deep in lactic acid and oxygen debt. A classic "pain event," it has its own legends. For years, Pierre Trentin's winning Mexico City Olympic ride was the model kilometer, and it's interesting to note that Trentin was unconscious for minutes afterward. "People were getting worried," remarks Oliver Martin, a U.S. competitor at the games, later an Olympic coach. "Trentin was out of it. What a ride—the perfect kilometer."

PURSUIT

This event is long enough that it pits track specialists against the faster road men, and it is a good general test of all-around ability. Riders start on opposite sides of the track and pursue each other; the one who completes the distance first, wins. The pursuit is a very tactical event, starting with a qualifying series of rides from which the eight best riders are chosen. The heats proceed with the slowest racing the next against the fastest, next-slowest against next-fastest, and so on. Distances are 3,000 meters for women and juniors, 4,000 for senior amateurs, and 5,000 for professionals.

Pursuiters is raced on a carefully planned schedule; a coach estimates what the winning time is likely to be and figures lap times accordingly; then he coaches from trackside, watch in hand, telling the rider to speed up or back off. Endurance is definitely a factor, as Russia's Vladimir Osokin found out to his dismay at the Montreal Olympics in 1976. Osokin had the fastest time of the Games in an early heat, but never fully recuperated, and finished out of the medals. Experienced Dutchman Herman Ponsteen calibrated his times perfectly and pulled out a silver without ever coming near Osokin's best effort.

TEAM PURSUIT

Contested by four-man teams, this is basically similar to the individual pursuit in its procedures, but the teamwork is crucial. Members

1983 WORLD CHAMPION WEST GERMAN PURSUIT TEAM
Strength and speed are basic, but this shot clearly indicates how important
aerodynamics and teamwork are to a seamless performance. Introduced to the
Olympics by Italy in the thirties, this event is a German favorite.

of a team take turns at the front, then drop to the rear in a tricky maneuver that sends them shooting up the banking, then swooping back
down onto the end of the line. A miscalculation here at forty miles an
hour means lost seconds or a bad crash. The event is an Eastern European specialty and requires a lot of practice; it's also pretty breathtak-
ing when the teams are smooth and evenly matched. Three members
of a team must finish, and the third man's time is the one that counts.

THE AMERICAN SCENE

BACKGROUND

The U.S. was a power in cycling from the late 1880s to the early 1900s, largely on the track. The automobile put an end to this, except for a revival in the form of six-day track racing in the late twenties and thirties, when it became a very hot item at Madison Square Garden and similar board-track venues. After World War II, the sport died here, except for small enclaves of Belgian, French, German, and Italian riders who kept it alive and waited for change.

They got a taste of it in 1974, when the U.S. Cycling Federation hired former Olympian Oliver Martin, who also happened to be the foremost black American in the sport since Major Taylor. With Martin as national coach, the U.S. took a best-ever ninth in the team time-trial event, and in 1975 Texan John Howard won the important Mexican Tour of the Baja. Only weeks later John Allis became the first American to break top twenty in Britain's much more important two-week Milk Race, and fellow American Dave Chauner won the final stage.

THE MONTREAL OLYMPICS

All of the above were major firsts for U.S. cyclists, and George Mount's even less likely sixth in the Montreal Olympics road race (best U.S. finish since 1912). It was handwriting on the wall; top-ten finishes are the stepping stones to medals. When Olympic road-captain Mike Neel turned pro and finished tenth at the Ostuni, Italy World Professional Championships (alongside the great Eddy Merckx), U.S. cycling people didn't know what to think; U.S. riders hadn't had results like that since before World War II.

It was obvious that Martin and his California Mafia (Mount, Neel, and most of the dominant riders were from California or lived there) were very different. "Fast and loose" was the criticism voiced by old-guard elements of the U.S. Cycling Federation, but their superior results in world class competition were obvious. Something was definitely happening. Then, in an unexpected move, the Federation hired a more conventional national coach, Eddie Borysewicz, formerly a coach in Poland.

Good results at junior level followed, but many top U.S. national team riders, oppressed by U.S.-style short-course criterium racing and the specialized low-mileage training, turned professional before achieving World Championship or Olympic results. Thus the best U.S. roadmen of the late seventies and early eighties were all professional—Le Mond, Mount, Neel, and Jock Boyer.

But the enormous financial input to the sport slowed the migration to pro ranks, and the food and lodging available at the Colorado Springs Olympic Training Center reduced the burden on riders financially. Better financing also allowed more European campaigning, and today a U.S. amateur, through team support and winnings, can afford to stay in the sport if he is adaptable to the system. The result was a vastly greater pool of talent—and the sensational 1984 Olympic results.

MIKE NEEL
Unofficial chairman of the "California Mafia," Neel was our first credible road pro, earning respect in Italy and elsewhere by riding to a very unexpected tenth place at the '76 Pro Worlds. This shot shows Neel (left) flanked by Magniflex teammate and 1976 Worlds bronze medalist, Tino Conti. Boxed in and partly obscured is the legendary Eddy Merckx. Neel went on to become an excellent manager here and in Europe.

AMERICAN PROFESSIONAL RACING

As recently as 1980, professional cycling was nonexistent in the U.S., and had been for years. Growth of the sport made pro racing attractive though, and for several years both the U.S. Cycling Federation (USCF), which governs amateur racing, and the Professional Racers Organization (PRO), founded by Belgian-born Chris van Gent, claimed jurisdiction. As the potential for pro racing became more clear, the battle for control became more bitter. Jack Simes, Art Greenberg and Dave Chauner (all connected with the Omni-Sports Group) joined forces with van Gent, and PRO (now U.S. PRO) took their case before the Union Cycliste Internationale (UCI). After a long battle they emerged victorious, and surprised many people with their quick moves to establish the sport. The 1982 PRO championship in Baltimore offered a prize list of $25,000; the following year it was up to $100,000, and got extensive prime-time TV coverage. Ironically, the winner was Colorado amateur and future Olympic medalist Davis Phinney, followed by Canadian amateur Steve Bauer—another Olympic (and professional) medalist-to-be. The Europeans had arrived for competition jetlagged and tired, and they got quite a surprise.

Internationally, too, professional cycling is moving into a new era in the U.S. Within a few years we had steadily improving Tour de France performances from Jock Boyer (a respectable 12th in '83) and then World Champion Greg Le Mond's very promising third in 1984.

"Greg has proved it can be done," remarks PRO's Dave Chauner, "and we owe him, all of us Americans in the sport. We hadn't seen a professional medal since 1899. . ." Equally important, 1983 saw the first professional stage race ever held here, the Tour of America, produced by World Tour Cycling and televised by CBS. In 1984, Olympic success was followed by the formation of several professional teams, of which G.S. Mengoni's was the first. Then Jock Boyer and SKIL put together a squad; both planned to race both U.S. and European events.

"When we started, we could only go up," said PRO

(continued)

president Simes after that well-staged, well-raced PRO Championship. "Now the situation is more complex. We have recognition, and we have options. Media and funding people are interested in the sport. Sponsorships are opening up. Before we were starting up a sport; now we're faced with the job of administering and promoting it well. The Olympics have been a big boost, and Steve Bauer's medal (a bronze in the road race) likewise. All the best American riders—e.g. Alexei Grewal—are turning pro. There will be Can/Am teams here and on the European circuit next year, and a strong professional U.S. national team to compete in the World Championships. It's not a dream anymore, it's happening." Write U.S. PRO at RD1, Box 130, New Tripoli, PA 18066.

THE U.S. WOMEN

If the climb to world class has been rocky for U.S. men, the opposite has been true for U.S. women. In 1969, Audrey McElmury set a magnificent precedent at the Brno, Czechoslovakia Worlds, winning the road race on a solo breakaway after crashing several times on a rain-slick course. Then, in 1977, red-haired Connie Carpenter took a silver medal in the road race, becoming the dominant U.S. woman rider while still in her teens. Soon there was a positive glut of talent, from which speedskater Beth Heiden clearly stood out, winning the World Championships road race in 1980, before her unexpected early retirement.

On the track, results were even better, as Sheila Young and Sue Novarra took a total of eight gold and silver medals during the mid- and late seventies in the match sprint event. There was little question that U.S. women were among the best, and at the 1982 Worlds, they stunned the competition. Connie Pareskevin and Young were first and second in the match sprint, with Rebecca Twigg and Carpenter first and second in the pursuit. Only lack of team cohesiveness kept U.S. riders out of the medals in the road race—and in 1983 Twigg took a silver here, Carpenter set a world record in winning the pursuit, and Pareskevin repeated in the sprint. The 1984 Olympics and World Championships confirmed all this as Carpenter, Pareskevin, and Twigg cleaned all clocks and Mary Anne Martin's Women's Tour de France win was icing on the cake.

U.S.-STYLE RACING: THE CRITERIUMS

U.S. racing is different from that in Europe, especially on the road. The short-distance (40–100 kilometers), short-course (1–2 kilometers) *criterium* is the most popular U.S. event, in marked contrast to the

DAVIS PHINNEY AND STEVE BAUER
At the 1983 U.S. PRO Championships 7–11's Phinney and Mengoni's Steve Bauer finished 1–2 against a field full of excellent pros, including Laurent Fignon, on his way to a Tour de France victory. The pair totally dominated the criterium circuit as well. Later Phinney took an Olympic bronze in Los Angeles, and Bauer a silver— after which he turned pro, took a Worlds bronze, and signed to ride with the famous Bernard Hinault's Vie Claire team.

minor part it plays in the European scene, where it serves mainly to present the stars close up in local appearances.

Criteriums are popular with promoters because the riders are very much in view, and purses can be fat—up to $100,000 for professionals. In addition, there are many "primes," cash awards offered by spectators for winners of a given lap. This short, flat racing brings road and track specialists together on more or less equal terms, which is a plus, but it tends to inflate some reputations, and does not develop the stamina needed for international road racing.

THE COORS INTERNATIONAL BICYCLE CLASSIC

Way back in 1975, before George Mount made his point at the Montreal Olympics, Mo Siegal's Celestial Seasonings Tea Company sponsored a weekend stage race known as the Red Zinger. By the time Mount won it in 1978, the Zinger had become a genuinely international

THE COORS
Professionals George Mount (left) and Greg Le Mond on a two-up breakaway at the 1981 Coors Classic—which is, oddly, a stage race rather than a Classic. Both began racing in the NorCal district and went on to professional careers; Mount took the Coors in '78, and this time it was Le Mond's turn.

race, and by far the most important American event, adding stages and attracting better riders each year. In recent years it has proved itself by the quality of its winners: Mount, Colombia's great "Patro" Jiminez, Le Mond, Boyer, Doug Shapiro, and Dale Stetina (twice).

By 1980 the budget had grown enormously, and the Adolph Coors Brewing Company stepped in to help, after which the ever-lengthening race became the Coors International Bicycle Classic. That year Jock Boyer won in a last-stage, last-ditch effort. In 1981 when Le Mond dismantled the Soviet Olympic squad, it was clear that both Le Mond and the race had definitely arrived. The following year CBS covered the event and in 1984 it was the final major tuneup for most Olympic road race hopefuls.

The impact of the Coors on the U.S. scene is reflected in a remark by former national road coach Mike Neel that the greatest resources of U.S. bike racing were "Greg Le Mond and the Coors"—a succinct and accurate observation. Both have maintained genuine international credibility long enough to fully establish themselves.

THE GREAT AMERICAN BIKE RACE

At the opposite end from a criterium race clearly, proving the media potential of long-distance competition, is the recently devised transcontinental Great American Bike Race, very successfully televised by ABC in 1982. The winner then and in 1983 was "Marathon Lon" Haldeman, who made it in just under ten days, averaging three or four hours' sleep per night. "It fried my brain," remarked Haldeman, who rode the final 24 hours nonstop to beat the ageless and very tough John Howard. It definitly appealed to audiences, getting the highest TV ratings of any U.S. cycling event until that time.

TRIATHLON

Even triathletes had to admit the Great American Bike Race was grueling, and they know about cycling from the bike leg of their very popular event. The Hawaii Ironman triathlon's much-discussed 112-mile cycling test is a time trial, and a very long one. Competitors ride alone against the clock for about five hours alongside sunbaked lava fields; it's serious competition by any standard. Viewers are impressed, but the real significance is that the triathlon is a "citizen's race"—a

TRIATHLON
With all the growth in cycling, it was the triathlon that really took it to the people; it is the essence of participant sport. This is champion Scott Tinley finishing the 100 + mile bike leg.

mass participation sport. Through it, many thousands of fitness buffs and serious endurance athletes had to learn about the bicycle in order to compete effectively. Those with special talent are starting to show up in Federation races.

FAT-TIRE FLYERS

BMX dirt-track racing for young riders, mostly ages 7–16, took the U.S. by storm in the seventies, and it has more active competitors than any other branch of the sport here. It is a sprinters' and bike-handlers' kind of racing, with heats that last around a minute. BMX is uncomplicated and fun to watch: five or ten kids start from a gate and go flat out on a downhill dirt track with lots of corners and jumps.

The adult spin-off has been ballooner downhill runs, out of which came the off-road bike. These runs are typified by the legendary Repack Run, disbanded, according to MountainBikes' Gary Fisher, "owing to uncontrollable group insanity." The Repack got its name from the fact that the overheated coaster brakes on early ballooners had to be repacked after a run. The annual Crested Butte Rally is another variation, an overland journey-cum-beer-bash that gathers up mountain bikers from everywhere for several days. The fast-growing National Off-Road Bicycle Association sanctions fat-tire races and rallies. Write Glenn Odell, 2175 Holly Lane, Solvang, CA, 93463, or call 805-688-2325.

THE 1984 OLYMPICS

A rising tide of participation, sponsorship, and international success indicated that Americans would do well at the '84 Olympics, but even the wildest enthusiasts of U.S. bike racing could not have predicted the crushing domi-

CONNIE CARPENTER (LEFT) AND REBECCA TWIGG

nance of American riders in Los Angeles. Of the eight cycling events, Americans won four; of a total of 24 medals, they won nine. It was unprecedented, breaking the record of seven medals set by the Italian team in Tokyo, 1964. Even allowing for the boycott by the Russians and some of their allies, it was amazing; all the best western Europeans were competing.

Colorado's Connie Carpenter opened the action with a flawless tactical race climaxed by a perfect photo-finish sprint in the women's road race. In second place by inches was teammate and long-time rival Rebecca Twigg. "I worked on my sprint with (husband) Davis Phinney, and it really helped," said Carpenter. Indeed it did—Phinney has been a virtually unbeatable road-sprinter for years. Carpenter, long neglected by the coaching staff in favor of Twigg (Carpenter was considered "too old" at 27 despite several previous worlds medals) was complete master of the situation. She timed her sprint perfectly and won by mastery

(continued)

of a technique known as "throwing the bike." Stamina, smarts, and experience prevailed, and her victory was no surprise. Since her 1977 Worlds silver medal on the road, Carpenter had been the dominant U.S. woman rider, with bronze, silver and gold World Championship Medals to her credit. Her World pursuit record in 1983 was the final clue. When she and the much younger Twigg buried the hatchet after several tense years, rivals were doomed; Afterward Twigg went to the Worlds and broke Carpenter's pursuit record, further substantiating the depth of U.S. cycling talent.

The men's road race was more of a surprise, and for some it was a shock. While Carpenter and Twigg had been acknowledged favorites, the U.S. men were just another strong team with a good chance to place. No American before or since Le Mond had performed at this level though. But midway through a cautious race, Colorado's Alexei Grewal sensed opportunity, took off on a characteristic solo flyer, opened a gap, then settled down to wait for reinforcements. Up came Canadian Steve Bauer, strong as a horse and a notoriously excellent sprinter. As Bauer came by, Grewal seemed to be coming apart completely in the hot Los Angeles sun. For most of the long breakaway the question seemed to be whether or not Grewal could hang on to Bauer's rear wheel for second place. Behind them were a pair of Norwegian riders, cutting into their lead. For reasons known only to himself, Bauer did not slow down and collect himself for the sprint. Never before had Grewal taken one from him. But when Bauer took off on his final dash, Grewal, who thrives on distance, had completely recovered from his earlier fatigue. He passed Bauer with startling ease, lanky arms, legs, knees, and elbows flailing like a windmill gone mad, and won going away. Grewal had been telling people for months that his sprint was improving, and it definitely surprised Bauer. A frequent victim of exercise-induced asthma, and no favorite of the coaching staff, Grewal rode a nervy and dominating race, proving himself once and for all. (Like Twigg, Bauer went on to prove himself another way: he turned professional for G.S. Mengoni, took a first-ever Canadian bronze at the pro Worlds, and signed a contract with

(continued)

Greg Le Mond in 1985.)

Behind this pair of gold medals were interesting personal stories. Carpenter and Grewal are intense individualists, not given to mechanical training-camp regimes, and Grewal was no shoo-in for the team. "If I hadn't automatically

(continued)

ALEXI GREWAL

qualified for the team, the coaches would never have selected me," he said at one point. Son of a Sikh Indian, direct and forthright, Grewal was regarded as too temperamental. His dominating '83 Worlds ride and consistent stage racing were discounted. Association with professionals like manager Mike Neel, Jock Boyer and Coors winner Dale Stetina had given him his own angle on things, and it did not follow the party line. Never quite at ease in training-camp situations, he had found a home with the Aspen-Dia Compe team. Too aggressive for the U.S. coaching staff to handle, Grewal took his best shot when others hesitated. Bingo.

Carpenter, who came to cycling after a speedskating injury took her out of that sport, actually left the bicycle to row one year. On at least two occasions National coach Eddy Borysewicz chose to work with Twigg in national and international competitions where the pair went head-to-head—a breach of the generally accepted protocol that younger riders must either defeat reigning champs on their own or wait their turn. But in her relationship to Phinney, Carpenter found something that brought her performance to the level of her talent.

In the team time trial Italy was supreme, a collection of perfectly trained bruisers riding state-of-the-art bikes with spokeless wheels of the type used by Francesco Moser in breaking the Hour Record in 1983. They won very easily. The U.S. team chose to use spoked wheels. In addition, the Americans were recovering from a feud between national and trade-team coaches that had resulted in cancellation of their '83 Worlds appearance. Nor were they properly peaked, by general consensus. In spite of all this they rode a maximum effort under difficult conditions. When Andy Weaver had to drop out of the race toward the end with a pair of broken spokes in his front wheel—an almost unheard-of mechanical failure in this event—Ron Kiefel, Roy Knickman, and Davis Phinney closed ranks and hammered through. Somehow they salvaged the bronze, and even came close to a silver, finishing only seconds behind favored Switzerland.

TRACK

This total of two golds, a silver, and a bronze in the road events was startling, and the track results were no less so. In the match sprint, Mark Gorski and Nelson Vails advanced through the early heats with unreal ease, to meet in the final event, where Gorski won easily, two heats to none. Midwesterner Gorski, who had been on course for this medal since the 1978 Junior Worlds, was no surprise; former Harlem bike-messenger Vails (shorn of dreadlocks the media had loved) definitely was. A late arrival to the sport, his 1983 Pan Am gold marked him as a threat, and he had taken heats from Gorski in the past. Together they were the most unlikely pair of riders to be found, but they came as close to

(continued)

MARK GORSKI AND NELSON VAILS

embodying the Olympic ideal as any two athletes you could name, maintaining friendly relations that were dropped only in competition.

The individual pursuit showed a supremely confident Steve Hegg, former downhill skier and friend of Winter Games gold medalist Bill Johnson, and the shrewd veteran California rider, Leonard "Harvey" Nitz, riding for the U.S. Nitz was clearly off the peak that won him the Olympic trials and set a U.S. record. He woke up with a stiff neck on the crucial morning, but worked his wily way through the heats to come up with a bronze few expected—by just five hundredths of a second.

Hegg was awesome, at an all-time personal peak, and he came alive with an Olympic (and U.S.) record ride that simply blew the doors off West Germany's Rolf Golz. Golz took it badly, stating that it would not have happened in Germany. The unperturbed Hegg pointed out that this was L.A. As a journeyman megatalent of two sports (he once competed for Canada on skis) Hegg was exuberant and droll. Asked by a journalist what he had in his water bottle, Hegg replied, "Anabolic steroids." But PRO's Jackie Simes, a former six-day racer, said that behind the clowning was probably the biggest young track talent in the U.S.

(continued)

STEVE HEGG

To say the U.S. team was on a roll was putting it mildly. Then came comic relief of a sort in the team pursuit, where the U.S. had a real shot based on Hegg, Nitz, Pat McDonough and Brent Emery. The team was on very light, special "funny-bikes" built by Raleigh, with 24" front wheels and Moser-type spokeless rears, with aluminum axles and nuts. But the staff botched the very basic chore of wheel-tightening before the qualifying round, causing Pat McDonough's crash after half a lap. "Don't your blokes check the bikes before competition?" asked an Australian.)

Next came a demoralizing spill for Hegg and Emery, caused in part by the pressure of competing with an in-complete team. This was followed by a rerun, still with only three members—a very severe handicap. Amazingly, they qualified fifth; at this point they looked golden. When crash victim Emery could not ride the later rounds he was re-placed by Pan Am gold medalist Dave Grylls, and the team—on its only full-strength run—easily defeated West Germany. Only the Australians were left between the U.S. and another gold. Then, at the start of the final, Grylls some-how pulled a foot out of his toe strap, ending this star-crossed attempt. Despite it all they took a first-ever U.S. sil-ver medal in the event.

The last, largely overlooked gesture came when Grylls told the crashed-out Emery to accept the medal at the cere-mony. Glitches and all, the pursuiters were amazing.

In the end, the U.S. took one or more medals in all but two events—the kilometer (where Rory O'Reilly set his bike up with the wrong gear) and the points race, where Danny Van Haute and Mark Whitehead never challenged seriously. West Germany's Fredy Schmidke (kilometer) and Belgium's Roger Ilegems (points race) were the beneficiaries.

The question that hung over the '84 Olympics generally could also be applied to cycling: with two of the three great amateur cycling powers missing, and with the home-turf ad-vantage, what did these results really signify?

A great deal, unquestionably. Coming on the heels of a strong amateur and professional U.S. showing at the 1983 Worlds, they were part of a general success at all levels and in all kinds of cycling competition. The results were too con-sistent to be accidental. Had only the favored U.S. women

(continued)

won, or if the U.S. had been held to bronzes and silvers, that would have suggested normal improvement; but in no other multi-event sport did U.S. athletes dominate more completely. They overcame conflicts with coaching and mechanical blunders, and they proved that the money pouring into this sport has had a direct effect. Investments by sponsors like 7–11, Aspen-DiaCompe, Levi-Raleigh, G.S. Mengoni, Murray and others had raised the level of competition higher than anyone fully realized. The 1984 Olympics were definitely the "great leap forward"—a truly amazing one, closely covered by ABC, full of unexpected heros and heroines who came through under ultimate pressure.

INDEX

Note: Name-brand equipment will be found under the name of its manufacturer

ILLUSTRATION CREDITS

Grateful acknowledgment is made to the following for their assistance in providing the photographs and drawings used in this book:

Kim Allis, for the photographs appearing on pages 27 (bottom), 50, 55, 57, 58, 60, 74, 77, 78 (left), 79, 83, 84, 86 (top), 88, 90, 95, 116, 117, 148 (all), 151, 160, 165, 167, 175 (all), 178 (top), 189, 192 (all), 199, 200, 204, 243, 253, 260, 261, 269, 272, 274 (lower right), 275, 276 (bottom), 279, 281, 291, 292, 293, 303 (bottom), 306.

Quin Bakaty for the drawings on pages 69, 72, 77, 100, 136, 140, 142, 143, 145, 147, 152, 155, 158, 166, 178, 184.

The Bettmann Archive, for the photographs on pages 327, 346, and 348.

Bicycle Sport, for the photograph on page 66.

Bikecentennial, for the maps on page 295 and the photographs on pages 169 (right) and 298.

Jim Blackburn Designs, for the photograph on page 303 (upper right) and the drawings on page 304.

Los Angeles Times photo by Mark Boster on page 344.

Dean Bradley and Fisher MountainBikes, for the photograph on page 86 (bottom).

Nancy Campbell, for her photographs on pages 9, 21, 26 (bottom), 35, 56, 78 (right), 80, 82, 87, 89, 91, 93, 94, 98, 99, 102, 106, 114, 119, 124, 134, 137, 159, 163, 170, 173, 174, 182, 195, 197, 201 (left), 219, 220, 221, 223, 224, 225, 227, 228, 229, 230, 231, 232, 233, 239, 240, 242, 243, 244, 249, 255, 264, 265, 267, 276 (top), 277, 282, 290. Copyright © 1985 by Nancy Campbell. All rights reserved.

Michael Chritton, for the photographs on pages 323 and 340. All rights reserved.

Cyclesports, Inc. and Angel Rodriguez, for the photograph on page 297.

Le Cycliste, for the photograph on page 45.

Eclipse Corp., for the photograph on page 274 (upper right).

Bud Light Ironman Triathlon World Championship and Ray Fairall, for the photograph on page 342.

Fisher MountainBikes for the photographs on pages 2 (top left), 52, 93, 288.

Robert F. George and Velo-news, for the photographs on pages 328, 329, 331, and 339. Copyright, Robert F. George. All rights reserved.

Paul Hilts, for the photograph on page 121.

Hine-Snowbridge, Inc., for the photographs on page 74.

The Hon Corporation International, for the photographs on page 61.

Johnson Camping Company, for the photograph on page 299 (top).

Green H. Liey and Ian Jackson, for the photograph on page 18.

Bruce Martin, for the photograph on page 67. Copyright © 1984 by Bruce Martin.

ABOUT THE AUTHORS

Basketball star BILL WALTON is best known for his national championships with UCLA and Portland Trail Blazers. Less well known to the public is the fact that he has also been riding and training on bicycles since he was big enough to get his leg over a top tube.

In recent years he has become increasingly involved in the sport of cycling, and has surfaced from time to time in competitive events, appearing several times as a guest observer at Colorado's two week Coors Classic race. As detailed in the introduction, the bicycle has long been a part of his general conditioning program for basketball, and a source of satisfaction in his personal life. He maintains road, track and off-road bicycles, as well as a clunker for knocking around the neighborhood, and attributes much of his overall fitness to their use.

BJARNE ROSTAING has been involved in many aspects of cycling for many years. As a journalist, his experience runs from coverage of the Tour de France, Olympics and World Championships to a monthly column in *Cyclist* magazine. His work appears regularly in cycling journals on both sides of the Atlantic, and he has also written for *Sports Illustrated, Outside* and other general interest magazines such as *Jazz Review* and *Soho News*. He novelized *Phantom of the Paradise* with film director Brian DiPalma in 1976.

As a lifelong cyclist, Rostaing maintains his own bikes, and his practical experience includes two years as manager of the West Hill Bike and Ski shop in Brattleboro, Vermont, where he led a kind of cafe-racer club known as the Woodchuck Randonneurs, who "always had a good time and didn't fuss with equipment a lot." He owns "more bicycles than can possibly be justified."